THE INVISIBLE PROFESSOR
THE PRECARIOUS LIVES OF THE NEW FACULTY MAJORITY

Practices & Possibilities

Series Editors: Aimee McClure, Mike Palmquist, and Aleashia Walton
Series Associate Editor: Jagadish Paudel

The Practices & Possibilities Series addresses the full range of practices within the field of Writing Studies, including teaching, learning, research, and theory. From Richard E. Young's taxonomy of "small genres" to Patricia Freitag Ericsson's edited collection on sexual harassment in the academy to Jessie Borgman and Casey McArdle's considerations of teaching online, the books in this series explore issues and ideas of interest to writers, teachers, researchers, and theorists who share an interest in improving existing practices and exploring new possibilities. The series includes both original and republished books. Works in the series are organized topically.

The WAC Clearinghouse and University Press of Colorado are collaborating so that these books will be widely available through free digital distribution and low-cost print editions. The publishers and the series editors are committed to the principle that knowledge should freely circulate and have embraced the use of technology to support open access to scholarly work.

Other Books in the Series

Aimée Knight, *Community is the Way: Engaged Writing and Designing for Transformative Change* (2022)

Jennifer Clary-Lemon, Derek Mueller, and Kate Pantelides, *Try This: Research Methods for Writers* (2022)

Jessie Borgman and Casey McArdle (Eds.), *PARS in Practice: More Resources and Strategies for Online Writing Instructors* (2021)

Mary Ann Dellinger and D. Alexis Hart (Eds.), *ePortfolios@edu: What We Know, What We Don't Know, And Everything In-Between* (2020)

Jo-Anne Kerr and Ann N. Amicucci (Eds.), *Stories from First-Year Composition: Pedagogies that Foster Student Agency and Writing Identity* (2020)

Patricia Freitag Ericsson, *Sexual Harassment and Cultural Change in Writing Studies* (2020)

Ryan J. Dippre, *Talk, Tools, and Texts: A Logic-in-Use for Studying Lifespan Literate Action Development* (2019)

Jessie Borgman and Casey McArdle, *Personal, Accessible, Responsive, Strategic: Resources and Strategies for Online Writing Instructors* (2019)

Cheryl Geisler and Jason Swarts, *Coding Streams of Language: Techniques for the Systematic Coding of Text, Talk, and Other Verbal Data* (2019)

Ellen C. Carillo, *A Guide to Mindful Reading* (2017)

THE INVISIBLE PROFESSOR
THE PRECARIOUS LIVES OF THE NEW FACULTY MAJORITY

Edited by Natalie M. Dorfeld

The WAC Clearinghouse
wac.colostate.edu
Fort Collins, Colorado

University Press of Colorado
upcolorado.com
Denver, Colorado

The WAC Clearinghouse, Fort Collins, Colorado 80523

University Press of Colorado, Denver, Colorado 80202

© 2022 by Natalie M. Dorfeld. This work is released under a Creative Commons Attribution-NonCommercial-NoDerivatives 4.0 International license.

ISBN 978-1-64215-158-9 (PDF) | 978-1-64215-159-6 (ePub) | 978-1-64642-380-4 (pbk.)

DOI 10.37514/PRA-B.2022.1589

Library of Congress Cataloging-in-Publication Data

Names: Dorfeld, Natalie M., 1976– editor.
Title: The invisible professor : the precarious lives of the new faculty majority / Edited by Natalie M. Dorfeld.
Description: Fort Collins, Colorado : The WAC Clearinghouse and University Press of Colorado, [2022] | Series: Practices & possibilities | Includes bibliographical references.|
Identifiers: LCCN 2022037202 (print) | LCCN 2022037203 (ebook) | ISBN 9781646423804 (paperback) | ISBN 9781642151589 (adobe pdf) | ISBN 9781642151596 (epub)
Subjects: LCSH: Universities and colleges—Faculty—Attitudes. | College teachers—Vocational guidance. | College teachers, Part-time—Social conditions. | College teachers—Tenure. | Education, Higher—Aims and objectives.
Classification: LCC LB2331.7 .I58 2022 (print) | LCC LB2331.7 (ebook) | DDC 378.1/2—dc23/eng/20220817
LC record available at https://lccn.loc.gov/2022037202
LC ebook record available at https://lccn.loc.gov/2022037203

Copyeditor: Karen Peirce
Designer: Mike Palmquist
Cover Image: Shutterstock #1513189949. Contributed by Halfpoint.
Series Editors: Aimee McClure, Mike Palmquist, and Aleashia Walton
Series Associate Editor: Jagadish Paudel

The WAC Clearinghouse supports teachers of writing across the disciplines. Hosted by Colorado State University, it brings together scholarly journals and book series as well as resources for teachers who use writing in their courses. This book is available in digital formats for free download at wac.colostate.edu.

Founded in 1965, the University Press of Colorado is a nonprofit cooperative publishing enterprise supported, in part, by Adams State University, Colorado State University, Fort Lewis College, Metropolitan State University of Denver, University of Alaska Fairbanks, University of Colorado, University of Denver, University of Northern Colorado, University of Wyoming, Utah State University, and Western Colorado University. For more information, visit upcolorado.com.

Land Acknowledgment. The Colorado State University Land Acknowledgment can be found at https://landacknowledgment.colostate.edu.

Thank you, my dearest husband William M. Bowden, for supporting me in every way possible during lean years and beyond.

Contents

Acknowledgments xi

Introduction. Hello, My Name Is Natalie, and I Am a Hypocrite 3
    Natalie M. Dorfeld

PART I. THE STRUGGLE IS REAL/ACADEMIA'S CURRENT
LANDSCAPE 13

Chapter 1. The Shadow of the Adjunct 15
    Michael Dubson

Chapter 2. From Tenure Track to Unemployment in Six Months 23
    Jeff Dories

Chapter 3. Becoming Lystrosaurus: Toxic Environments, Mass Extinctions,
and Other Cautionary Tales for Academics 31
    Dustin Michael

Chapter 4. Adjunctivitis: The Plague of Academia 41
    Marjorie Stewart

Chapter 5. Closing of My College Department and Swingline Factory 51
    Constance H. Gemson

PART II. THE DEBILITATING EFFECTS OF DISPOSABILITY 59

Chapter 6. A Dark Night and a Brighter Day for Adjuncts 61
    Maria Shine Stewart

Chapter 7. Statusism: How Adjunct Exploitation Isolates and Divides
College Faculty 71
    Christian L. Pyle

Chapter 8. Between a Rock and a Hard Place on a Deserted Island:
Negotiated Mental Health on College Campuses Through the Lens of
a Rebellious Adjunct Professor 79
    Belle H. Foster

Chapter 9. Unheard Voices and Unseen Faces: The Experience
of Adjuncts 87
    Nooshan Ashtari and Pamela Minet-Lucid

Chapter 10. Ignorance Is Bliss 95
    Ann Wiley

PART III. KNEE-DEEP IN THE TRENCHES/WHAT NOW? 103

Chapter 11. This is What Solidarity Looks Like: A Model of Thick Solidarity at the University of Illinois 105
    Andrew Bowman, A. Kay Emmert,
    Shawn Gilmore, and Bruce Kovanen

Chapter 12. Where to Start? An Overview of the (Ab)use of Contingent/NTT Laborers and a Call for Radical Transparency to Assist the New Faculty Majority 113
    Katie Rieger and Sarah Lonelodge

Chapter 13. "Ten . . . Toil Where One Reposes": Stories of an Adjunct Faculty Organizer 123
    Anne Balay

Chapter 14. Alternative to Nothing: Rejecting "Alt-Ac" Success Stories and Acknowledging Failure 129
    Daniel S. Brown

Chapter 15. Reconsidering the Status of Contingency: Are These Really the Trenches? 137
    Jennifer K. Johnson and Nicole Warwick

Chapter 16. From Being One to Hiring One: Both Sides of the Adjunct Phenomenon in Higher Education 149
    Kimberly M. Miller and Joanna Whetstone

Chapter 17. Adjuncting without Anguish: A 21st Century Roadmap to Success for Contingent Faculty 161
    Devan Bissonette

PART IV. BYE, FELICIA 169

Chapter 18. Breaking Up with Higher Ed 171
    Lee Kottner

Chapter 19. Where the Pipeline Ends: Teaching High School Equivalency in a Medium-Security Prison 181
    Andrea Verschaeve and Jason Porath

Chapter 20. Contracting and Consulting: Crafting a Career 187
    Ian S. Ray and Brandi Wren

Chapter 21. After Adjuncting: Questioning Academia's "Big Club" 195
    Steven Yates

Chapter 22. We Are the University.................................203
    Debra Leigh Scott

Chapter 23. Escape This Neoliberal Shit Show Now 211
    BC Dickenson

Conclusion. Labor-Informed Graduate Education 217
    Amy Lynch-Biniek

Contributors 223

Acknowledgments

The idea for this collection originally came from Joe Fruscione and Lee Kottner's narrative project *Teaching Poor: Voices of the Academic Precariat*. Both have left academia for greener pastures, but they were kind enough to share rough drafts and contact information, which aided this collection tremendously. And although we have never met in person, I know we would all become fast, rabble-rousing friends.

I admire each and every one of the contributors of this book: Michael Dubson, Jeff Dories, Dustin Michael, Marjorie Stewart, Constance H. Gemson, Maria Shine Stewart, Christian L. Pyle, Belle H. Foster, Nooshan Ashtari, Pamela Minet-Lucid, Ann Wiley, Andrew Bowman, A. Kay Emmert, Shawn Gilmore, Bruce Kovanen, Katie Rieger, Sarah Lonelodge, Anne Balay, Daniel S. Brown, Jennifer K. Johnson, Nicole Warwick, Kimberly M. Miller, Joanna Whetstone, Devan Bissonette, Lee Kottner, Andrea Verschaeve, Jason Porath, Ian S. Ray, Brandi Wren, Steven Yates, Debra Leigh Scott, BC Dickenson, and Amy Lynch-Biniek.

Your stories are brutally honest and vulnerable, and we need to hear more like these in order to move forward.

A huge shout out goes to Seth Kahn and Amy Lynch-Biniek, whose humble natures and activism in the field I have respected for years.

Lastly, thank you to Florida Institute of Technology for granting me a sabbatical to work on this collection. It was a labor of love and very eye opening. Moving forward, I hope I can be of more assistance to my peers in the field.

~~~

Portions of Constance H. Gemson's essay were originally published as "Adjunct Blues and Class Notes" in the book *The Children of the People: Writings by and About CUNY Students on Race and Social Justice*.

Portions of Maria Shine Stewart's chapter were originally published by *Inside Higher Ed* as "The Plight of the Nonrenewed" (under the author name Anonymous) and "A Kinder Campus for Adjuncts?"

Portions of Christian L. Pyle's essay previously appeared in *North of Center* and the *Bluegrass Courier*.

They have all been reprinted with permission.

THE INVISIBLE PROFESSOR
THE PRECARIOUS LIVES OF THE NEW FACULTY MAJORITY

Introduction. Hello, My Name Is Natalie, and I Am a Hypocrite

Natalie M. Dorfeld
FLORIDA INSTITUTE OF TECHNOLOGY

As I write this introduction, I imagine sitting around a circle of academics. Small chat is being made. The coffee is stale. We awkwardly take turns introducing ourselves to the fellow educators and, more importantly, the readers of this collection. When it comes to me, I brush off my corduroy pants and say, "Hi, my name is Natalie. I teach composition and literature at Florida Tech. I am the biggest hypocrite in the world. My practice and preaching are not aligned. In fact, they are not even close. You should probably take your cheese platter and leave now." But for this to make any sense, we must start at the beginning.

I graduated from Slippery Rock University in 1998, double majoring in philosophy and English with a specialization in writing. The running joke amongst my friends was I wanted to make myself as unemployable as possible. For the next few years, I bounced around between odd jobs in my dismal Rust Belt town (book seller at Borders, head lifeguard, alpaca shaver, housecleaner, and chiropractic assistant) before heading back to SRU for graduate studies.

From 2001–2002, I worked in the writing center at SRU. By day, I tutored undergraduate students. At night, I took composition and literature classes. I found this work deliriously intoxicating because, like most students who major in the humanities, (1) I love to read and write, and (2) I was told I write well. To say I was green about the academic landscape would be putting it mildly. Naively, I followed the advice of my professors, who had entered a more merciful job market, to keep on going. Get that brass ring. Obtain the almighty piled higher and deeper terminal degree.

In 2003, I started my part-time teaching journey while simultaneously pursuing a Ph.D. in English with a concentration in composition and TESOL at Indiana University of Pennsylvania. I worked in northwestern Pennsylvania and was a freeway flyer between multiple campuses: private institution, state school, and community college. In my most productive year as an adjunct professor, I made a whopping $13,500. No medical benefits. No retirement contribution. I only survived because I was living with my future husband at the time, who had a full-time job with benefits.

Like most on this dysfunctional merry-go-round, I became severely depressed. I sent out what felt like a million resumes, and I quit collecting the rejections after 100. And, like every adjunct out there, I can empathize with the struggle:

- I was denied flu shots from the health center because I was part-time, even though I had more student contact (sometimes double) than full-time faculty.

- I was given classes one day before they started, and then I was chastised by the dean because I was disorganized.
- I didn't have a first or last name. I was "that adjunct in the hall."
- I would attend every math meeting on campus because they served free pizza, and I could not afford a meal plan.
- I furnished my apartment by dumpster diving and made bookshelves out of milk crates and leftover plywood from the lumber yard.

Fast forwarding to today, 2021, I am now a tenured associate professor of English at Florida Institute of Technology, which is a private research university located on the Space Coast. Am I a genius? Hardly. I sometimes misspell cat. Am I well published? Not really. There is always room for improvement. I am simply one of the lucky ones, for I was in the right place at the right time. I have no false illusions of grandeur or superiority. So, why this adjunct collection now, and why do I feel like a giant fraud?

Because I tell my first-year students to follow their passions. I love the English major with every fiber of my being. It's deeply embedded in my soul. Hell, I even show *Dead Poets Society* in class, but I discourage students from hoisting me on their shoulders with my bad back and all. However, when a promising writer comes up to me and says, "I want to be an English professor one day," I want to punch that student in the face. Hard. This would be done out of love, naturally, but the administration would probably frown upon it.

But it also brings up larger and uncomfortable questions in higher education, such as how did we get here? How can one obtain a Ph.D. in English yet make more money as a manager at Burger King? What the hell went wrong? When did it go awry? And perhaps most importantly, how can we help the next generation of academics? Options are desperately needed and a lot more than one of them.

Historical Context

I often wondered why my professors did not warn me about the bleak job market in humanities, but things were very different when they started their careers, the so-called golden ticket days of academia. According to Marc Bousquet, author of *How the University Works: Higher Education and the Low-Wage Nation*, more than half of the faculty in public institutions were unionized in the 1960s (187). Furthermore, Bousquet notes, in the 1960s–1970s, part-time faculty made up only 20 percent of the total population. They were used as more of a stopgap measure, i.e., if a full-time faculty member took a sabbatical and/or an emergency hire was needed for whatever reason. The rest, 80 percent, were either tenured or on the tenure track (201). And then the 1980s rolled in with a vengeance.

In the era of Reaganism and trickle-down economics, buzzwords like "flexibility" and "supply vs. demand" and "alternative perspective" began to swirl around college campuses (Bousquet 198–99). Couple that with anti-union rhetoric from politicians, and things started to decline rapidly. Higher education became more of a business, one designed to make money and cut any and all humane corners. What was one easy way to accomplish this? Deny all the bells and whistles that come with full-time employment. In 1987, part-time faculty rose to 40 percent of the faculty in higher education (201).

Today, this system of exploitation has almost completely inverted itself in one working generation. According to New Faculty Majority, which cited data available from the Department of Education, as of 2009, 75.5% of college faculty are considered contingent, "meaning they have NO access to tenure." That is 1.3 million out of 1.8 million faculty members across the United States. Of those, 50% are adjuncts, which is a part-time professor. For all intents and purposes, they are the backbones of every department but the Walmart laborers of the college: low pay, no retirement contribution, and zero medical benefits ("Facts about Adjuncts" 1). Think it cannot get worse? It does.

According to recent statistics from both New Faculty Majority and Coalition on Academic Workforce:

- Over 1/3 have no office space or phone.
- Ninety percent receive no formal campus or departmental training.
- Class assignments are often received just one or two weeks before classes begin.
- With no health coverage, many are forced to sign up for Medicaid (Douglas-Gabriel).
- Some are paid as little as $1,500 with the median pay being $2,700 per class ("Facts about Adjuncts" 1).

To put it bluntly, as stated earlier, you can earn a Ph.D. in English and make more as a manager of a fast-food chain.

And this inequity does not discriminate from college to college. It's a nationwide epidemic of sorts. According to Scott Jaschik, citing an American Institutes of Research study, between 2003 and 2013, the share of faculty members who were off tenure track increased from:

- 45 to 62 percent at public bachelor's degree-granting institutions.
- 52 to 60 percent at private bachelor's-granting colleges.
- 44 to 50 percent at public research universities.
- 80 to 83 percent at community colleges.

To those on the ground floor, this is common knowledge. Outside of the ivory tower, however, this dirty little secret is widely unknown. As Douglas-Gabriel similarly notes, many individuals (students, parents, education policymakers, and journalists) think college professors live a life of the mind: raking in six figure salaries, working twelve-hour weeks, and having the summers off. In fact, it wasn't until the tragic death of Margaret Mary Vojtko that mainstream media decided to sit up and take notice.

Professor Vojtko taught French for 25 years at Duquesne University, grossing just $10,000 per year; when she was 83 years old, the school decided not to renew her contract, and she subsequently passed away, impoverished and close to homelessness (Sanchez). The national backlash, which sparked anger and outrage, left many asking, "How can schools that make millions of dollars and be so heartless and greedy? Moreover, if this is widespread, why do working professionals put up with it? Why don't they fight back?"

The good news is some people are doing just that. In *Reclaiming the Ivory Tower: Organizing Adjuncts to Change Higher Education*, Joe Berry highlights successes at the University of Illinois and Roosevelt University in Chicago. By laying out clear plans—make a committee, go public, recruit allies, act like a union, and spread the word via websites, flyers, and emails—the Coalition of Contingent Academic Labor (COCAL) has been moving the needle steadily there and elsewhere (Berry 118–129). According to its website:

> They achieved major gains in June 1998, including the reclassification of PT faculty teach two sections as salaried half-time employees with full medical, dental, and retirement benefits, and a floor of $4000.00/course. These successes inspired other faculty in the Boston area where there are 58 separate institutions of higher education. However, since most of these colleges had no union, part-time faculty from other colleges began to join with those at UMB [University of Massachusetts Boston], making the April 1999 conference a base for the Boston Project, now in its second year of demonstrating the success of regional coalition. ("History of COCAL" 1)

Likewise, as discussed by Colleen Flaherty, in *The Gig Academy: Mapping Labor in the Neoliberal University*, authors Adrianna Kezar, Daniel T. Scott, and Tom DePaola, detail how this shift from employing full-time to part-time workers isn't limited to just faculty employment. It's a canary in the coal mine for postsecondary education as a whole.

The text "notes that academic and support staff members, librarians, curators, archivists, and postdoctoral fellows have all suffered steep cuts to their ranks in recent years, as well" As a result, Flaherty notes, many office and administrative staff are either part-time employees or outsourced, which can lead to poverty-like wages, unrealistic overloads, and demoralizing mental health effects.

For those working at state schools with strong unions that have the ability to organize and strike, change is happening. It may seem painfully slow, but it is occurring nonetheless. For others, specifically those in locales without union protection, the battle for equality can feel like two steps forward and one step back. And in a right to work state, such as Florida, where I work? Things become gray and murky. Tread lightly, my friend. If one is too vocal, he/she runs the risk of being dismissed.

Contingency, Exploitation, and Solidarity: Labor and Action in English Composition, edited by Seth Kahn, William B. Lalicker, and Amy Lynch-Biniek, touches upon this delicate balancing act, with a call for full-time faculty to advocate and stand behind their peers in the trenches.

In one chapter noted in their collection, "Adjuncts Foster Change: Improving Adjunct Working Conditions by Forming an Associate Faculty Coalition (AFC)," Tracy Donhardt and Sarah Layden discuss how the AFC at Indiana University-Purdue University Indianapolis (IUPUI) was created to improve working conditions for contingent faculty, secure funding for conferences, obtain office spaces, and win modest raises. Through much back and forth with administrators, small gains were made, including:

> We were invited to serve on the committee to plan the campus-wide orientation for part-time faculty for fall 2011, the first such offer ever made. We increased membership in the Coalition to nearly 250 part-time faculty, full-time faculty, staff, and students. We gained additional media coverage ... Where no raises for part-time faculty had been approved in years, the Coalition lobbied for and won raises for those working in the School of Liberal Arts ... We held a "Coffee with the Coalition" event to promote our existence and remind students, faculty, and staff of our mission and the need to get involved. We held a third-annual teach-in. We gained professional development funds for all part-time faculty across campus who presented at conferences. (194–195)

Such stories reveal why multiple voices, angles, and solutions are needed at this time in higher education. As others have noted, on the most basic level, adjuncts should be given access to professional development, decision making votes regarding their classes and policies, adequate meeting spaces with students, instructional resources, fair and transparent renewals, and a place at the table during department meetings (Heitsch, Levine, and Madison 96). But we can do better. We must do better for all parties involved.

Purpose and Organization of the Book

With the onset of the recent pandemic, academia is at a crossroads. 1. Enterprising graduate students are in limbo because of departmental cuts and new caps on M.A. and Ph.D. programs. 2. Adjuncts are being forced back into the classrooms, many lacking adequate insurance, while COVID-19 spreads like wildfire. 3. Chairs and deans are running around with their heads cut off due to projected enrollment and budget woes. Some smaller institutions may be forced to close their iron gates forever. People are angry and rightfully so.

What makes this book a different animal? I like to think of this narrative collection as a Target store—because it is classier than Walmart—for academics.

There is something for everyone. Likewise, because ages and living situations vary a great deal, individuals need a Plan B. Its goal is to reach faculty members in three phases of their careers:

- those thinking of entering the profession
- those knee-deep in it and looking for ways to improve conditions
- those who have vacated academic positions for more humane alternative tracks

There is no one-size-fits-all scenario when entering academia. Individuals, especially in the humanities, are expected to make great personal and professional sacrifices. The stories are brutally honest, raw, and vulnerable. Furthermore, it gives a platform to voices that are often silenced, giving readers a sneak peek into what being a college professor really entails.

Part I: The Struggle is Real/Academia's Current Landscape

The first part of this collection isn't meant to dissuade anyone from reaching for their goals, but it is a precautionary warning about the current academic landscape, which involves hiring freezes, campus closings, and the restructuring of departments. Educators know "retrenching" is a pretty word for cutting staff and faculty across the board. As mentioned earlier, 75 percent of faculty members have no access to tenure, leaving them vulnerable and disposable every semester. Statistically speaking, the odds are not in your favor.

Marjorie Stewart, author of "Adjunctivitis: The Plague of Academia" discusses the woes of the "freeway flyer" lifestyle in her piece. To those outside of the academy, this term is widely unknown, but adjuncts know it all too well. The term is used to describe a part-time professor who travels to multiple institutions, often within one day, to piece together some semblance of a full-time job due to the minimal salaries provided by adjunct positions. In addition to the hustle being exhausting, it becomes downright confusing when the days and different schools blend together like a kaleidoscope. She states:

> But not all was right in my world. I had three classes at PCU [alias for a private city university], two at a local community college, and two with another private college in the suburbs. I had three book bags: a Monday/Wednesday/Friday bag, a Tuesday/Thursday bag, and a Wednesday night bag. If I pointed my car in the wrong direction and didn't realize it within a few miles, I was late for class.

And others in this section, the ones who have so-called "made it" by securing full-time jobs, note that the part-time struggle often affected their finances and family dynamics, with most not landing stable employment with benefits until they were well into their 40s, 50s, or 60s.

Part II: The Debilitating Effects of Disposability

Piggybacking on Part I, this section reveals the darker undercurrents of academia, the not so pretty version we don't share in the glossy brochures or with prospective parents on group tours. Because the system prides itself on cheap labor, even the greatest and most energetic of faculty members will inevitably feel one (or all) of the following: mental, physical, and emotional exhaustion. And the kicker of all this? Adjunct faculty members are often assigned first-year courses, so they are the people most students will meet first, the ones who are expected to "be happy" and "alert," as one nameless dean encouraged.

For instance, Maria Shine Stewart, one of the contributors featured in Part II, is currently an adjunct faculty member at two colleges. As noted in her chapter, her teaching experience includes 27 continuous years in adjunct capacities at up to four colleges simultaneously, with her introduction to adjunct life coming shortly after completing her first master's degree (in English). She has served on two MLA committees dealing with adjunct labor, one as the result of an appointment and one through member election. She also has a master's degree in counseling and is concerned with community and campus well-being.

She has been a popular columnist at *Inside Higher Ed* from 2011 to the present, and her writing reveals she knows the isolation that goes hand-in-hand with contingent life. As the heart of any department, with over 50% of its faculty being part-time in most liberal arts' programs, her chapter describes the feelings of being underappreciated and often underutilized within the campus population: migrant, marginalized, expendable, and invisible. As she writes of what non-adjuncts sometimes think about adjuncts, "You must be a good teacher. You teach at three different schools." Little do they know the sheer exhaustion that goes on behind the scenes.

If one adds the COVID-19 domino effect (parents teaching from home and Zoom burnout) to the situation, it's not hard to see why the last two years have been overwhelmingly draining, leaving many academics wanting to jump ship all together. Not to mention, a majority of part-time faculty members are not given health insurance by their universities. Many were not given the option to teach remotely while tenured professors had choices. Academia portrays itself as a beacon of fairness and principles. It is not. It is simply a broken system of haves and have-nots.

Part III: Knee-Deep in the Trenches/What Now?

Part III is meant for those who are knee-deep in the academic trenches, including faculty members, administrators, and chairs, from a variety of different institutions and locales. They have completed their graduate or doctoral courses. Perhaps they are happy where they are, or they are quietly looking elsewhere. Already in for the long haul, they are seeking solutions on how to improve their current situation and/or the health of their department.

Anne Balay, author of "Ten Toil... Where One Reposes": Stories of an Adjunct Faculty Organizer" in this section, organizes adjunct faculty members for SEIU Local 1 in St. Louis, Missouri, at the Community College level, the would-be Ivy level, and the urban Catholic level. Missouri is not a state that facilitates public sector bargaining at the best of times, but during the pandemic and accompanying recession, her members will bargain new contracts in the summer of 2021.

Circumstances like these are not rare, but as Balay stated in her chapter, these schools treat contingent faculty "like missionaries who will get their reward in heaven." She noted that since adjuncts don't want to wait that long, they develop strategies, organize their fellows, and fight to keep hope alive. More than anything, she said, they yearn to feel like their work—their sacrifice—is meaningful, which they hear in spades from students but from few else at the institutions that employ them.

As their organizer, Balay said her main task is to get out of their way. She relies on her experience as an oral historian and background in queer theory to use the power of the adjunct faculty members' stories—their embodied, visceral experience—to expose the corrosive norms that bind us all. Only then, she said, can we challenge the regimes that render their work invisible and irrelevant to the real work of the schools where they teach and imagine ways to insert them in the center where they belong.

Other authors in this section offer guidance on a tactile level (student, full-time faculty, and administration advocacy) while still others call for radical systematic reform. This includes the restructuring of academic departments, dividing composition and literature, and either cutting down on the overproduction of doctoral students or providing more stable, well-paying positions that specifically require their qualifications.

Part IV: Bye, Felicia

Part IV is for those who are considering pursuing greener pastures via alternative-academic careers. The authors in this section either advise taking jobs outside of academia and/or have left the field themselves. The one common thread is being an adjunct is not a dead-end job. For working professionals with advanced degrees, there comes a time to say enough is enough. As a result, many of the contributors have moved on to better positions with improved salaries, medical benefits, and retirement contributions.

Ten years ago, Andrea Verschaeve had a full-time, non-tenure track teaching position at a university, and she was receiving a small stipend as the part time director of the school's writing center. As she notes in her chapter, she was enrolled in a Ph.D. program at Indiana University of Pennsylvania, had completed the required coursework, and was conducting research on her dissertation. She also felt trapped and miserable.

Jason Porath, co-author in this collection with Verschaeve, began his educational journey toward a doctoral degree while working as a special education teacher at a juvenile detention/treatment center in Michigan. He enrolled in the doctor of educational leadership program at Central Michigan University and, Porath explains, upon completion of the coursework, he entered the dissertation phase eager and enthusiastic to earn the doctoral degree and advance his career. However, a three-year delay in the approval process for data he was interested in using, on top his mother's diagnosis with multiple sclerosis (MS) and quick decline, derailed his dissertation progress.

Today, both Verschaeve and Porath teach felons in a medium-security North Carolina state prison. They never expected part of their workday to include sally ports and pat downs. They never envisioned their classes being interrupted by correctional officers performing inmate counts, nor did they think their classrooms would be completely devoid of internet access. But they both believe that the educational roadblocks in their lives, which often felt like personal failures, have resulted in fulfilling professional detours. The prison classroom is rewarding in ways that may not be immediately obvious to academic professionals "out in that world." Together, Verschaeve and Porath discuss why they were drawn to a career in education, what their paths looked like over the course of their twenty-plus-years of teaching, and how and why they began—and plan to continue—this gratifying teaching career behind bars.

Conclusion

Being an adjunct professor is hard, more soul crushing than most can imagine. Those who never go through it don't understand what it's like to be a freeway flyer across different states, to teach while sicker than a dog because there is no health insurance for folks like you, and to send hundreds of applications out into the void, only to hear nothing back 75 percent of the time. I admire the honesty and bravery of every narrative in this collection. I also understand what it is like to have a love/hate relationship with the field.

While I encourage students to follow their dreams and throw caution to the wind, I often feel like a hypocrite. If I had the chance to do it all over again, would I? My heart says yes, but my head says no. Hell to the no. It's simply too difficult. The hard truth is that tenured positions are diminishing at record speed. Few faculty members find their way into those positions, despite years of strong academic service and experience. The shame many feel about not being able to support themselves can be paralyzing, trapping non-tenure-track faculty in hopelessness and poverty. It robs them of time and energy to change their situations.

Will this collection provide all the answers? No. That text doesn't exist. Teaching is a deeply personal decision, and I wouldn't want to dissuade anyone from his/her dreams. But every adjunct should know this: it's not you. If you are struggling and feel invisible, know the system tends to eat its young, old, and everyone in-between. 1. So, know the field. Know what you are getting into on day one. 2. If you can unionize and strike, do so. If you hold any position of power and can help contingent faculty (with curriculum overhauls, administrative positions, online options, class schedules, and so on), speak up. Do so often. 3. Be cognizant that there are exit strategies. This is not a sign of defeat. It is simply the highest form of self-care.

At the end of the day, the new faculty majority are the backbone of every department. If they all walked out at the same time, every higher learning institution in the nation would be brought to its knees overnight. It's high time we hear them (*truly* listen to their valid concerns), support their emotional and financial well-being, and treat them with the respect and dignity they wholeheartedly deserve.

Works Cited

Berry, Joe. *Reclaiming the Ivory Tower: Organizing Adjuncts to Change Higher Education*. Monthly Review Press, 2005.

Bousquet, Marc. *How the University Works: Higher Education and the Low-Wage Nation*. New York UP, 2008.

Donhardt, Tracy, and Sarah Layden. "Adjuncts Foster Change: Improving Adjunct Working Conditions by Forming an Associate Faculty Coalition (AFC)." Kahn, Lalicker, and Lynch-Biniek, pp. 183–97.

Douglas-Gabriel, Danielle. "This Photo Essay Shows What It Really Means to Be Adjunct Faculty." *The Washington Post*, 24 Oct. 2016, https://www.washingtonpost.com/news/grade-point/wp/2016/10/24/this-photo-essay-shows-what-it-really-means-to-be-adjunct-faculty/.

"Facts about Adjuncts." *New Faculty Majority*, 2020, https://www.newfacultymajority.info/facts-about-adjuncts/.

Flaherty, Colleen. "The Gig Academy." *Inside Higher Ed*, 10 October 2019, https://www.insidehighered.com/news/2019/10/10/you%E2%80%99ve-heard-gig-economy-what-about-gig-academy.

Heitsch, Dorothea, Glenn Levine, and Karen Lentz Madison. "What You Can Do: A Position Paper by the MLA Committee on Contingent Labor in the Profession." *ADE Bulletin*, vol. 153, 2013, pp. 92–97. MAPS: MLA Academic Program Services, https://doi.org/10.1632/ade.153.92.

"History of COCAL." *Coalition of Contingent Academic Labor*, http://www.cocalinternational.org/about-us.html.

Jaschik, Scott. "When Colleges Rely on Adjuncts, Where Does the Money Go?" *Insider Higher Ed*, 5 Jan. 2017, https://www.insidehighered.com/news/2017/01/05/study-looks-impact-adjunct-hiring-college-spending-patterns.

Kahn, Seth, William B. Lalicker, and Amy Lynch-Biniek, editors. *Contingency, Exploitation, and Solidarity: Labor and Action in English Composition*. The WAC Clearinghouse/UP of Colorado, 2017. WAC Clearinghouse, https://doi.org/10.37514/PER-B.2017.0858.

Sanchez, Claudio. "The Sad Death of An Adjunct Professor Sparks a Labor Debate." *NPR*, 22 Sept. 2013, https://www.npr.org/2013/09/22/224946206/adjunct-professor-dies-destitute-then-sparks-debate.

Part I. The Struggle is Real/ Academia's Current Landscape

Once upon a time, as most dark fairy tales begin, being a college professor was considered a respectable job. In the 1960s–1970s, more than half of the faculty in public institutions were unionized, and part-time faculty only made up 20 percent of the faculty population (Bousquet 187, 201). These full-time lines also came with all the bells and whistles one would expect with six to eight years of higher education: office space, medical benefits, and retirement contributions. The future looked promising, even bright.

Today, academia's current landscape is grim. According to New Faculty Majority, citing data from the Department of Education, as of 2009, 75.5% of college faculty are now on renewable tracks, meaning "they have NO access to tenure." Of that percentage, 50% are part-time professors ("Facts about Adjuncts"). While they often carry heavy teaching loads in introductory courses, their wages are dismal, and insulting at best. Some are paid as little as $1,500 per course (Douglas-Gabriel), with the median pay being $2,700 ("Facts about Adjuncts"). The so-called new faculty majority, the very professors instructing your children, may quality for food stamps.

Part I of this collection shares vulnerable, behind-the-scenes looks at professors' experiences in the academic market, which has now been disrupted with the onset of the COVID-19 pandemic, disruption that has included hiring freezes, the closing of small college campuses across the nation, and restructuring of academic departments. The authors share their stories with brutal honesty. Some are funny. Some are tragic. All are worth hearing.

- In "The Shadow of the Adjunct," Michael Dubson, also the editor of *Ghosts in the Classroom: Stories of College Adjunct Faculty—and the Price We All Pay*, discusses the long-term effects of what it was like to be a career adjunct for 15 years, when he always carried fear. Fear of not getting work. Fear of enrollment declines. Fear of not gaining enough income to scrape by from one semester to the next. He chronicles the long-term effects of what this lifestyle does to academics.
- Jeff Dories, an assistant professor at Florida Institute of Technology, details his roller-coaster ride to full-time employment in "From Tenure Track to Unemployment in Six Months." He relays the often unseen and/or unspoken struggles of parents working in the humanities in academia, including long commutes from home, retrenching within higher education systems, and elimination of entire departments due to politics.
- "Becoming Lystrosaurus: Toxic Environments, Mass Extinctions, and Other Cautionary Tales for Academics" by Dustin Michael is a humorous

but somber take on a husband and wife (both with Ph.D.s in English) trying to find meaningful work in the same area. He states, "Academic jobs have to be open and posted, and even if you happen to beat the dozens and sometimes hundreds of other applicants for one of those, the hiring process takes a long time—half a year or more sometimes." In the meantime, bills and student loans are relentless. Someone or something must give.
- In "Adjunctivitis: The Plague of Academia," Marjorie Stewart highlights the freeway flyer experience and explains that when living this reality, "I had three book bags: a Monday/Wednesday/Friday bag, a Tuesday/Thursday bag, and a Wednesday night bag. If I pointed my car in the wrong direction and didn't realize it within a few miles, I was late for class." She did eventually land a tenure-track job after many ups and downs, but she's quick to note she was 57 years old when she did so.
- Lastly, Constance H. Gemson examines what happens when college departments simply disappear. Not only are adjunct professors left scrambling to teach at various campuses with no certainty of future assignments, but the rich interactions that students who would otherwise never meet in real life had with one another, including students of different ethnic and racial backgrounds, simply dissipate into thin air.

These tales are not meant to dissuade anyone from their dreams. The call to teaching is a passion, which often is not motivated by financial considerations. But make no mistake about it—the current academic landscape is changing to a contingent, disposable model, and not for the better of the educators or students. Those with idealistic notions of landing a tenure-track job right out of doctoral studies in the humanities, with a three- to five-page CV, are simply naïve. The system is broken.

Works Cited

Bousquet, Marc. *How the University Works: Higher Education and the Low-Wage Nation*. New York UP, 2008.

Douglas-Gabriel, Danielle. "This Photo Essay Shows What It Really Means to Be Adjunct Faculty." *The Washington Post*, 24 Oct. 2016, https://www.washingtonpost.com/news/grade-point/wp/2016/10/24/this-photo-essay-shows-what-it-really-means-to-be-adjunct-faculty/.

"Facts about Adjuncts." *New Faculty Majority*, https://www.newfacultymajority.info/facts-about-adjuncts/.

Chapter 1. The Shadow of the Adjunct

Michael Dubson
BUNKER HILL COMMUNITY COLLEGE

For 15 years, I was a career adjunct, and my constant companion was fear.

Adjuncts working full-time elsewhere, who only want adjunct work, or who continue to work after retirement may be subject to adjunct maltreatment, but because their economic and work situations are different, the maltreatment does not bring the same fear.

I walked hand-in-hand with fear every academic year. There was the fear of not getting enough work—enrollment declines or new full-time faculty (not me) would affect available classes. Because not enough work meant not enough income, I took everything offered—in case a course was cancelled or taken away. (Colleges will hire anybody to have a body in a classroom. If the teacher doesn't do well, tough bananas. Not re-hired!) But too much work could create other problems, such as a double-booked class meeting time at two different colleges or tight travel time between schools. What's worse? A breakneck commute or telling a department chair or dean you can't teach one of their classes?

There was the fear of not being re-hired (fired). The fear of some slight, real or imagined, by some administrator. The fear of getting bad course evaluations in one course after years of good ones. Or the fear of a real or trumped-up complaint from a student. It only took one to end my "tenure" at a college I had successfully worked at for years. Fear, like the overflowing boxes in the back of my car, the whirling numbers on my odometer (I wore out two cars driving in "Adjunct Land"), the fatigue from teaching eight classes a semester at four colleges, constant driving, constant grading, and seeking respect and validation in a profession that had ripped it away, was always there.

Then there were the ever-present existential fears. Another academic year and still traveling on the course contract road, plateaued in adjunct limbo. Still living paycheck to paycheck, worrying about rent, utilities, food. Worrying about health insurance, whether not having it or paying too much for it. Worrying about the future. Will I still be driving to multiple campuses in my 70s because I can't afford to retire? Another year older and still no better off. Another year of life—worrying about what I am doing, where I am going, what is going to become of me.

But fear was not my only constant companion. There was also abuse. Like fear, abuse took many forms. Snubbed by full-time faculty members in the hallway. They were in my department; they knew who I was. If I didn't speak first, they wouldn't speak. If I did speak first, many did not respond, or their response was perfunctory.

Abuse occurred when I accepted the "adjuncts always welcome" invitation to attend department or division meetings. I heard full-time faculty lament about "the adjuncts" teaching in the department, the implication being that we didn't know what we were doing and certainly were not achieving precious course objectives. When I shared my thoughts, whatever I said was ignored or dismissed by many of my full-time "colleagues." Eyes rolled, and snickers occurred. Someone even said, "What do you know? You're just an adjunct." Even when laughter and dismissal did not occur, I learned very quickly that I had no say in anything—whatever decisions were made, I was denied a voice.

Abuse came in promises not kept, or never intended to be kept. "Oh, yes, we would love to hire you full time." Love to, but I can't. Or, "We'll never hire you, so don't bother applying." Sometimes job openings actually occurred. I worked hard on that cover letter and résumé, feeling it reflected who I am, what I have done, what I can do. I sent it off enthusiastically. Then came the kiss-off letter from human resources. No interview—after working at the college for years and building up an impressive work record.

There were those occasions when I was called in for an interview. I sat and answered questions directed at me from full-time faculty members who knew me and my work. They picked over me like vulture over carrion and decided that my work record just couldn't compete with the 50-minute interview a sparkling outsider gave. The sparkling outsider(s) got the job(s). Another kiss-off letter from human resources, and another year on the adjunct trail—the wheels of my car rolling down the highway, spinning my fate, adding echoes to the existential chant. Why am I not getting hired full time? Why are fancy strangers so much better than I am? If I'm not good enough, why are they letting me teach in this school? Why am I not good enough? What is wrong with me?

These questions went unanswered, but other truths were crystal clear. As an adjunct, I worked for less than minimum wage. I worked with no safety net provided by my employer. Although I was sometimes called "part-time," I had more classes, more students, and more schoolwork than any full-time faculty member and very little support from the institutions where I worked. I was a member of the working poor, an academic migrant worker, an intellectual sweatshop factory slave. Yet I had advanced degrees awarded by these colleges, degrees that promise the way to professional and financial success, to the respect of others and to a full and fulfilling life. My college degrees didn't bring any of the above.

As a career adjunct, I experienced additional abuse above and beyond the norm. I learned to become hard and cold in order to survive. I was fired from one college because I was assigned a class I could not accept. I requested two Tuesday-Thursday morning classes, what I'd been teaching for years. I was assigned ONE 8:00 a.m. Monday-Wednesday-Friday morning class. MWF mornings were when I taught at other colleges, MWF morning classes I might not get back, work I couldn't afford to give up. When I told the chair I couldn't do the MWF class, she went ballistic. Not intellectual, not academic, not even an understanding liberal, she morphed into a howling monster. "Do you know how HARD I WORKED on this schedule?" she yowled. "If you don't do this class, YOU ARE OUT!" The only thing missing in this Hollywood producer cliché was an ugly, thick cigar clenched between her teeth.

At another school, I had a disruptive student who periodically threw tantrums and stormed out of class whenever she did not get her way. What she wanted or didn't want was never clear; tantrum time was unpredictable. This student was a 30-year-old woman and mother of a young boy. (Yikes!) Seeking support, I went to the dean who immediately took the student's side. The student's paroxysms were my fault because I had "lost control of the class." What of this student's responsibility for her own behavior? The other students were fine. I was not offered work for the next term. If I had been, I would have turned it down. Ironically, this was the first college that hired me after I sent out my post master's degree résumés.

A dean at a different college, who also offered me one of my first jobs, couldn't praise me enough throughout my first year. "Your students' work is so good!" she gushed at one portfolio grading session. When they hired their next full-time person, she promised it would be me. She even put that in a recommendation letter she wrote for me.

One year later, four jobs opened. I was interviewed twice but not hired. I asked this dean why she had promised me a job and not hired me. After a laundry list of petty grievances, she told me that I was not "smart enough" to teach at her college.

I was angered by this comment. This was her cruel way of backpedaling away from her high-to-Heaven praise and promise of a full-time job, and we both knew it wasn't true. Even though I was not "smart enough," I continued to get two, sometimes three, courses a semester. What bothered me the most was that I was unable to respond. She could have chalked it up to "insubordination," and that could have been it. This college was one of my major jobs, and I couldn't lose it—not with her as a reference. I had to silently swallow it.

I also had to silently swallow it when deans joked about how adjuncts were freeway flyers, gypsy teachers, road scholars, and campus nomads; when I accepted prorated pay for an under enrolled class—though colleges easily recover the money of a full salary from fully enrolled courses; when a full and waitlisted class was taken from me and given to a full-time faculty member whose classes did not fill.

My final account of abuse is the worst and representative of the dumpster fires that are being passed off as colleges in this country. I was offered a journalism class, from which I was to produce a newspaper of student work. The department chair knew I had substantial newspaper experience. The offer included a sweet, albeit hypothetical, promise. If the newspaper succeeded, a journalism department might be created, and I would become its full-time director. Why did I do this? I had been a career adjunct for almost ten years; I was desperate to get a permanent position. This roulette wheel of a chance was worth spinning.

However, I was given no office, no computers, no telephone, no staff, and no budget. In the class, we discussed journalism, journalistic standards and news, and feature and editorial articles. The students created a considerable body of work, but neither the department chair nor any administrator offered me any resources to do a newspaper. One day, I ran into the college vice president. "How's that newspaper coming?" he demanded expectantly. He did not ask if I had everything to make this miracle happen. He knew there were no resources. Nevertheless, somehow, I was to produce a newspaper. I had become the miller's daughter from *Rumpelstiltskin*. Produce gold from straw; I didn't even get any straw.

I should've told them to give me resources and support or forget it. That would have been the end of it. I would not have been re-hired . . . and the hypothetical full-time director of a journalism program would never happen. So, I typed the articles on my home computer, on my own time, then took that to the school's copy center. It wasn't a newspaper, but it was a publication. The department chair was delighted. The distributed copies were gobbled up by the students. So, we did a second issue. Then I asked the administration for funding. The reply was swift: "The college will not support this publication because it is not of professional quality." But it was not of professional quality because the college hadn't supported it!

The fall semester ended; I was offered the same journalism class in the spring, with the expectation of continuing the publication. Having not learned my lesson, I agreed to teach it. I enjoyed working with the students' writing, enjoyed seeing the pleasure and the pride they experienced in seeing their words in a publication distributed college wide. We did one more photocopy version, and then I went to the administration again to ask for money. This time they said yes.

Our final publication was a slick, beautiful book. The cover was in the school colors with a comb spine. Once distributed around campus, like its primitive counterpart, the book went like hotcakes. Then the school refused to pay the printing bill. The printer filed a lawsuit against the college and threatened to file one against me. The school sent me a registered letter telling me that I was responsible for the $2,000 bill. I went to the union; the bill was paid immediately.

The administration did not want a student newspaper. They wanted to toss some bones to the students, and when nothing, or nothing of quality, was produced, they could blame me. And the full-time job as director of a journalism program—a lost fantasy. I left this toxic waste dump.

Semesters rolled on. Soon, I'd been a career adjunct for 15 years. There had been so many interviews, so many "pass overs" for a "real" job, it wasn't worth applying anymore. Nevertheless, I did—applications, interviews, not hired. Adjunct teaching was all I would ever have. I would have to settle for teaching 16 classes a year. I would have to prepare for my own retirement. I would have to find other sources of recognition and fulfillment.

And then . . . I finally landed a full-time job. After a May 15 interview, I expected ye old adjunct backstab. Instead, I was called in for an interview with the vice president on July 3. Producing a paper, he grandly announced, "Your starting salary will be. . . ."

I had crossed the great divide. No longer adjunct, now full time. I was thrilled, speechless, incredulous. My name would be in the school catalog, on an office door, and in the course schedule next to my classes. I was real, I existed, I mattered. My full-time job began September 1, 2006, a monumental day in my life.

Because I had given up on this ever happening, this job was one I almost didn't apply for. At this school, I had already been through five other applications and three interviews. Just before the closing date, I applied. I put enough best feet forward into my letter and résumé to be a centipede, and when I got passed over this time, I was going to make sure to let them know they'd passed over one damn good candidate who could have done so much and been so much, someone who could have brought so much to the college and the campus life. Except I wasn't passed over.

Everything was so different after that. Immediately, I was caught up in the swirling world of campus life. I became the advisor of two student clubs. I developed two new courses. I was welcomed in department and division meetings, and I was no longer dismissed as irrelevant or inferior, even when I said the same things I'd said before. Full-time faculty members who formerly snubbed or dismissed me now warmly welcomed me.

Within a year, I was the chair of the academic affairs committee. I was elected to be the speaker at the end of the semester honors ceremony. I was awarded a citation for outstanding performance. In my fourth year, I was invited to join a national research project sponsored by the Bill and Melinda Gates Foundation. I went from assistant professor to associate professor to full professor. I was awarded tenure in 2012. My employment status had changed and my life with it. These were experiences an adjunct would never have.

Something that did not change was adjunct contempt. At statewide union meetings, I saw adjunct faculty derided and dismissed as they put forth inevitably voted down proposals. When I served on search committees, I saw how internal adjunct candidates were treated. In one case, three previously hired sparkling outsiders adamantly opposed the candidacy of an internal adjunct who had worked at the college for ten years. "This person isn't going to know how to work with our students," they all said. How could someone who had worked with our students for ten years not know how to work with our students? At department meetings, there was the familiar lament about "the adjuncts" teaching courses the wrong way, as if they were in classrooms on the moon.

Something else did not change. The fear. I had a six-year climb to tenure. During the first three years, I could be dismissed without cause and dismissed with cause in the second three years. I was terrified of being found wanting and fired. Therefore, I was afraid to say no to anything asked of me. Because I was afraid to say no, I said yes to everything. What would happen if I couldn't manage everything, made mistakes, screwed up, lost control? Sometimes I even feared that, as a former adjunct activist, I had been hired only to silence me, and they were going to dump me after a year or two—after I had abandoned my other adjunct jobs and lost the position I had in those colleges.

After tenure, the fear began to recede, and I comfortably hit cruising altitude until I was appointed director of an academic program at the college. I worked under an unsupportive, know-nothing, hands all-over-the-place dean, which became one of the worst experiences of my working life. The dean WAS the director, and I her administrative assistant. She was unreasonably demanding, condescending, and often outright abusive. She loved to have meetings and talk everything to death, but there was no continuity from one meeting to the next.

Decisions were made about the program by the administration. I was neither consulted nor informed until after the fact. My own ideas and vision for this program were ignored, dismissed, or mocked. The dean presented herself and the upper administrators as a court judging me and finding me wanting. When everything was at its most impossible, I went to the union. The chapter president at that time directed a program that was also under the auspices of this dean—a major, immobilizing conflict of interest. The union president gave me advice but offered no intervention on my behalf.

I didn't handle this well. As a tenured, full professor, I could have stood my ground from the beginning. I am the director; I could have said, "*You* are here to support *me*, not the other way around," and called her out on every act of abuse. But as this nightmare began, a great, dark shadow fell upon me, taking me totally by surprise. The shadow of the adjunct. It was as if I had traveled back in time. Suddenly, I was a powerless, poorly paid faculty member sitting across from an all-powerful, well-paid dean, and I just had to take what was dealt. And if I didn't—the fear of being fired surfaced, from the program, from the school. I have been told how difficult it is, if not impossible, to fire a tenured professor, but I've never tested that—not out of capriciousness and not when there were real things worth fighting for, but because of the adjunct fear. I resigned from the directorship. In 20/20 hindsight, this was a mistake, but staying and fighting would have been a stressful, difficult experience, and as I had been repeatedly told, "This is not *your* program, Mike."

I have never felt the same about my college, the college leadership, my job, or my place in this school after this experience. I'd had gotten a bird's eye look into the soul of my college, and what I saw horrified me. The irony of it all is that when I was an adjunct and had this experience many times, I could stay on the periphery of the school and easily find other jobs. As a full-time faculty member, when the bottom fell out, I was trapped in a hopeless, negative place.

This past year of teaching remotely has been the worst. Isolated, working at home without colleagues or support, being at the mercy of technology with a mind of its own, feeling the distance between me and my students, experiencing the increased rudeness and demands of students, noticing an increase in student complaints and my fear of complaints, and feeling like I just wasn't doing a very good job, the shadow of the adjunct was always there every day. I constantly expected the certified letter telling me I was through.

Do I regret following this path? I graduated from a community college, and because of that, I wanted to teach in a community college. I went to college and to graduate school pursuing this goal. I was thrilled when I was a TA in grad school, then when I was teaching my own class and, finally, being out there, master degreed, teaching. Despite the adjunct status, pay, and abuse, I believed I was doing something of value and something I truly enjoyed. I knew I would have to work as an adjunct for a few years, but I never thought it would be 15 years. I've gotten everything I wanted; I am one of the "lucky" ones. I do wish I had known then what I know now. I would have planned and prepared accordingly. If I had not gone into teaching, who and where would I be today? I could be much better off; I could be much worse off. It is "The Road Not Taken."

The survival of the U.S. higher education system rides on the backs of adjunct faculty, who teach the majority of classes. Yet, adjunct faculty receive the poorest pay, the lowest status, and the worst treatment. These are evils adjuncts share with those in other professions who are paid poorly and treated badly, yet they are the essential workers who keep the system running and the corporate profits coming. This is the nature of greed, economic exploitation, and economic terrorism, the green slime of Christian capitalism.

Many overpaid administrators are out of touch with the work of teaching and the needs of students. Many are only interested in their own careers, their own power, their own perks, and in building up their résumé while hiring more administrators whose six figure salaries drain school budgets. Ultimately, many administrators sail off to another job, leaving behind a smoking ruin that another administrator will have to fix.

While colleges continue to treat adjuncts poorly, administrators on every level continue to spout liberal platitudes about fairness, workers' rights, respect, kindness, decency—you name it. The stream of liberal humanitarian sentiment flows eternally, perpetually hypocritical as the liars and the cruel continue to run the henhouse.

Is the problem funding? If so, then government and academic leaders, who profess how important education and students really are, need to find support for colleges so the majority of classes won't be taught by overworked, underpaid, stressed out, abused adjunct faculty. But it isn't about funding. There is always money for more administrators and administrator raises when there is no money to hire new full-time faculty and when union contract negotiations drag on for years. This is about the lopsided power of the haves vs. the have-nots, the desire to divide the faculty from each other, to create a frightened, powerless underclass, to corrupt higher education, so it lurches farther away from the ideals and values the leaders continue to profess.

Today, I have been full time longer than I have been adjunct. Nevertheless, the insecurities and fears that developed from years of adjunct abuse live on. And I continue to cringe as a tenured, full professor beneath the shadow of the adjunct.

Chapter 2. From Tenure Track to Unemployment in Six Months

Jeff Dories
Florida Institute of Technology

My first full-time teaching job was at a public university in Pennsylvania. It paid well. I was able to walk to work and maintain a strong family life. In February of 2014, I was given a contract for the 2014–15 school year. Then, in May of 2014, I was sent a letter that the university had cancelled my contract due to "unforeseen budget factors." Fifteen other full-time contingent faculty were also let go at the same time. It became clear to me then that faculty contracts are only written with one party in mind—the university.

The public university in Pennsylvania reassigned the classes from full-time contingent faculty to graduate students who would work for much lower pay. Nationwide, universities pay 80 percent less for adjunct instructors and graduate student labor than for full-time, tenure-track faculty (Bettinger and Long 598). Because of this, it is not a surprise that contingent faculty are frequently replaced by lower-wage adjuncts. However, this practice often starkly contrasts with extravagant spending in other parts of the university, from construction projects to high-paid administrators and management.

Throughout my time teaching at this public university in Pennsylvania, news articles regularly described the profligate spending on things like driveway lighting, flowers, and other personal expenses by the president of the university (for example, Guza and Wojcik). The campus was also undergoing massive construction projects, including new privatized dorms, at a time that the number of students was decreasing because of demographic trends. As I left my office on my final day of employment, I passed a million-dollar marble staircase that had just been built. I also passed a tour group as the guide was bragging to parents that the university had over "90 percent full-time faculty." I thought to myself, *not anymore*. In the seven years since I left this school, it has eliminated over 200 full-time faculty jobs through retrenchment and by not replacing professors who have left (Gardner). At the time of this writing, the school remains in a financial crisis with many more jobs at stake.

Losing my job at this public university in Pennsylvania resulted in difficulties that reverberated throughout my personal life. Because I was laid off in May, I was unable to secure a position for that fall due to the short time before the start of the fall semester. Luckily, my spouse had a steady job, but that also meant my job search was location-bound. Because we could no longer afford childcare, we made the decision that I would focus on searching for academic jobs and caring for our children rather than taking a job outside of academia. I spent most of those days searching and applying for jobs, making lunch for the kids, changing diapers, and trying to avoid depression about submitting over 100 applications without any success. In most cases, I did not even receive an email rejection from the colleges. The applications merely disappeared into a void.

My experience of struggling with balancing an academic job with family life and then having a job search with family obligations is common. Nationwide, according to a Harvard University Graduate School of Education Collaborative on Academic Careers in Education (COACHE) survey, 52.6 percent of faculty members are parents, and 12.3 percent are "caregivers for a dependent adult" (qtd. in Mathews). And, according to the COACHE survey, 40 percent of women and 32 percent of men who are parents "somewhat disagree" or "strongly disagree" with the statement, "My institution does what it can to make personal/family obligations (e.g. childcare or eldercare) and an academic career compatible" (qtd. in Mathews [table]). Balancing work with family obligations is often difficult in academic careers. This difficulty is compounded by other challenges adjuncts face including the pressures of an academic job search. Personally, I found myself regularly struggling with guilt for either spending too much or too little time on my job search or with my family.

At first, as I stayed home, I felt lucky. I was able to be with my children at an important time of their childhood. I had security that many adjuncts do not have—a spouse with a good job. Though, after a few months, we realized the situation would be more difficult than we had originally thought. My student loan companies would not allow me to consolidate my loans, nor would they let me defer them, so we ended up in severe economic trouble. I had to cash in my small retirement savings from the public university in Pennsylvania and take out three different personal loans that would take five to six years to pay off. This created extreme financial and emotional stress. Many adjunct and contingent faculty members face a similar struggle balancing student loans with the low wages from their employment.

My family also struggled with health-related bills. While we had health insurance through my spouse's job, we could no longer afford the copays, prescription costs, and deductibles because of my lost salary. Because of this, some of my health problems that need maintenance quickly deteriorated. Struggling with obtaining healthcare coverage is common among those employed as contingent and adjunct labor. According to a press release by the American Federation of Teachers (AFT) that detailed a survey the organization conducted, "fewer than half of survey respondents have access to employer-provided health insurance; nearly 20 percent rely on Medicaid," and, similar to my predicament, "about 45 percent of faculty surveyed have put off getting needed healthcare, including mental healthcare" ("'Army of Temps'"). Over time, often these neglected health issues compound, leading to increasingly worse outcomes. Many contingent faculty end up leaving the field as a result of health difficulties, being a caregiver, and other health-related financial stress.

These problems are widespread in higher education. Contingent and adjunct faculty often do not have job security, lack benefits, and are regularly paid wages that do not support basic living expenses. According to the AFT survey of contingent and adjunct college faculty, "41 percent struggle with job security, reporting that they don't know if they will have a teaching job until one month before the beginning of the academic year," and 75 percent do not know if they will have employment from one term to the next ("'Army of Temps'"). Job insecurity has been proven to have negative impacts on mental health, physical health, and general social well-being (Menéndez-Espina et al.). With contingent faculty in a constant state of physical and emotional stress, often this impacts all areas of their personal and professional lives.

After an extensive job search, I was able to secure my second full-time contingent teaching job at a private university in Pennsylvania. It was two-and-a-half hours away from home, but my spouse and I agreed it was too good of an opportunity to turn down. After being hired, I learned that the branch campus where I was employed was under threat of closure. Because of this new information, my spouse did not relocate to the area. With two small children, this created many problems. We raced to find childcare, transportation, and a small apartment to rent near the new school. This created a lot of unexpected costs. At one point, because of these unexpected expenses, I determined that my family would have been better off financially if I had worked at a minimum wage job closer to home. Because, like many in the teaching profession, I had a passion for being in the classroom, my family made many sacrifices for me to continue teaching.

This job at the private university was the most difficult and the most rewarding job of my career. There was a hiring freeze at the branch campus where I worked. Because of this, every time an employee left the university, the rest of the faculty and staff pitched in to make up for the loss. At one point, the academic dean was doing the job of four people who had left for other jobs. Many contingent professors, including myself, regularly served on three to four academic committees, advised, supervised clubs, helped with orientation, tutored, and had many other duties as well. Most of us were thankful to have a teaching job, so we served in any way that we could in order to retain our jobs.

Personally, I ended up working 25 or more hours a week with service-based assignments on top of my teaching schedule. This did not leave much time for professional development. While I am proud that I did maintain a research agenda throughout this period, my output paled in comparison to other faculty members who did not have extensive teaching and service expectations. Also, because of the school's financial problems, younger professors were given the title "visiting" even though we were considered full-time continuing professors. This allowed the university to pay us less money and to easily eliminate our positions at any point. The "visiting" title also served as a place marker of when we were hired. Many of the "visiting" professors had terminal degrees, extensive research experience, and more teaching experience than some permanent faculty; however, because of when we were hired, we were given this status as temporary.

It would not be until years later, with some reflection, that I realized how difficult this experience at the private university had been. I was passionate about the service assignments I was given. As chair of the campus' committee on diversity and inclusion, I was able to work with students and colleagues to create a more equitable college on many levels. I regularly volunteered as a tutor in the campus' learning center and frequently stayed beyond my required hours to help students. I was on other committees that did valuable work, served on the faculty senate, and regularly advised 20 or more students each semester. I truly loved this work. However, teaching a 5-4 load on top of these service assignments and working two-and-a-half hours from home impacted my physical health, mental health, and family life. Overall, I am thankful to have had the experience, but it was a costly one in many ways.

The job at this private university ended up lasting for five years. In my fifth year, the school decided to essentially eliminate the liberal arts. All liberal arts classes would be transitioned to distance learning or farmed out to a community college consortium. This meant my position would be eliminated. Even though this was a difficult ending, given the circumstances, the university treated us relatively well. The university gave us one-and-a-half years' notice of the transition and a small payout at the end of our contract. Cynical colleagues viewed this as an attempt to prevent lawsuits. However, given my experience at my first university of being fired after signing a contract, I knew that universities have no obligation to give contingent faculty advance notice or a payout. While the payout seemed generous for someone who had served five years like me, for those who had worked 30 years and were near retirement, it seemed like a small consolation.

Once again, I entered the job market. After filling out over 100 applications, the call that I had been waiting for came—a tenure-track job interview. A few weeks later, in March 2020, I was offered a tenure-track job near St. Louis. Then, within days, the country began shutting down because of the COVID-19 virus. I received a phone call from the school explaining that they were still planning on hiring me, but the paperwork would have to wait until they had a better picture of the impact of COVID-19. From March until July, the phone calls were the same— *We need you. Every person on campus is still committed to hiring you. We are just waiting for the governor to approve some educational funds.*

While my family and I were waiting for the contract, we were fixing up our house to put it up for sale, packing, and looking for houses in the St. Louis area. At the same time, I was teaching online and trying to negotiate problems associated with the pandemic. My spouse and I were helping our kids with online school, checking out schools in the St. Louis area for our kids, talking with our kids about the move, and trying to make sure they were doing well throughout the pandemic. Then, in July, the final call came—the school in St. Louis retracted the job offer because of COVID-19. We were devastated and relieved at the same time. While we were extremely disappointed about the loss of the job, we were relieved that we would not have to move in the middle of a pandemic.

This experience of losing a job due to the pandemic was not unique to me. According to Dan Bauman, writing in *The Chronicle of Higher Education* in April 2021 and citing U.S. Department of Labor statistics, "Since the World Health Organization declared a pandemic in March of 2020, institutions of higher education have shed a net total of at least 570,000 workers. . . . Put another way, for every nine workers employed in academe in February 2020, at least one had lost or left that job a year later." As a different article from *The Chronicle of Higher Education* noted in February 2021, "Colleges have lost about 12 percent of their workers nationwide during the pandemic" (Gardner). Experiences like my own, having a job offer retracted, are more difficult to quantify. However, it is clear that these retractions happened frequently as well. Many social media accounts, as well as podcasts, chronicled these experiences, including the podcasts *Teaching in Higher Ed* with Bonni Stachowiak and *The Professor Is In* with Karen Kelsky. Kelsky, on behalf of *The Professor Is In*, posted to *Twitter* on the subject multiple times, with hundreds of replies from professors who had job offers retracted.

Even though it was July when I lost the tenure-track job offer in St. Louis, I was lucky enough to find employment on a contingent basis for the following fall at another public university in Pennsylvania. While teaching at this university, I encountered struggles similar to those faculty were facing all over the country. However, because I was in a contingent position at this university, often the challenges were more difficult. For example, for most of the summer, the faculty at this school were told to expect to be teaching in person for the fall semester, although, because of the pandemic, we anticipated being moved online at any time. Because of this situation, all new faculty members were expected to take a four-week class focused on teaching online. What I did not learn until later was that we were not compensated for taking this class. While I could understand this being a part of the service expectation for tenure-track faculty members, for those of us who were only teaching for a semester or two, it seemed reasonable to expect compensation.

Unfortunately, the enrollment at this second public university decreased in the spring, so there were no classes for me to teach that semester. In a little over six months, I went from having a tenure-track job offer to negotiating unemployment. My experience is not unusual. I have many colleagues and friends who have had it much worse. The problem is that struggle, instability, student loan debt, and lack of healthcare coverage are the norm for most contingent labor. Currently, contingent faculty members are the core of the university; under current conditions, universities cannot run without this labor force. Unfortunately, contingent faculty are often invisible and expendable.

After six months of being unemployed, I began looking for jobs outside of academia. I spent a lot of time researching how to make a living through freelance writing. I was excited about and fearful of this prospect. I knew that I could make some money through writing, but I did not think it would be enough to support our family. Regularly, I would waver back and forth from excitement about the possible change in career to sadness about leaving academia. I would get angry at myself for spending so much time on a Ph.D. and putting my family into incredible debt, only to be forced out of the profession. However, I had started to come to terms with this transition. In many ways, I experienced each of the stages of grief throughout this experience.

Then, in May of 2021, I received another important phone call. It was from a private university in Florida. After I had viewed my academic career as dead, I now had a job interview. Academic job interviews are normally stressful. This stress was compounded by the pandemic. I had spent the previous year teaching on Zoom and isolating with my family, so the idea of flying, interviewing in person, and doing a presentation and a teaching demonstration was unnerving. After a long process, I was hired for a continuing position.

While my story at the private university in Florida is just beginning, I find myself hopeful and fearful. In the pre-COVID-19 era, academic jobs were already precarious. Now, they are even more so. I am conflicted thinking about my friends and colleagues who are still struggling as adjuncts. Most of them have worked just as hard as I have. Many of them have a more impressive curriculum vitae. Yet, they are still struggling. I find myself thankful for my position and feeling guilty about their struggle. While my current job has more stability than my previous positions, it is still contingent. Because of this, already I have been struggling with how to balance advocacy for adjunct and contingent labor with maintaining my current position. It is an invisible and unclear line to negotiate. Only time will tell if I can do it well.

Works Cited

"'Army of Temps' Report Reveals Grave Plight of Contingent College Faculty." *American Federation of Teachers*, 20 Apr. 2020, https://www.aft.org/press-release/army-temps-report-reveals-grave-plight-contingent-college-faculty.

Bauman, Dan. "Here's Who Was Hit Hardest by Higher Ed's Pandemic-Driven Job Losses." *The Chronicle of Higher Education*, 19 Apr. 2021, https://www.chronicle.com/article/heres-who-was-hit-hardest-by-higher-eds-pandemic-driven-job-losses.

Bettinger, Eric P., and Bridget Terry Long. "Does Cheaper Mean Better? The Impact of Using Adjunct Instructors on Student Outcomes." *The Review of Economics and Statistics*, vol. 92, no. 3, Aug. 2010, pp. 598–613. *MIT Press Direct*, https://doi.org/10.1162/REST_a_00014.

Gardner, Lee. "The Great Contraction: Cuts Alone Will Not Be Enough to Turn Colleges' Fortunes Around." *The Chronicle of Higher Education*, 15 Feb. 2021, https://www.chronicle.com/article/the-great-contraction.

Guza, Megan, and Andrew Wojcik. "Atwater's Personal Expenses Exceed $1.6 million Over Five Years." *The HawkEye*, 23 Apr., 2010. https://thehawkeyeonlinenews.wordpress.com/2010/04/23/atwaters_personal_expenses_exc/.
Kelsky, Karen [@ProfessorIsIn]. *Twitter*, https://twitter.com/ProfessorIsIn.
Mathews, Kiernan. "Childcare for Faculty: The Babar in the Room." *Blog*, Harvard Graduate School of Education Collaborative on Academic Careers in Higher Education, 10 Aug. 2020, https://coache.gse.harvard.edu/blog/childcare-faculty-babar-room.
Menéndez-Espina, Sara, et al. "Job Insecurity and Mental Health: The Moderating Role of Coping Strategies from a Gender Perspective." *Frontiers in Psychology*, vol. 10, 2019. *Frontiers*, https://doi.org/10.3389/fpsyg.2019.00286.
The Professor Is In, hosted by Karen Kelsky. https://theprofessorisin.com/podcast/.
Teaching in Higher Ed, hosted by Bonni Stachowiak. https://teachinginhighered.com/episodes/.

Chapter 3. Becoming Lystrosaurus: Toxic Environments, Mass Extinctions, and Other Cautionary Tales for Academics

Dustin Michael
SAVANNAH STATE UNIVERSITY

There are basically two kinds of species: specialists and generalists. Generalists come equipped with a set of evolutionary adaptations with broad applications, and they can eat a lot of different types of things and withstand a broad range of environmental conditions. They will do anything to stay alive and are more resistant to extinction than specialists, who usually have one or two highly advanced adaptations that can be used only for a single purpose. Because specialists often can live only in certain types of places and eat certain kinds of food, they are highly vulnerable to extinction; they will starve if they can't eat what they want.

~~~

My wife, Neesha, is about to lose her job. She has a Ph.D. in English. Her specialty is creative nonfiction memoir. She's brilliant, efficient, professional, and fair, but she and a bunch of other professors who teach at the school where I teach are on contracts that cannot be renewed past three years. It isn't the school's fault, necessarily. My wife knew from the beginning this was going to happen. Also, it isn't just this one school. It's like this all over. Still, there's a certain coldness to it, the idea that even though this highly qualified and diligent person's performance reviews and student evaluations are consistently excellent, she's going to be let go in less than a month because that's what her contract says has to happen, and in the fall, she will be replaced by a new professor who will get to teach here for three years before being let go, regardless of how well he or she does.

And apparently this is sort of the thing now. It's happening more and more. You show them your Ph.D., and they give you a contract that's like a camping permit. After three years, they kick you out, you pack up your tent and go to the school across town, maybe camp there for three years, then they kick you out, you pack up, and come back. The teaching diet on this lifelong camping trip is invariably freshman composition. Neesha never complains about her rations. It's almost as if she's forgotten she's a specialist.

~~~

I've been thinking a lot about specialists and generalists, about animals that survive extinctions. Inevitably, that thinking leads to an animal called Lystrosaurus.

Lystrosaurus was not a dinosaur—it lived before the dinosaurs—but it *was* a generalist. Two hundred fifty million years ago in the Permian period when it arrived on the scene, it must have looked like the biggest dork—a chunky little doofus with teeny tiny hips and hind legs that packed gigantic Popeye forelimbs and with a face like a bucktoothed landscaping tool that tapered into a beak for shearing tough vegetation. Lystrosaurus probably got picked on, pushed around, and eaten all the time, and with no known natural defenses—no quills or armor, no claws or horns, or chomping teeth, or venom, or size, or speed—there wasn't a lot that Lystrosaurus could do about that.

All Lystrosaurus could do, really, was to keep doing its thing and hope that maybe everybody else on the planet would suddenly die, which, of course, happened, because the Earth's atmosphere turned to poison gas at the end of the Permian period, and, maybe due to its ability to dig holes or breathe underground or eat whatever plants were left, Lystrosaurus, the dork, suddenly ruled the entire world.

~~~

In my current position (which is slightly more permanent than the one with the three-year contract Neesha has, but which is by no means a sure thing), I was hired to be a generalist, to live low to the ground, to eat whatever happens to be available, to be ugly. This was not what I had imagined for myself in grad school. I went to grad school on a fellowship to specialize in creative nonfiction, specifically the personal essay, and I quickly transformed into a cuddly little personal essay writing koala who envisioned a future spent swaying lazily in branches of some private liberal arts college and teaching two creative nonfiction courses a semester with plenty of free time to write and enough money left come summertime to take my wife and kids on vacation.

This was delusion. From inside the sealed bubble of my doctoral program, I was unaware that the atmosphere outside had turned to poison. I hadn't noticed that almost every other creature like the one I had become had walked off the graduation stage, drawn a labored, wheezing breath, and then crawled to the edge of the campus to die a slow, gasping death at the fringes of an endless job market wasteland.

~~~

Sometimes, when dealing with matters regarding academia, there is a disconnect between expectation and reality. For instance, I can report there is never any time to write. I am currently teaching five face-to-face courses and one online course. There is a lot of grading. This is the first essay I've written in years, and I am writing it on my phone in the free seconds between answering emails, force-feeding my four-year-old, and trying to stop my other two kids from crushing themselves with furniture. As for summers off, to all teachers except for a select few, the phrase evokes terrible ambivalence because while yes, summers off means a break from the teaching and grading, it also means no paycheck from May until September.

It is a time for burrowing underground, lying still, and taking only very small sips of air. For those on the tenure track, or for me, anyway, it is sometimes possible to teach up to two classes during summer break, but for the most part, "summers off" means I get to tell the people at my second job that they can schedule me for more hours through the week for three straight months. I get to say to a person who is only slightly older than my students, "My availability is wide open, dude. Load me up."

~~~

Some paleontologists speculate that the proliferation of Lystrosaurus into the most abundant and widespread animal to ever have walked the Earth was due to nothing more than dumb luck—that it just happened to plod into conditions that were welcoming to it but deadly to everything else.

~~~

When I first became an English major, nobody told me what my new life would be like, but I should have known something was up with the field from how badly all the faculty in the English department seemed to want me to be there. I was an unremarkable, undeclared sixth-year senior who had just walked out of the college of education after a dismal program assessment exam and a lackluster set of teaching evaluations. I needed to declare a new major, and the only two stars guiding my course at that point were "something I already had some credits in" and "something that didn't require any math."

I'd taken a bunch of literature and writing courses because the professors teaching them were mostly laid-back and cool—except for a couple who were dicks—and anyway I thought I could mostly avoid the ones who were dicks and just take a couple of more courses and graduate, so I strolled on over to the English department in my flip-flops and asked if I could be an English major, please. This was a crumbling department that could barely afford toner for its decrepit copier, but if there had been any money in the budget for champagne and balloon drops, they would have burned through every cent that day.

In the background of all this, a massive budgetary shortfall at the university had necessitated the closure of a bunch of programs. These were the George W. Bush years, the first extinction pulse in what would be seen later as a great dying. Whole departments faced annihilation—big programs that before then everyone had assumed were some of the load-bearing beams holding the university up: philosophy, French, geological sciences. Deans and department chairs were told they had to justify their existence with numbers. The English department was at DEFCON 1. Any newly declared major, no matter how stupid, meant a decrease in the likelihood that the whole department would be dissolved and all the faculty would be shitcanned.

Right after I signed the English major declaration form, the chair of the English department high-fived me. It would be the last time I would receive a high-five from a chair of an English department, although, sadly, not the last time I would offer a high-five to the chair of an English department. Pro tip: English department chairs are much stingier with their high-fives when you're on the faculty.

~~~

Lystrosaurus did not high-five English department chairs. Lystrosaurus laid low, stayed out of everyone's way, and tried not to be killed and eaten. Lystrosaurus dug itself a hole, took tiny little breaths, and hunkered down while 96 percent of life on Earth choked volcanic ash and methane gas—a great strategy for success, and one I've adopted as my own in faculty meetings.

I was telling one of my classes about my strong admiration for Lystrosaurus recently when a student exclaimed, "It's like the honey badger!" I nodded eagerly, and we high-fived, the student not being the chair of an English department. In truth, though, he was wrong. Lystrosaurus was not like the honey badger. Although the honey badger is a generalist like Lystrosaurus, the honey badger does whatever it wants. Lystrosaurus did whatever it had to.

~~~

Before I was allowed to graduate as an English major, I was required to sit with a career counselor and discuss job opportunities and my future. The woman behind the desk opened a binder to the word "English" and told me I could be anything I wanted to be.

"You can do anything with an English major," she told me. "Maybe you'll be a journalist or something." She stamped my form and sent me out the door.

Now, as my wife neared the end of her three-year term and we stood on the threshold of financial apocalypse, I paused to wonder what other English majors' lives are like and whether anyone with this degree has really gone on to do "anything." I took out my phone and zipped off a request to my English major friends asking them to check in and report what jobs their degrees had allowed them to get.

More than 60 responses poured in over the next few hours, and I have to say I was surprised. I expected a lot of them to say they were unemployed or receiving income assistance, but only one did. Some said they were working part-time jobs in retail, and several wrote that they had recently returned to school to pursue different or advanced degrees. If the responses were arranged like a solar system, the central star being "English degree," then there would be large planets consisting of middle school and high school English teachers and college professors; medium planets consisting of editors, copyeditors, copywriters, writing center staff, and librarians; small planets consisting of office managers, consultants, accountants, and insurance salespeople; and a vast asteroid belt of other kinds of careers: software developer, bookstore owner, storage facility manager, equipment technician, costume designer for film and TV, paralegal.

It was by no means a comprehensive survey, but it prompted some considerations. First, conspicuously absent from the results were journalists. Among my friends, it appears, the English major-turned-journalist is extinct. Second, the English major's range is global. The posts came from Japan, Korea, Europe, and all over the US, representing a snapshot of a vast English major diaspora. Third—and I only note this because of my theory that almost every English major secretly fantasizes about writing a bestselling novel—no one in my little survey was making a living writing books.

~~~

On weekends, I work my side hustle. I sling books at a big-box bookstore. Recently, as I was punching out for my lunch break, I asked my boss how many books the store could hold.

"What do you mean, how many can it hold?" she asked.

"You know," I said, "like, if I were to shelve a book in every possible place in this whole store, how many would there be?"

My boss raised an eyebrow. "What is this for?" she asked.

"Nothing," I said, physically feeling the minutes of my break passing, each one high-fiving me in the face as it went. "I'm just curious."

Another long moment passed.

"Would you say," I tried, "that there are about a million books here?"

Slowly, my boss nodded.

"Awesome," I said. "Thanks."

According to one reliable source then, the bookstore where I work has a capacity of about a million books. Each year, according to several online sources, more than 300,000 new titles are released. That means that stocking one copy of each new title released each year would fill my entire store in less than three years—and that's not counting all the books that are already in print—not the four bays of shelves just for Bibles, not the *Iliad* or Ellison or Twain or the 66 individual James Patterson titles that each have multiple copies. And next year, there will be more than 300,000 more new titles. And the year after that. And the year after that.

During a slow moment at the customer service kiosk in that same shift, I did a few quick searches for authors I knew—anybody I knew who had ever published a book. Between my store and the nearest one—which are the two biggest bookstores for hundreds of miles—I found exactly one copy of one book by one person I knew, written by the professor who directed my doctoral dissertation. The book is a literary journalism exploration of antique collecting. We stock it because we have an "antiques" section and, there being very few books about antique collecting, pulling the book would leave a hole on the shelf.

~~~

All throughout my studies in English—through undergraduate, master's, and doctoral coursework—I was mysteriously content to not know what my life would be like once I had the degrees I was working toward. The only reason I can conceive of for this is that my professors were too overworked and distracted to tell me, and I was too stupid to ask. But everyone seems to agree now that, at least in academia, the situation is untenable.

There is abundant evidence that it's getting worse, too, as more universities slash tenure lines, grind them into teeny little bits, and toss them down to the throngs of adjunct instructors who are so desperate and demoralized that they'll snap them all up without fail, so that in the end, the university gets to staff the same amount of courses at a fraction of the cost without having to pay as many employees' health benefits. This is how it is now, but I wondered if life in the ranks of academia was always so tough.

I remembered reading that not long ago, under Cambridge University, archeologists had discovered hundreds of anonymous scholars' skeletons from the Middle Ages. The story featured a lot of photographs of grinning skulls and bones sticking out of dirt and a lot of text. I didn't get a chance to read the whole thing because that was the day my ENGL-1102 students turned in second drafts and 50 students were emailing me at once to try to get an extension, but I just so happened to have gone to grad school with a woman who specialized in medieval studies, and we stayed friends. So, I zipped off a message to her asking what a medieval scholar's life would have been like.

"You're the only person I know who would know," I added. She wrote back immediately.

"I have a campus interview early next week, and I'm scrambling to prepare. Do you mind if I reply when I get back? I'm in panic mode."

Indeed, this was an exciting moment for her. She had been employed sporadically since she'd gotten her doctorate, despite applying to pretty much every college-level teaching job anywhere in the English-speaking world for three years straight. As a medievalist, she was a koala, but she was out there saying, "Feed me whatever. Koala don't give a shit anymore. Forget the eucalyptus." The particular position she was interviewing for was for a medievalist—her eucalyptus. She had every reason to be in panic mode. I thanked her anyway and apologized for bothering her.

Another reason she had to be in panic mode, I recalled, was that the previous week she had been on the local news because a bullet had burst through the exterior wall of her house and ricocheted around inside until it landed, finally, a few feet from her baby's crib. I had watched part of the video from the story because it appeared in my newsfeed, but I hadn't gotten to see the whole thing because the night I saw it, grades for response paper seven had to be turned in for my online course. But I knew the gist—bullet, crib, scary. It occurred to me that because she was my friend, I should probably have said something supportive, and that maybe now was the right time to do that. I typed a reply:

"By the way, sorry about the bullet," but I erased it because I didn't want her to think I was the one who fired it.

"Heard about how your house got shot up. Crazy!" I typed, but then I erased that, too.

I was an English professor after all; I should be able to eloquently express concern and solidarity for this person I care about. I studied words, after all. Words were supposed to be my life. Other people are supposed to learn how to do this kind of thing from me.

The cursor blinked in silence. I could almost feel her watching the screen on her end, watching to see if I said anything else, watching the walls for more bullets to fly in from outside—sitting, watching, being in panic mode.

Finally, I just wished her luck on her interview. She didn't write back.

~~~

Sometimes, when dealing with matters of English degrees—particularly graduate ones—there's a disconnect between expectation and reality. People expect that if you have a master's or a Ph.D. that you always have a job or that you can always get a job whenever you want. The reality is that it's always really hard to get any job. Academic jobs have to be open and posted, and even if you happen to beat the dozens and sometimes hundreds of other applicants for one of those, the hiring process takes a long time—half a year or more sometimes.

Meanwhile, bills keep coming in, bills for the rent and the lights and the car and the student loan I'll be paying until I'm in my mid-60s, but if you have a graduate degree and you apply for a regular job—like the pizza delivery job I am applying for in the hopes that working a third job will help offset the loss of my wife's teaching position—well, people tell you you're overqualified. Thus, many scholars who are just trying to keep the lights on and the rent paid find themselves in this weird employment purgatory of being not qualified enough to be gainfully employed long term at a college and too qualified to punch the clock anywhere else.

Everyone I asked about this told me that when they fill out applications for nonacademic jobs, they don't even list those advanced degrees they spent years toiling away in seclusion to get. I'm not putting my master's or Ph.D. or my professor job on my pizza delivery application, but that means there's a huge gap in employment. What am I supposed to tell them I've been doing for the last decade and a half? I once asked a fellow Ph.D. about this. "You're a creative writer," he said. "Make something up."

~~~

Lystrosaurus waddles out of its burrow and raises its scaly countenance toward the orange sky of morning. The moon, still visible against the dawn, hangs like an exhausted tear on the cheek of the new day. Lystrosaurus grunts, scuffs his foreclaw in the dirt, and tilts his heavy, tusked head downward. There are no longer any predators to worry about here, but there is plenty of competition for resources, and it's getting harder for Lystrosaurus to feed his young. The whole world is drying up and chafing like an exposed root in the sandpaper air.

Wearily, Lystrosaurus plods across the dusty landscape once more in search of food, hoping the digging will be light today, that the soil will be loose and moist and full of fibrous bits of plant matter, because Lystrosaurus, who was kicked and jostled by his young all night in the burrow, is starting to feel the slow crush of years in his bones, and he could use an easy day for a change, because it's pretty much been one damned thing after another for Lystrosaurus lately, what with the trouble with the Subaru last week, the nasty virus that came home from the kid's preschool, the landlord who won't deal with the termites . . . plus, how long did Lystrosaurus bang away on that stupid committee spreadsheet, and now they aren't even going to use it? Scraping harder at the surface layers of soil with his powerful tusks, Lystrosaurus can't even believe this shit anymore.

How did I even get here? Lystrosaurus muses, thrusting his beak into the newly made hole to explore it for shreds of vegetation. Finding no food, Lystrosaurus snorts and begins to dig again with motions worn into muscle memory through endless hours of mindless repetition. *Am I depressed?* Lystrosaurus wonders casually.

~~~

At the breakfast table the other day, my wife and I spoke about finances. The loss of her income will represent a 45 percent decrease in our yearly household budget unless she gets hired right back in the fall at the school across town, but she doesn't want to get hired right back. She doesn't want to get hired back ever. She is about to go wandering right off the continent of being an English professor. She says she likes the students and the work, but that she's going to learn how to do something else. She says it's unfair to expect her to live this way, losing her job and having to beg for another one somewhere else three times a decade.

"I think," she said, "I could make a difference doing something else."

I nodded. The "something else" she was referring to is medicine—a complete career shift. She will go back to school, starting all the way over, taking the basics. Statistics. Calculus. Introductory chemistry. I could feel the atmosphere shifting. The air in my lungs seemed tighter. I summoned my long experience as an English major, English grad student, and English professor, because I knew this was an important moment, and I wanted to say just the right thing.

"I mean, yeah, like, go for it or whatever," I said.

She looked at me, and I gave her a look that told her I loved her, told her I support her, told her I couldn't agree more.

Then I looked down at my bowl of cereal and sighed. I dug my spoon into the bowl. It made a soft, crunching sound, and I pictured a primordial claw digging through the ancient, barren Earth.

Chapter 4. Adjunctivitis: The Plague of Academia

Marjorie Stewart
Glenville State University

> To be contingent means not to know if you'll be teaching next semester.
>
> – Kevin Birmingham

> Love means never having to say you're sorry.
>
> – Erich Segal

Long, long ago in a university far, far away—let's call it Private City University (PCU)[1]—there was a writing program director who came complete with the appropriate costume—tweed jacket with elbow patches, gray flannel trousers, a slightly rumpled oxford cloth shirt, and a decidedly stained necktie. Long and lean, 60-ish, graying—an English professor from central casting by way of the costume shop.

Unfortunately, in addition to the costume, he came complete with the appropriate instructions. Our writing program director—let us call him Dr. Director—was forced, through the economic circumstances of the university, to rely more and more heavily upon adjuncts to teach composition courses, and he accepted those circumstances. Although he occasionally taught composition, he was, first and foremost, a literature specialist, a medievalist to be precise.

Secure in his own tenure, with about five years until retirement, he saw composition and the need for adjuncts as nothing more than a nuisance. Instead of merely assigning schedules to full-time faculty, he now had to recruit, interview, and hire adjuncts, then struggle to match their availability to the scheduled courses. He had to give them an orientation. He had to observe their teaching and meet with them to discuss it. He had to meet with them yet again to discuss the student evaluations of their teaching. He had to include them in the portfolio review meetings to assess the writing program itself. And he had to pay them a $50 stipend and feed them lunch out of his budget for those portfolio meetings. In all fairness, at least he did those things. Many schools merely throw adjuncts into the classroom with no support or preparation.

Enter our second character, an adjunct with five years of teaching experience when she came to PCU—me. I was already aware of the precarious lifestyle—low

---

1. All names have been changed. And changed again. The guilty are protected. The innocent not so much.

pay; no health insurance; and no control over my syllabus, textbook, or teaching methods.

I had applied to the university once before but had not been contacted. The second time, I asked a friend in the registrar's office if she knew anyone. She did. Our hero. She spoke to him; he called me in for an interview.

When the day of my interview came, I took a portfolio of writing assignments, student evaluations, and recommendations. I dialed Dr. Director's extension from the lobby and waited. Soon I saw a man in a tweed jacket with suede elbow patches approaching.[2]

After a long, awkward wait for an elevator, Dr. Director led me to his office. We sat. He asked me how I knew my friend. He asked why the writing program director at a school where I had taught had changed her name—had she gotten married?

The seasons change. Two years pass. I teach six courses. Dr. Director observes my teaching twice and enthusiastically endorses it. He meets with me to discuss my student evaluations, which exceed the university average in every category and include a number of positive comments. He offers me three Composition I sections for fall 2006, including one honors section.

All is right with the Private City University world.

But not all was right in my world. I had three classes at PCU, two at a local community college, and two with another private college in the suburbs. I had three book bags: a Monday/Wednesday/Friday bag, a Tuesday/Thursday bag, and a Wednesday night bag. If I pointed my car in the wrong direction and didn't realize it within a few miles, I was late for class.

> It wasn't just me. Kevin Birmingham describes the profession this way:
>
> It looks like the miles ticking away on her shabby car's odometer. . . . It is coming to terms with the appalling fact that you have spent the better part of the last decade applying for a seat at this table, trying to convince committees in hotel suites that you would be a more effective member of this particular team. It is the painful recognition that it never fully outraged you until the jobs didn't work out.

This had to end.

Then, unfortunately, a local community college advertised a full-time job in composition. Like all of us, in or out of academia, I longed for a living wage and benefits. Even more, I wanted to know where to go every day. I wanted to give up my "If this is Wednesday, it must be Private City University" way of life. I didn't want three book bags lined up in the dining room.

In short, I wanted a real job.

---

2. Really. I couldn't make this up. A decade earlier he would have been smoking a pipe.

I began to scramble about, gathering information for the application. One requirement: name and contact information of a current supervisor for reference.

No problem, right? My department heads knew the way of the adjunct world—surely they will support me in this extremely long-shot attempt to settle down. All I had to do was to pick one. Choose the department chair who would understand my situation and give me the best recommendation.

I chose Dr. Director. I could certainly rely upon him for a reference, he said. In fact, he said it in an email May 3:

> Hello, Marjorie—I'll be glad to recommend you. Please let me know right away if you have to change your teaching assignments here.
>
> Thanks,
>
> Dr. D

In retrospect, the "let me know right away" might have been a warning. Another email arrived about a week later:

> Thanks, Marjorie—I am sure you will get the job. Would you still be able to teach the fall Monday afternoon honors ENGL 101? Could you ask to keep this time open? Maybe you could still do the other two classes I mentioned?
>
> Your teaching has been great, and I would hate to lose it.
>
> Thanks,
>
> Dr. D

When I got the email, I had one foot out the door to go out of town. Since I didn't know quite how to answer it, I decided to wait until I got home. After all, I could hardly walk into a new job dictating my schedule. Because Dr. Director seemed encouraging, I didn't worry. After all, he valued my teaching. He said so.

Unfortunately, Dr. Director's idea about how to avoid losing that teaching was puzzling. I received another email on May 16:

> Margie, I'm sorry, but at this point I need to ask someone else to teach the fall classes we discussed. I appreciate your letting me know early in the summer about your application to Rural County Community College, but I can't wait until June or July to complete the fall hires. I will be on vacation for most of June, and I want to take care of fall classes now.
>
> I appreciate your excellent work for us, and of course I will be glad to write recommendations, answer questions, etc. Also,

if you become available for fall classes, please let me know—something may well be available.

Thanks,

Dr. D

I could lose my house, I thought—after all, those courses represented almost half of my income for the fall term. I couldn't see the bank understanding Dr. Director's need to fill his classes and therefore waiving my mortgage payments. Ironic that much of the literature about adjunctcy discusses the "homelessness" of adjuncts. I was not only homeless in the university, I now ran the risk of being literally homeless.

At least he said he was sorry.

Shock turned to fury. I ranted a bit.[3] I reminded myself of my own rule: Never answer an email that makes you angry until at least 24 hours. This one would take 48.

Then I noticed that he had spelled my name wrong. My name, a part of both my family legacy and my teaching legacy.

> My aunt, the aunt for whom I was named, Marjorie Best (who also spelled Marjie with a "j"), died about five years before I started teaching. She left her nieces and nephews a bit of money. Wowie, as we called her, never married. She lived with her mother—my grandmother—and alone after grandma died.

> Wowie always rented. She wanted to buy a house, but single women didn't do that—in fact, legally they couldn't do that. When the house where she had lived in a quirky third floor apartment was torn down, Wowie found another great place to live—an apartment with two bedrooms, a formal dining room, and an attic she converted into a studio. When people asked her why she rented such a big apartment, she would say, "Do they think that just because I'm single I should hang on a hook?" When she died, my sister and I, both single women, bought houses using the money she had left us as down payments.

> I wish she had known that she bought two houses for single women. I wish she had known I became a teacher. She spent 43 years teaching primary grades, starting in the midst of the Depression with a two-year degree from the Indiana State Normal School, then finishing her bachelor's and her master's

---

3. A 2014 study by psychologists Gretchen M. Reevy and Grace Deason points to venting as a potentially negative coping mechanism used by contingent faculty when they find themselves in stressful circumstances. I could have saved them the trouble of research and just written them a letter.

degrees—both while teaching full time, and the master's while caring for her elderly mother. Her first contract said that teachers would be paid their salary "when the school board had the funds," a not-unusual clause in the 1930s. Sometimes they waited several months for those funds to become available. Teaching salaries improved, though, so that about five years after she retired, new teachers were starting out at more than she had ever made in her career. I grew up with stories of how teachers are treated unjustly. I grew up with stories of a great love of teaching in spite of that injustice.

The shock, anger, and sadness at Dr. Director's decision provided something I needed, though: the powerful motivation of panic. I obsessed over the application for the Rural County Community College job (they required a three-page cover letter addressing a variety of pedagogical issues) and got it in—pronto.

I remembered a meeting I attended in my second year at PCU. A dean announced an increase in adjunct pay. "Not enough, of course," he said. "It's not even a salary, really. It's an honorarium."

Well, I'd rather be honored by a living wage and benefits, thanks just the same.[4]

The American Association of University Professors issued a report, *The Annual Report on the Economic Status of the Profession, 2020–21*, that shows the percentage of faculty working on a contingent basis has remained relatively stable at about two thirds since 2006–07. Their report attempts to trace the effects of the COVID-19 pandemic but states:

> Any researcher who tries to quantify the economic impact of COVID-19 on contingent faculty members—particularly adjunct faculty members—will quickly discover an ugly secret in higher education: colleges and universities are not required to report detailed employment data on contingent faculty members. (12)

The report goes on to refer to a "dearth of basic information" regarding the demographics of contingent faculty members (12). Given the "data-driven" nature of today's institutions, it's hard to make a case to them for improving the conditions of a group about whom the data are unknown.

And those conditions for adjuncts exist for a reason. As Birmingham states:

> Amid competing budgetary pressures, classroom instruction is the easiest expense to cut. And part-time employees aren't just cheap; they also provide curricular flexibility. Unpredictable course enrollments encourage administrators to find faculty who can be hired and fired just as unpredictably.

---

4. Am I whining (a term that will return soon)? Let's move on and look at the literature—it will be a relief for everyone.

And such was the case at PCU.

Shortly after this, the plight of adjuncts was brought to light in the story of Margaret Mary Vojtko, a 25-year adjunct at Duquesne University in Pittsburgh. After her death in 2013 at the age of 83, *The Pittsburgh Post-Gazette* published an op-ed piece by Daniel Kovalik, an attorney for the United Steel Workers, which was attempting to organize adjuncts at Duquesne, and the outrage about working conditions in the academy finally left the hallowed ivy-covered ivory tower and went viral. Kovalik pointed out that adjuncts have no job security, no severance, and no benefits.

Vojtko's story has been fleshed out in more in-depth articles, including one by L.V. Anderson in *Slate*. Even that story, which discusses her hoarding, her frequent refusal to take charity, and her mental health issues, concludes that the university behaved badly, and that the continuing culture of contingent faculty is "a scourge." Anderson declares that underpaid adjuncts are bad for students, bad for taxpayers, and bad for the universities themselves.

As Vojtko's story faded from the public eye, discussions continued to rage within the academy. One particularly unfortunate piece was a letter to the editor of *The Chronicle of Higher Education* headlined, "Is That Whining Adjunct Someone We Want Teaching Our Young?" Written by Catherine Stukel, a full-time professor of business technologies, it entirely ignores the facts of both Vojtko's life and death and the corporate-model systems that have created the adjunct crisis in American education.

Stukel suggests that adjuncts should quit whining and "put on [their] big-girl panties." She reasons that part timers may not be selected for full-time jobs because they are annoying, they are not likeable, they are mediocre, or they don't fully engage their students. I have certainly known both part-time and full-time professors that fall into one or more of those categories. But I have known far more competent, engaging, and likeable professors, again, both in full-time and part-time positions.

Although Stukel does hand out tough but practical advice, it isn't easy. I spent seven long years trying to make the adjunct lifestyle work.

After I didn't get the job at Rural CCC,[5] I enrolled in a doctoral program in composition. When I was ABD, I got a full-time job with benefits on a one-year contract. I moved from that position to running the writing center at an art school not far from Private City University. I spent four years there, received my doctorate, and then moved to a tenure-track job. Many of my friends and former colleagues have not been as lucky. When I mentioned at a party that I was leaving my job at the art school, half a dozen recent Ph.D.s in literature or composition sent applications in the next day.

As I write that, I know that I am incredibly lucky. I am not smarter, more experienced, or better educated than my contingent faculty friends and colleagues.

---

5. Really, is anyone surprised?

When I finally decided that enough was enough, I took an enormous risk by investing time and money preparing for a career that might not exist in an environment that was angry, alienated, and alienating.

As early as 1995, Anne Cassebaum asked:

> How did our profession become so divided? Why are we in such a weak labor position? The answer goes beyond our own profession as full-time positions get splintered into part-time ones all over the U.S., but the reason for our vulnerability also lies in the attitudes of our fellow educators. (2)

She continues, "How can those who value education exploit educators?" (7).

Unfortunately, neither she nor anyone else has provided an answer to that very good question. Cassebaum does not naively assume that adjunctcy will disappear; she merely argues for fair pay and job security. She points to several "attitude problems" among full-time faculty that work against those goals. Like Dr. Director, most of the faculty members she characterizes are blithely unaware of the plight of adjuncts. They mask their harmful attitudes in benevolent platitudes: "They're lucky, they don't have to do all the committee work and extra stuff we do" (2), and "They're surprisingly professional" (7). I heard that "surprisingly professional" or "surprisingly scholarly" many times.

> My friend Chuck is an actor. Once the drama critic in our city's major daily newspaper described one of his performances as "surprisingly good." No amount of explanation about how the critic meant that Chuck was cast against type, giving a strong performance in a very different role than he usually plays softened the blow. Chuck has not forgiven the critic to this day.

It might seem as if this essay would have been depressing to write. It wasn't.[6] Seeing the weight of stories of adjuncts—nameless, homeless people who bear the responsibility for teaching most of the first-year composition and basic writing courses in colleges today—made me feel less alone. The most frustrating part was understanding that much of the problem exists because full-time faculty members like Dr. Director remain oblivious.

To make changes, full-time faculty members need to learn to speak the language of the adjunct rather than that of the academy on the subject of adjunctcy. I've often heard full-time faculty members claiming, "We treat our adjuncts well here." I used to believe that was true, especially at Private City University.

Until that email, that is. Then I began to believe that there is no way to treat adjuncts well. I believe that the overreliance on part-time instructors has created a system where it is impossible to treat adjuncts well—their very adjunctcy is a symptom of ill treatment. It is part of the discourse of the academy that leads

---

6. Well, not too depressing.

full-time faculty and administration to believe otherwise. It is how Dr. Director can sleep at night.

> Wowie never owned her own home, but for her 70th birthday we gave her a dollhouse kit. She became an accomplished miniaturist, first assembling, painting, and wallpapering the house, then crafting tiny furniture for it: a Chippendale highboy, a delicate Queen Anne dining room set, petit-point Persian rugs.

Wowie might have settled for a miniature house, but I am not willing to settle for a miniature career. Once, when I was bemoaning my adjunct lot, my sister pointed out that when I got a "real job," I could work for better conditions. It is a rocky road. My current college does not have adjunct representation on the faculty senate. When I have advocated for it, I hear the same things I heard as an adjunct: They're not like us. They just teach their classes and go home. They don't do research. They won't want to serve. How would they keep in touch with their constituents? (The same way I do, I suspect—by email). And then, the concession: some, however, are "surprisingly professional."

It is us-and-them all over again. I still hold the belief that the faculty is all in this together. The divide between tenured and tenure-track faculty, full-time contract faculty, and adjunct faculty must be healed if higher education is to survive this plague.

Perhaps the best cure for adjunctivitis is for the academy to go cold turkey—totally eliminate all adjunct positions, replacing them with full-time tenure-track jobs.[7] If, after a few years, it turns out to be true that some of us *liked* being second class citizens, *wanted* part-time work, *enjoyed* being nameless and homeless, *refused* representation in shared governance, then exactly that number of adjunct positions could be recreated. Since that is unlikely at best, the next choice would be for all faculty to band together to fight for good working conditions—and the good teaching they might inspire—for all.

Works Cited

Anderson, L. V. "Death of a Professor." *Slate*, 17 Nov. 2013, http://www.slate.com/articles/news_and_politics/education/2013/11/death_of_duquesne_adjunct_margaret_mary_vojtko_what_really_happened_to_her.html.

The Annual Report on the Economic Status of the Profession, 2020-21. American Association of University Professors, July 2021. *American Association of University Professors*, 2021, https://www.aaup.org/file/AAUP_ARES_2020-21.pdf.

Birmingham, Kevin. "'The Great Shame of Our Profession': How the Humanities Survive on Exploitation." *The Chronicle of Higher Education*, 12 Feb. 2017, https://www.chronicle.com/article/the-great-shame-of-our-profession/.

---

7. What drugs am I on, you might rightly ask.

Cassebaum, Anne. "Adjuncts with an Attitude?: Attitudes Encountered in the Struggle for Fair Pay and Job Security for Adjunct Faculty." 46th Annual Meeting of the Conference on College Composition and Communication, Mar. 1995, Washington, DC. Paper. *ERIC*, http://files.eric.ed.gov/fulltext/ED385853.pdf.

Kovalik, Daniel. "Death of an Adjunct." *Pittsburgh Post-Gazette*, 18 Sept. 2013, https://www.post-gazette.com/opinion/Op-Ed/2013/09/18/Death-of-an-adjunct/stories/201309180224.

Reevy, Gretchen M. and Grace Deason. "Predictors of Depression, Stress, and Anxiety among Non-Tenure Track Faculty." *Frontiers in Psychology*, vol. 5, 2014. *Frontiers*, https://doi.org/10.3389/fpsyg.2014.00701.

Segal, Erich. *Love Story*. 50th anniversary ed., HarperCollins, 2020.

Stukel, Catherine. "Is That Whining Adjunct Someone We Want Teaching Our Young?" *Letters: Correspondence from* Chronicle *readers*, *The Chronicle of Higher Education*, 25 Aug. 2014, https://www.chronicle.com/blogs/letters/is-that-whining-adjunct-someone-we-want-teaching-our-young/.

Chapter 5. Closing of My College Department and Swingline Factory

Constance H. Gemson
LaGuardia Community College

It's over.

In 2014, my adjunct college teaching assignment ended after 17 years. I taught for-credit classes on choosing a career at LaGuardia Community College's cooperative education department, and oversight of students' internships was reassigned to other programs. College teaching was a meaningful addition to my life, but I was never compensated for much of my time.

My trip to the college took over 45 minutes from my Upper West Side, Manhattan home. Across the street from my school was the Swingline factory: massive, dusty, red. Once, this place was home to 450 jobs where workers produced staples and staplers. The brand name Swingline is still well known. Years ago, a factory job meant steady work, a set paycheck, and a chance for the workers' children to do better. Then these factory jobs went to Mexico.

American workers were stranded without employment. My college provided training for these workers. I felt empathy for their lives. The Swingline building continued to be empty. It could be a disco with flamboyant nights or affordable housing. The closed doors served as a symbol of the need for education. The present and future are clear; worker security is an illusion in the disposable employee economy.

Adjuncts' status seems similar to the "Uberization" of the gig economy. Car drivers and part-timer academics share a similar lack of stability about wages. We serve at the pleasure of those on top. Part-time faculty members see their careers as limited rather than idealistic; many scramble to teach at various campuses with no certainty of future assignments.

Unions are a viable solution. The Professional Staff Congress (PSC) is a local union affiliated with the American Federation of Teachers that has over 30,000 members, and PSC includes part-time and full-time academics, librarians, and higher education officers. Union members are usually advocates for both part-timers and full-timers ("About Us").

Remembering the Neighborhood/Hearing about the Job

My college job meant a commute to the new destination of Long Island City, once a hub of factories, now eat and run territory. Queens, where Long Island City is located, is the most diverse community in the United States, and all ethnicities are found in one ever-changing borough, yet the stores and restaurants in Long Island City felt generic.

In 1997, I got this job the old-fashioned way: through the switchboard. I was looking for an in-service educational program being offered to the organization where I worked. I called LaGuardia Community College. The anonymous switchboard operator transferred my call to Paula in the cooperative education department.[1] It was the wrong number but the right time! She shared recollections of the many new immigrants who enrolled at this college. Paula was enthusiastic about those enrolled in the varied programs.

She lived right near where I worked, and we met for dinner a week later. We discovered we were both social workers. Paula told me told me that when the college opened in 1971, most students were from Queens. Later, students came from Poland, Argentina, India, Greece, the Dominican Republic, China, or Nigeria. Paula gave me the dean of the department's name and number to contact about classes for the spring.

The following week I met Cathy, the department's administrator, to discuss part-time teaching. I was hired for the next semester to teach Fundamentals of Career Advancement. A department professor wrote an excellent text that I would use.

Exploring Class Content

My students interviewed each other during the first session. To decline to answer was acceptable. After 9/11, I was concerned about how Muslim students, who made up a significant portion of the student body, would be identifiable based on their clothing, but I did not need to put on the brakes. Classmates were kind. My school produced the play *The Vagina Monologues*. I saw the production on HBO, and I wondered if this was the right choice when most Muslim students valued modesty, which meant most students came to class casually dressed in jeans and lively shirts.

Class content included the Myers-Briggs Type Indicator assessment, which highlights traits such as extroversion versus introversion, sensing as contrasted to intuition, and thinking compared to feeling. The Holland Code profile, which we also covered in class, details qualities such as artistic, social, enterprising, and conventional. I used TV characters to illustrate these themes, and I also defined emotional values—my examples of different people who display differing values included a cloistered nun and a corporate leader.

I also used the text *Gateway to the Workplace*, which details the initiation into the world of work. We examined the ideas of John Dewey and other philosophers, and we discussed the new workforce and the necessary skills for success.

---

1. Pseudonyms are used for students; all other names are unchanged.

Discovering Career Autobiographies

Many students worked at LaGuardia Airport. Two African American students shared their airport stories. Pamela, a flight attendant, dreamed of becoming a psychologist. "I want to handle bigger problems," was her remark. For a class assignment, she interviewed a member of the Black Panthers. Would others believe "Black Panther" was the name of a car or a movie? Jack, a former football player, checked all the dead bodies when they arrived at the airport in the special boxes. He wanted a new job. Other students in my classes who were home health aides reported they had limited money and limited time to seek out new alternatives.

The college was perceived as a post-high school vocational choice. A few students began attending four-year colleges, then changed directions. Some were over 40. Suzanne worked at Aqueduct Racetrack and "had been everything but the jockey." She wanted to become a public interest lawyer. Julia from Nigeria, now a home health aide, was unsure about her future. Neal wanted to open a tattoo parlor. Based on TV shows, forensic psychology became a career of interest for some.

For many new arrivals, their educational orbit was narrow. They made the transition from around the globe to this country's challenges and contradictions. Many wanted security, and several chose business careers. Their dream school was Baruch College, in distant Manhattan. Rare students discovered academic opportunities at Barnard or Vassar. Al showed me with pride his acceptance letter to Morehouse College, where Martin Luther King, Jr., studied.

Most students had fewer choices. Students became curious to see if a career fit and if they wanted to wear it. Fieldwork provided this opportunity. At times, my students found they were regarded as a better source of information about technology than older staff. They also discovered health internships did not include clinical work. Students' work titles were administrative assistant, teacher assistant, and legal assistant at places such as Lenox Hill Hospital, Queens Community House, Black Entertainment Television (BET), MetLife, advocacy groups for immigrants, or local public schools.

This academic life lacked the romance of a rural campus setting; the campus buildings were those of a former candy factory. Work, school, and families were the familiar triad. Babysitting plans seemed to crash once a semester. The overworked parent brought the offspring to class. Youngsters were given crayons to color on paper. Children were respectful in this special place.

Understanding My Family's Story and the Connection to the Present

When I was in college, my responsibility was to be a student. My heroes were Michael Harrington, author of *The Other America* about U.S. poverty, and Cesar

Chavez, the farmworker activist in California. I met both leaders. I received my master's degree in social work at Stony Brook University. A four-year college and graduate school were affordable choices for my parents, who were both teachers. My younger brother went to medical school and became a doctor. My family's financial responsibilities were manageable. I aimed to be a social change agent to create new personal and political realities. Many friends were first-generation college students. Their lives expanded at college. The City University of New York (CUNY) had free tuition until 1976, when the city almost declared bankruptcy. This temporary charge for education became permanent.

My situation was unusual. My ambitious grandfather, Irving, my father's father, arrived as a Russian newcomer at age two and graduated from City College of New York at 19. Even with free tuition, higher education was a financial stretch. He tutored immigrants in English for 25 cents an hour, a high rate of pay. My grandfather's education bumped my father's family into the middle class. City College was a vital lifeline for immigrants, then and now. My grandfather taught at Boys High School in Brooklyn, a top-notch public school. My father and uncle were proud alumni.

My mother's mother, my grandmother Evelyn, completed two years at Adelphi College in Brooklyn, now Adelphi University on Long Island. She taught kindergarten for over 40 years. Under her college yearbook photo was the wonderful saying, "Independence now, independence forever, Evelyn knows what she wants!" I cherished my legacy of three generations of teachers.

My mother's middle school history class interviewed the neighborhood's old-timers and published their work in an elegant booklet. My father loved teaching high school English and told me we never know what Willy Loman sells in *Death of a Salesman*. My family regarded teaching as a noble calling, one that provided security during the Great Depression. Both families owned children's camps: my father and his father owned Camp Berkshire in Winstead, Connecticut, where Ralph Nader's family owned a restaurant. My maternal grandmother's camp was Camp Algonquin in upstate New York, on the Canadian and the United States borders. She taught her campers both national anthems, and I still know the first lines of "Oh Canada!" For all my family, teaching and owning a camp were both necessary for financial stability. They would understand the situation of adjuncts at the university.

Today, the working world is becoming a world of mini-jobs or "jobettes" with little security or benefits. Uncertainty was a familiar factor at my school for students and part-time faculty as well. Many adjuncts have become the new poor as wandering Ph.D.s search the college dust bowl for new opportunities and work. Some part-timers sought full-time opportunities in foundations, research, and publishing. We knew this reality before COVID-19.

I remembered when jobs listings were defined by gender. Engineer and lawyer were male-only. Clerical jobs were for women. Donald, a Black male student of mine, was aware of racism but was surprised to find out about gender-defined roles. *The New York Times* ended this practice in 1967.

Assessing Student Interviews

I gave a classic assignment: interview someone you admire. Students wrote about immigrants on extended visas, supportive supervisors, and respected colleagues. When I was selected as the subject, I declined. It felt too personal. A volunteer for John McCain's first campaign for president interviewed him. Julian interviewed a Legal Aid lawyer and admired her idealism. Suzanne selected an assistant teacher of children with special needs. One male student chose a police officer. This officer would not reveal the name of the officer who had been killed when he was present, and he still felt devastated. My student's brooding essay read like a Raymond Carver story. Another paper detailed a production assistant for the film *Malcolm X*. One subject was the owner of a karate studio. High school and college teachers were recognized.

Tom examined the organizational chart at MetLife, where he was an intern. He saw his dream job: CFO, the chief financial officer. Tom did not know this executive but arranged to interview him. Tom wore a jacket and tie for this meeting while the administrator did not.

Anish from India admired a doctor. The physician shared a quote from Hillel, a Jewish sage: "If I am not for me, who will be? If I am for myself alone, what am I? If not now, when" (Rosen)? My student was moved by this saying.

One class session was held in a computer lab. At first, a tech support colleague taught the group. This once intimidating session became my favorite. I became the solo driver and led my students to explore computer learning. I knew what it was like to have a beginner's mind and be a new learner.

Recalling Post-9/11 Memories

The classroom experience changed after 9/11. Before that time, many students wanted to use their language skills and work as travel agents or at the front desk at hotels in the future. Maria was disappointed about her hotel experience.

"I'm twenty-three; I've wasted so much time. So many customers are demanding and challenging, and I hate to work all different shifts," she said.

"Now, you are clear about what you don't what to do," I replied.

She looked relieved and began researching other professions.

After 9/11, police and accounting jobs were regarded as steady and secure. The once-friendly skies of airport work seemed frightening and dangerous.

Joe worked in a men's clothing store and was the only employee born in Queens. He stated, "I am the only one who can speak Spanish to the customers, and everyone else is Muslim." The class suggested he read about his colleague's traditions.

Recalling a Special Meeting

One semester, Rosa spoke with me after class. "Professor Connie, I know you worked with cancer patients as a social worker. My mother died of cancer when I was eight. My dad never told me she was sick, and he just told me to go out and play. Why did he do that? I just wanted to spend more time with her, and I didn't know she was dying."

I said, "Rosa, your dad didn't want to worry you. Now parents are encouraged to share more openly when a family member is sick. Your dad was doing the best he could."

Rosa looked unconvinced. "I'd like to give something back, and maybe I could volunteer for one of those marches against cancer," she said.

"Rosa, that would be a great idea," I replied.

The following week, she told me that joining the march meant asking participants to contribute money and to attend this event. She was too busy with her college classes, and additional expenses were not practical for her tight budget.

Valuing Small Groups

To encourage informal interaction, I sometimes divided the class into three groups, asking them to consider factors in choosing a senior college and determining its suitability as a match for them. I created roles: the leader to keep the conversation on track, the recorder to document the findings, the speaker to summarize the results, and the writer to take notes on the blackboard. The most frequent criteria for choosing a senior college were convenience and cost. With its low tuition and nearby location, CUNY was a contender for both American newcomers and blue-collar participants born in the United States.

One student stated to her small group, "My friend said he wouldn't want to go to Brooklyn College because there were too many Jews there." This remark was accepted by her seven group members. How could I deal with this situation? I had an ethnically neutral name, and I did not discuss my religion in class. I needed to make the student aware and yet not make her uncomfortable.

"That's an interesting perception," I said softly. "What is the percentage of Jews in the United States?"

One class member stated confidently, "Oh, at least twenty to thirty percent." The others nodded their heads in agreement.

"No, the Jews are less than three percent in this country," I replied. "I am Jewish and feel uncomfortable with that remark." At first, the group was quiet, and then the animated discussion continued.

In 15 minutes, sharing ended. For the entire class, I emphasized diversity both at this college and in New York City. I wrote a James Baldwin quote on the blackboard: "The role of the artist is the same as the role of the lover. If I love you, I have to make you conscious of things you don't see" ("Quotable Quote"). The class ended, and students left. I was busy packing up my books and belongings in my backpack.

The student who made this remark about the Jews entered the room. "Professor, I am so sorry I hurt your feelings. My friend said that remark about Brooklyn College. I didn't." I looked her straight in the eye.

"Coming to see me took a lot of gumption. I accept your apology."

I held out my hand, and she offered hers. We shook hands firmly. She felt she was respected as well.

Walking out of class on a spring morning, I saw a group of students who moved their hands like dancers. All the students were deaf, and I saw the joy and exuberance in their communication. My college had a well-known program for deaf individuals where a high school diploma can be earned in a collaborative setting for those who lack hearing.

I felt like an anthropologist studying work. When I got a mammogram, I spoke to the technician about her training. I heard a woman in a hard hat at a deli as she told her friend about her day. I wondered what it was like in the fashion industry or working as an accountant.

Understanding Adjunct Options

Now, my adjunct life is over. As an adjunct, I relished meeting new immigrants. I learned to be a more worldly city resident. Teaching expanded my life but did not determine my future. What recommendations can I offer to others? Explore personal options during your entire career. Develop multiple income streams and ideas. Activate your colleagues to unionize and work for better conditions for all. Realize that even a simple raindrop can enrich the slow growth of a tree, but the power of a storm or a union can be mighty and fierce.

When my time ended at the college, I wondered about my students. Will work be a source of satisfaction or disappointment for them? How will new technology change their world? I assessed how much I had learned and shared in this box-like setting that was once a candy factory. I thought about the Swingline factory, an empty shell; years later, it sold items for theater productions. I remembered the pre-COVID-19 story of LaGuardia Community College and the unknown destinations for us all.

Works Cited

"About Us." *PSC CUNY*, 2022, https://psc-cuny.org/about-us#:~:text=The%20 PSC%20is%20a%20%E2%80%9Clocal,affiliated%20with%20the%20AFL%2DCIO.

"Quotable Quote." *Goodreads*, 2022, https://www.goodreads.com/quotes/611633-the -role-of-the-artist-is-exactly-the-same-as.

Rosen, Emily. "If not now, when?" *Pittsburgh Jewish Chronicle*, 13 May 2020, https:// jewishchronicle.timesofisrael.com/if-not-now-when/.

Part II. The Debilitating Effects of Disposability

During the COVID-19 pandemic, there has been an uptick of interest and concern about students' mental health. And for all intents and purposes, this is a good thing. It seems there is a weekly email circulating on college campuses about stress relieving activities to participate in, including petting puppies during finals week, doing yoga in the quad, and making arts and crafts in the library. But what about the professors teaching these students? Is anyone really checking up on them?

Building upon Part I, this section pulls back the curtains on what the system does to individuals. Even the youngest, most bubbly of professors will eventually experience one (or all) of the following in this rat race: mental, physical, and emotional burnout. And let's not forget financial exhaustion. It has been said that "forty-four percent of new teachers leave teaching within five years" within the K-12 system (qtd. in Will). Within colleges, word of mouth indicates it's not much better.

- In "A Dark Night and a Brighter Day for Adjuncts," Maria Shine Stewart deconstructs assumptions those outside of academia hold about professors working at multiple campuses. As she points out, a plumber once said to her, "You must be a good teacher. You teach at three schools." She shows that little do such individuals know that teaching at more than one institution is a matter of survival due to the low salaries, not a love affair with the current inverted setup in which more than half the faculty work part time.
- Christian L. Pyle, an adjunct English professor at Bluegrass Community and Technical College in Lexington, Kentucky, discusses the sometimes unfortunate disconnect between members of the full-time faculty and part-time faculty and how this disconnect further ignites classifications of segregation, disenfranchisement, and marginalization within the academy.
- In "Between a Rock and a Hard Place on a Deserted Island: Negotiated Mental Health on College Campuses Through the Lens of a Rebellious Adjunct Professor," Belle H. Foster cheekily details the four parts to the mental health roller coaster of an adjunct professor: "(1) the new adjunct honeymoon phase, (2) the denial and disillusionment stage, (3) the forget* it milestone (* forget may be replaced with other 'f' words), and (4) panic." She illustrates that while colleges invest thousands of dollars on the mental health of students, which is important, they also need to turn their lens inward because the mental health of the part-time faculty is not OK by a longshot.

- Nooshan Ashtari and Pamela Minet-Lucid convey how the academic system eats its young, making individuals feel bad when they struggle, as if they failed. However, as they note, it's the machine itself that's the problem. They relay what most of us in academia already know: If you have another source of income, or a partner that can help you out, life is easier. If you must take care of someone else, such as a child, an adult, or an elderly person, being a contingent faculty member is virtually impossible.
- In "Ignorance is Bliss," Ann Wiley (pen name) explores the obliviousness in the decision-making processes of academic institutions that is caused by an absence of adjunct perspectives. She shares three different yet overlapping views of this phenomenon: those of students, full-time faculty members, and administrators. As she points out, when individuals are in the dark, whether knowingly or simply because they are out of touch, they cannot and will not help the most exposed populations within their very own department.

The Great Resignation from teaching is a dismal reality. For young people just coming out of college, obtaining a Ph.D. in the humanities is becoming less desirable by the minute. Why? Because they know applying for 100 full-time jobs and receiving 100 rejections will affect a person. It will eventually lead to mental and physical burnout, not to mention hardships when trying to pay back mounting school loans on a shoestring budget. And while dealing with all of this, the new faculty majority are the first professors most students will meet. That speaks volumes.

Work Cited

Will, Madeline. "5 Thing to Know About Today's Teaching Force." *Education Week*, 23 October 2018, https://www.edweek.org/leadership/5-things-to-know-about-todays-teaching-force/2018/10.

Chapter 6. A Dark Night and a Brighter Day for Adjuncts

Maria Shine Stewart
Cuyahoga Community College

Though I may be just one adjunct in academia, I have lived at least nine lives within it. And perhaps my trajectory resembles other adjuncts' lives:

1. Adjuncting for the first institution while completing a master's degree in English.
2. Adjuncting for a second university while working full time (in a very secure writing/editing job) on that campus in a neighboring department.
3. Adjuncting for two other departments in that second university—summer programs for underserved students and continuing education—to purposefully gain versatility.
4. Returning to adjuncting full force at two schools after giving birth to a medically frail child and "temporarily" surrendering full-time employment.
5. Discovering that even working at three schools simultaneously could be balanced as a child grew stronger and finding a way to align processes (not curricula) across institutions. Also began teaching memoir writing and gained awareness of writing across the lifespan, which became a focus.
6. Adapting to becoming a disabled instructor after an auto accident left significant physical repercussions. (The accident occurred after checking the driving distance to a prospective fourth institution.)
7. As health returned, morphing into an adjunct who believed a full-time teaching job was still within reach, vigorously applying and interviewing, applying and interviewing.
8. Continuing to be an adjunct while fulfilling a one-year stint as a full-time, non-tenure-track faculty member, a big break that broke when that NTT position was not renewed.
9. Remaining an adjunct in the autumn of life, collecting scant retirement income that is further slashed by the Windfall Elimination Provision that seems counterintuitive after years of substantially paying into both state retirement and Social Security systems.[1]

Along the way, I earned a second master's degree, in counseling, and discovered that adjunct labor occupies a substantial part of that field's staffing as well. I do not begrudge adjuncts who "made it," finding a way to secure employment. These have included talented faculty much younger than I am whom I cheered on

---

1. For more information, see "What Is the Windfall Elimination Provision?"

when they were in graduate school, and I was mid-career. Their work, earnings, and visibility have ascended. I have remained behind.

Yes, I have been fulfilled from working with the hundreds, likely thousands, of students who have crossed my path; from working with some extraordinary colleagues; and from the joy of witnessing students' growth and engaging in a genuinely creative profession. However, I have felt the ache of scant opportunity to share what I've learned about teaching and about writing—and about colleges and universities, for that matter. I have presented at some conferences and written for publications about higher education, but that sense of camaraderie of working on a project is short-lived. Also, I have faced ongoing economic consequences of my part-time employment, such as those engendered by having two surgeries for cancer.

And, for all intents and purposes, I wear a durable, all-seasons invisibility cloak at my colleges. For adjuncts, there can be no career closure, no retirement status, no title of Adjunct Emeritus—even if our files are bursting with student papers, our minds percolating ideas, and our wallets and purses and phones holding bills (the kind you pay, not the other kind).

Others like me could not have imagined such an outcome when we fell in love with our profession, our calling. A plumber observed: "You must be a good teacher. You teach at three schools." If only that perception of adjuncts were more widespread instead of the harmful stereotypes that persist within academia.

Though on a cheerful day my life might overflow with optimism, as represented in a piece I wrote called "A Kinder Campus for Adjuncts" (reprinted with modifications in this essay as "A Brighter Day"), realistically, less upbeat moments do gather. "The Plight of the Nonrenewed," another piece I wrote which is also reprinted with modifications here, this time titled "A Dark Night," emerged in a very dark time.

"Some professors soar; adjuncts flap and dive and flap again—until they can't flap anymore" (Harris). I hope if you are an adjunct reading this piece, this moment finds you aloft, and if you are a tenured ally or administrator, I hope you might venture forth to help us all fly together, in formation, with the power of unity, purpose, and strength.

I. A Dark Night

Dear Academic Department:[2]

I hadn't intended to write one of these letters, ever. I thought that loyalty was part and parcel of being a colleague; however, I wasn't put on the course schedule after two decades of teaching here.[3]

---

2. Thank you to Doug Lederman and Scott Jaschik, editors at *Inside Higher Ed*, for their support of my writing over many years and permission to reprint this section, which has been modified slightly from the original. It was published initially as Anonymous, "The Plight of the Nonrenewed" in *Inside Higher Ed*.

3. The sudden absence from the schedule had happened once before, also (initially) without explanation.

You let me discover this by myself—with no explanation. And the timing could not have been worse. My spouse is unemployed; our child is in college. We may have to leave our home.

I know: There are hard times all over. Why should it—or could it—be different for my family?

When nonrenewals happen, one's imagination runs wild. If there was some perceived deficiency for which I was nonrenewed, it's probably better to know, though my self-esteem is currently flattened. And if it were simply an error, it would seem natural that an error could be quickly fixed. Instead, I am in limbo.

If my nonrenewal was (as someone close to me suggested) due to adjunct activism, that could be devastating—but true. "Oh, now I understand why that topic was important to you," a family member said.

Alternatively, you may not be mulling over any of this. As a distant member of the busy department, I am probably not on your radar. Perhaps the department never really knew me fully as a teacher or scholar. The few times I tried to discuss my own intellectual life or community activities or writing, tenured colleagues appeared uninterested. A friend was even told, "Don't talk about your ideas to colleagues too much."

Like others in academia, some readers may assert that responsibility for sustaining or creating positions lies above or beyond—the dean's office, the provost, the VPs, the president, the board of trustees, even trends around the country. But while I am wondering how I will meet next year's expenses and pursue what I consider my vocation, I am also wondering if readers can help stem the erosion of positions. You might be able to create better working conditions: if not for my generation, then for the next. You do have the power (Keenan).

Perhaps you can show me that my bad-day comparison of the role of adjuncts in the university "family" as comparable to forgotten kids in the homes of the distracted rich is not valid. Perhaps you can show me that fierce battles you fight elsewhere in the university arena and within your scholarly discipline can be fought for less visible colleagues. Perhaps you can go to the mat for your department as a whole and possibly the future of your . . . our . . . academic discipline.

Some people think instructors of a certain age have lost their currency, in every meaning of the word. I may find it hard to buy groceries and may need to take out a loan to buy required health insurance—I lack that currency—but I never lost my intellectual currency. If you think your adjuncts are stagnant or too tired to excel, do something. Evaluate, provide in-service . . . and be prepared to discover that you might be wrong.

An energetic, dedicated colleague with 40 years as an adjunct was extremely depressed one fall. I had never seen her as anything other than capable and charismatic. Nonrenewed. No perceived deficiency in her skills—rather, new colleagues, new chair. Another colleague has left the country, tired of not knowing how she would pay her bills. I am now down at least one-third of my anticipated

$30,000 income in a good year for teaching 10 to 13 courses annually at various schools. Ultimately, there is no Machiavelli guide to being an adjunct (Carroll), though one might strive to be strategic.

Personally, I rolled with the course assignments and never fussed when things didn't go my way. It has been suggested to me by someone outside of academia that too smooth an employee may be perceived as disengaged. Want two classes? Get one . . . or expect two, then get one, if that. Always be prepared to be "bounced," no matter what your load. Risk overload at multiple schools rather than not being able to pay bills. Teach morning, noon, night, weekend, online.

Some may be thinking: *Get a real job?* Jobs are not abundant in my region. *Publishing?* Dwindling. *Libraries?* Shrinking. *Bookstores?* Nonexistent. *Human services?* Despite rhetoric about our society's mental health needs, few openings. *Alt-ac jobs* on campus or lectureships at two-year schools? Have tried. *Private high schools?* Few slots, no go.

Overheard: *I can't imagine why an adjunct would keep at it after three years.* My imagined comeback: I tried to find other paths. Ironically, every time I applied for a full-time job that did not come through, full-time and part-time colleagues have said, "But you don't really need the job. You have a spouse." Is this the 21st century?

A well-meaning friend offered the platitude that a door shutting might mean a window opening. It feels, to me, like the door is shutting and the windows are painted shut.

Exit strategy and career plan are, of course, ultimately one's own responsibility.

While I figure out what I can now do for myself: Can there *please* be forward thinking in colleges or universities on how to cultivate, advance or utilize existing talent without strategies that boot talented instructors out—deliberately or accidentally—in our maturity? Other industries value retention and experience. And when it comes to classroom management, literacy acquisition, writing skills, minority outreach: Believe me, adjuncts can enter a campus discussion, given the chance.

Those on this path should be careful. One may end up vulnerable while critically ill or in chemotherapy[4] or—as I sense myself becoming on other dark days—dejected. As the case of Mary-Faith Cerasoli retaught me, I may be one mishap from the street ("Homeless Professor"). This century may see things getting worse for adjuncts. In the unsolicited words of a former full-timer who left for greener pastures, "Don't get caught" in the part-time pool. But one could get caught.

Or be set free at the absolutely worst moment.

Sincerely,
Saddened

---

4. For a description of one infamous case, see Colleen Flaherty's "#iammargaretmary."

II: A Brighter Day

It was as a secretary in a busy English department at a large state university 40 years ago that I first learned that full-time and part-time faculty occupied different worlds.[5] Although these worlds intersected in the classroom—and at times in my very small office—I wondered even then if better communication and mutual recognition were possible. I saw students served by both forms of faculty. I handled instructional materials created by everyone, and I sensed the degree of commitment—or frustration—that both groups brought to their jobs. From this initial vantage point, expanded by the varied roles I have had on- and off-campus since then (including full-time, non-teaching work plus many years as an adjunct at multiple institutions), I propose three questions for colleges to consider while reflecting on teaching conditions of adjunct faculty members:

- Are adjunct faculty members at your school being treated like professional people?
- Are they supported in the places on campus where they work?
- Are they given things they need to do their very best, even in difficult economic times?

If your answers are already in the affirmative, you may not need to read on. But I urge you to anyway.

Acknowledge Professional People

People, all of us, possess goals and needs and talents. And you know the line belted out by Barbra Streisand—"People who need people are the luckiest people in the world" (Styne and Merrill). I still remember the shock when I first heard that phrase. Not necessarily, Barbra: If someone needs someone, and no one else is around, that individual is not so lucky.

Mishaps occur to everyone, regardless of job title. But if the copier is broken, and no one is there to help (and an adjunct faculty member drove a long distance to prepare materials), that's not lucky. If a contingent faculty member has completed a creative project in the community—and no one on the campus acknowledges it—that's not lucky. If a student needs astute advising and administrative offices are closed (while an adjunct instructor is teaching very late), that's not so lucky. And if one dozen capable adjuncts are terminated at the end of the academic year, and no one protests, does their disappearance make a sound?

Memos or emails that go to some people, not all, erode communication. In my experience, when full-time faculty members join a department, only rarely

---

5. Thank you to Doug Lederman and Scott Jaschik, editors at *Inside Higher Ed*, for their support of my writing over many years. This section, which has been modified slightly, was published originally as "A Kinder Campus for Adjuncts?" in *Inside Higher Ed*.

are any adjunct colleagues part of that welcome. Adjuncts themselves may be hired without fanfare, under the wire, with scant preparation time. And policy issues, curricula, debates, textbook decisions . . . Why exclude the full teaching force who might be able to help?

The very adjectives—adjunct, term, contingent—themselves can be dispiriting. "Just an adjunct" is a sad mantra. Every human being needs to feel valued. But let me affirm the upbeat intention of the song "People" (Styne and Merrill). If we are interdependent and rise to the challenge of supporting one another, it *is* an amazing feeling: "You were half, now you're whole." A spirit of camaraderie helps all of us, especially under pressure.

A vivid memory: On one campus where I have regularly taught, an IT staffer quickly talked me through a computer program over the weekend, which was both sanity saving and in the best interest of my students. That is best practice. Often, the savviest campus personnel are status-blind. Can we all strive for that?

Lee Kottner, longtime social media director of New Faculty Majority, has suggested, "Get to know adjunct faculty members, make them visible in the rest of the department. If there's a web page or poster in the department identifying faculty, include adjuncts" (qtd in Stewart).

Provide Proper Places

Not every campus has individual offices for faculty members, but having a buffer zone around the classroom with even a degree of privacy can greatly improve pre- and post-class communication with students. When you have to rush out of a classroom before the next scheduled teacher approaches—without any space nearby—it can be unsettling. Campuses can incorporate spots of reflection where full- and part-time, tenured, and contingent faculty members can congregate. Sharing ideas, even just smiles and nods, is not a bad thing.

Yes, cyberspace is an important place. But human contact counts. Being separated from full-time faculty can be isolating. If more visible, all faculty members can be part of transformative conversations and collaboration. One campus exiled a large group of part-time faculty to a space the size of a walk-in closet. It was doubtful that this was done on purpose. In any case, full-time faculty converged to express dismay and got action on that issue—fast.

A colleague in another department was a fellow adjunct for nearly two decades; we met at a gathering of a professional association though we had spent all that time one floor apart, never knowing we shared interests. And one student at a community college seemed surprised to learn that department members occupying different floors of the same building might not talk, except for awkward moments in the elevator.

"Why doesn't everyone just bring a dish and have a potluck?" she asked.

That was so sensible. Let's do it.

Supply Required Things

I remember the happy surprise of sticky notes, dry-erase markers, and a pen in my mailbox at one institution at the start of the term. The well-stocked supply room that I had access to as a departmental secretary decades ago is long gone, so like most people, I carry my own supplies. In Kottner's words: "Treat adjunct faculty like you'd treat your tenured colleagues. Support them with offices, supplies, access to copiers" (qtd in Stewart). And then think bigger. She writes, "Help support their research, too. Make funds for conferences and travel available to adjuncts. In fact, giving adjunct faculty first crack at the funds would be a great idea to balance out pay inequity" (qtd in Stewart).

Joe Fruscione, a freelance editor, cofounder of PrecariCorps and former adjunct, offered further tips on professional development and job satisfaction. "Allow adjunct faculty to teach upper-level courses in their areas of expertise," he suggested. And he added a thought germane for any adjunct who feels his or her shelf life has expired, urging campuses to provide a "meaningful path to promotion and raises—i.e., reward experience. Don't punish it" (qtd in Stewart). Opening the doors to workshops, teaching awards, and summer seminars to all faculty members can strengthen the entire institution.

According to Douglas Martin, Herbert Freudenberger first used the word "burnout" in psychology in the mid-1970s, notably in his book examining mental health professionals. It is "the extinction of motivation or incentive, especially where one's devotion to a cause or relationship fails to produce the desired results" (qtd. in Martin). As described by Scott Plous and Paul Sephton, Christina Maslach and her colleague Michael P. Leiter later defined the antithesis of burnout as engagement. I first heard the word "burnout" from an adjunct faculty member when I was a secretary, and I was startled. Among the team I served, she appeared dedicated and well regarded by students. In time, I learned that idealism does not inoculate one from burnout. Incidentally, that colleague went on to a distinguished career in Montessori education.

A good fit between the institution and those who work for it—along with competent supervision and support—promotes well-being. Furthermore, if people, places and things do not work together to promote a healthy workplace, it creates a palpable domino effect. All faculty members potentially suffer if the talents of their peers are not fully engaged. And students respond to what faculty embody, from exhaustion to exhilaration. Positive morale is contagious. And can't problem solving involving more perspectives reap dividends as-yet unenvisioned?

A cynical reader might reflect that it's good to keep adjunct faculty uncertain about everything—from available courses next semester to whether the copier will be unjammed before classes start. *Let's keep them on their toes, lest they become slackers.* After all, we are in competition for scant resources. I disagree.

For three years, I served on the Modern Language Association's Committee on Contingent Labor in the Profession and learned about conditions at many colleges and universities. A report titled "Professional Employment Practices for Non-Tenure-Track Faculty Members: Recommendations and Evaluative Questions" that was written by previous members of the committee is available in PDF form (Committee on Contingent Labor in the Profession). If various institutions took even a few questions and worked them through to constructive answers, it could transform conditions for adjunct faculty.

Although some people may still assert that adjunct labor is a given, a low priority, or the rage of the future, the discussion need not stop there. It is within the power of colleges and universities to lead with better professional practices.

> Dedicated to the memory of David Wilder, Artist, adjunct, and activist, 1956–2017 (See Farkas; MacDonald to learn more about Wilder.)

Works Cited

Anonymous. "The Plight of the Nonrenewed." *Inside Higher Ed*, 16 May 2014, https://www.insidehighered.com/view/2014/05/16/plight-one-adjunct-and-many-essay.

Carroll, B. Jill. *Machiavelli for Adjuncts: Six Lessons in Power for the Unempowered*. Aventine, 2004.

Committee on Contingent Labor in the Profession. *Professional Employment Practices for Non-Tenure-Track Faculty Members: Recommendations and Evaluative Questions*, Modern Language Association, June 2011. *Modern Language Association*, 2011, https://www.mla.org/content/download/3368/81826/clip_stmt_final_may11.pdf.

Farkas, Karen. "Part-Time College Faculty to Educate Others about Their Plight on Wednesday." *Cleveland.com*, 24 Feb. 2015, https://www.cleveland.com/metro/2015/02/part-time_college_faculty_to_e.html.

Flaherty, Colleen. "#iammargaretmary." *Inside Higher Ed*, 19 Sept. 2013, www.insidehighered.com/news/2013/09/19/newspaper-column-death-adjunct-prompts-debate.

Harris, Adam. "The Death of an Adjunct." *The Atlantic*, 8 Apr. 2019, https://www.theatlantic.com/education/archive/2019/04/adjunct-professor-higher-education-thea-hunter/586168/.

"Homeless Professor Protests Conditions of Adjuncts." *PBS News Hour*, 31 March 2014, https://www.pbs.org/newshour/nation/homeless-professor-protests-conditions-adjuncts.

Keenan, Elizabeth. "How to Be a Tenured Ally." *Bad Cover Version*, 30 Oct. 2013, https://badcoverversion.wordpress.com/2013/10/30/how-to-be-a-tenured-ally/.

MacDonald, Evan. "Cleveland State University Adjunct Professor Killed in Shooting Was Passionate Artist, Nephew Says." *Cleveland.com*, 27 March 2017, https://www.cleveland.com/metro/2017/03/cleveland_state_university_adj.html.

Martin, Douglas. "Herbert Freudenberger, 73, Coiner of 'Burnout,' Is Dead." *The New York Times*, 5 Dec. 1999, https://www.nytimes.com/1999/12/05/nyregion/herbert-freudenberger-73-coiner-of-burnout-is-dead.html.

New Faculty Majority. http://www.newfacultymajority.info/.

Plous, Scott. "Christina Maslach." *Society Psychology Network*, 4 Aug. 2016, https://maslach.socialpsychology.org/.

PrecariCorps: Agents for Higher Ed. https://precaricorps.org/.

Sephton, Paul. "Dr. Michael Leiter on Combatting Burnout and Promoting Engagement at Work." *Sound Bar*, Jabra, 14 April 2021, https://www.jabra.com/blog/dr-michael-leiter-on-combatting-burnout-and-sparking-engagement-at-work/.

Shine Stewart, Maria. "A Kinder Campus for Adjuncts?" *Inside Higher Ed*, 21 July 2016, https://www.insidehighered.com/advice/2016/07/21/how-improve-teaching-conditions-adjunct-faculty-members-essay.

Styne, Jule, and Bob Merrill. "People." *Second Hand Songs*, https://secondhandsongs.com/work/54816.

"What Is the Windfall Elimination Provision?" *Retirement: Social Security Resource Center*, AARP, 27 Dec. 2021, https://www.aarp.org/retirement/social-security/questions-answers/what-is-the-windfall-elimination-provision.html.

Chapter 7. Statusism: How Adjunct Exploitation Isolates and Divides College Faculty

Christian L. Pyle
Bluegrass Community and Technical College

For six years, I thought daily of death, not as an end to be feared but as a consummation devoutly to be wished.[1] Life seemed hopeless and humiliating, and oblivion seemed a sweet release. Every time I heard that someone had died, I thought, "Lucky bastard." Whenever I heard that someone had committed suicide, I'd think, "Was he an adjunct? If so, I get it." My wife still describes her dread coming home every day, worrying that she would find me dead. Her love kept me alive, and her health insurance allowed me to get treatment. I eventually crawled out of the dark pit of depression and have learned skills to protect myself from falling in again.

My fall into depression began in 2008 during my "adjunct awakening." Prior to this, I had not lamented my contingent status. I began teaching English as a teaching assistant when I started grad school at the University of Kentucky in 1990, and I moved on to work as a part-time instructor at what was then called Lexington Community College, now Bluegrass Community and Technical College (BCTC), in 1997. Prior to 2008, confidence in my ability and work ethic convinced me that I was on the road to full-time employment.

Then came the Great Tenure Debate.

In late 2008, the board of regents for the Kentucky Community and Technical College System (KCTCS), the parent of BCTC, tried to remove the possibility of tenure for new full-time faculty. My initial impulse as a college teacher was to support tenure, even though I was not eligible for it. However, reading the arguments about the issue by full-time faculty members shook my sensibilities. Without tenure, they argued, the college's full-time faculty would all be . . . gasp . . . adjuncts. Adjuncts were described as "rootless," despite the fact that many full-time faculty at BCTC came there from other places while many adjuncts, me included, were native to the area.

Furthermore, we were depicted as unreliable. One associate professor claimed, "Every academic coordinator has a story of the adjunct who bails out the day before the semester begins (or during the midterm)." While that may be true, I suspect there may be even more stories of adjuncts who've gone beyond their job

---

1. Portions of this essay previously appeared in *North of Center* and the *Bluegrass Courier* in articles I wrote about adjunct life. Both were published with the support of tenure-track professor Danny Mayer.

descriptions in service to their departments: serving on committees, aiding with ongoing projects, and jumping in to take over those abandoned classes at the last minute.

Prior to this, I had noticed that when there were full-time openings available, hiring committees in my area either imported someone from another school, or they chose someone who had only been an adjunct at BCTC for a couple of years (as opposed to a couple of decades). I also noted that the pro-tenure arguments stressed that removing tenure would keep the college from "recruiting" new faculty. Finding potential full-time hires seemed easy to me, as adjuncts at BCTC outnumbered tenure-track profs by more than double.

I could see that there was a stigma attached to being an adjunct.

Systems of segregation, disenfranchisement, and marginalization not only are bred by biased mythologies (such as racism, sexism, etc.) but also breed such mythologies. The caste system of employment in higher education has created a mythology I call "statusism." I suspect it is the result of cognitive dissonance: The minds of good people see the unfairness of the system and try to find a justification for it. No one likes to think he or she has benefitted from an unjust system. If full-time, tenure-track teachers are treated better than their part-time colleagues, they must *be* better.

Psychology has shown how even randomly applied labels can affect how people see each other and themselves. In the infamous Stanford prison experiment, for example, college students were randomly designated as "guards" and "prisoners." Soon the "guards" became authoritarian while the "prisoners" submissively accepted the abuse. Thankfully, statusism is not that dramatic, but it is just as real. It is subtle, and it silently creeps into how people who should be colleagues see each other: full-time or part-time, essential or non-essential, voiced or voiceless, permanent or temporary, and tenured or disposable.

One effect of statusism is blaming adjuncts for their status. For example, Catherine Stukel, a full-time professor at Morton Community College, dismissed adjunct concerns as "garbage" in a letter to *The Chronicle of Higher Education*. Why are adjuncts not full-time? She said:

> Perhaps the position is filled, or the tumblers in the universe just didn't fall into the right place for you. Or maybe you aren't aware that you are annoying your colleagues with your opinions about everything, at every meeting, and at every event. Perhaps your full-time colleagues wouldn't select you for full-time work because you are not likable. Perhaps you have a reputation for mediocrity, or you don't fully engage your students. Did you ever think of another profession? Would you advise your own students to work part time with no benefits when there are plenty of full-time opportunities in this world just waiting for them?

To Stukel, the system is a just meritocracy. You didn't get an interview for a full-time job at the school where you've been teaching for years? Obviously, you are either unlikeable or a bad teacher. Psychologically, tenure-track professors have a strong motivation to defend the system that elevates them. "Did you ever think of another profession?" Adjuncts willingly take jobs as adjuncts and don't quit even though their continued adjunct status should tell them they are unsuited for the job, someone like Stukel would say. Thus, adjuncts' exploitation is their own fault for being so exploitable.

Note that Stukel thought an adjunct might be passed over justly for expressing an opinion that, presumably, tenured colleagues did not like hearing. Statusism provides a handy club with which to pound the few adjuncts who are willing to speak out about the injustice of the system. I had a debate with a tenured professor at BCTC whose views were similar to Stukel's. The arena was a Facebook group for BCTC faculty, and the topic was a blog entry by Nick DeSantis about how Delgado Community College changed its pay system so that adjuncts would receive their first checks sooner than seven weeks into the semester. BCTC had a similar delay that made adjuncts wait two to four weeks longer than full-time faculty to receive the first check of the semester, and the delay had proven difficult to fix. (One department chair who tried to fix the problem reported to me that the college president replied, "Aren't the adjuncts used to being screwed over?").

A tenured professor, whom I'll call "TP" from here on, responded to the DeSantis blog entry by posting, "It will be done as long as people are lining up for their abuse?" I replied, "I wouldn't blame the victim for the abuse. With most colleges in America exploiting adjuncts, it's either play the game by their rules or go home." TP was not having any of that: "How many years would it take until it was too much? That is how many years they will exploit adjuncts' labor (which seems forever as they accept whatever is thrown at them). That is not 'me' blaming the 'victims'—just a cold reality drawn from radical labor history."

The discussion got a bit heated, and I did my part to stoke the flames. I fired back, "The privileged, pampered, and paid off teaching class exists as a buffer between the administration and the masses of adjuncts—that's a cold reality, too. Like it or not, you're part of the equation, too." (I was very pleased with the alliteration.) Like, Stukel, TP asked why I didn't do something else with my life, but he also chastised me for inaction, writing, "You don't like it, it is abusive, do something about it." But I am, I protested. I was speaking out about the injustice, which, as a lone adjunct, was about all I could do. TP knew that I had published articles about the adjunct issue and had raised adjunct issues on the college email list.

Then came the catch-22. Like Stukel, TP didn't want to hear adjunct opinions: "This is the problem in regards to you, not adjuncts as a whole. You blame others that in no way exploited you for the fact you have worked as an adjunct for 17 years." He says the exploitation of adjuncts is the fault of adjuncts silently accepting the exploitation, and that we should "do something" about it. However, that "something" should not be to criticize the system, especially if that means pointing out the role the more privileged class plays in the system.

Notice how TP mentioned the number of years I had worked at BCTC? He did that seven times in the conversation. He had done the same thing in a previous discussion when I had been there 14 years. Over and over, he flogged me with the number. (In both cases, I mentioned my years of service simply to establish my ethos, as we say in freshman comp.) For a long time, I was puzzled that long-serving adjuncts were rarely promoted to full-time status when the rare full-time job was available. Full-time profs expect their years of service to be rewarded with tenure and promotions, so why wouldn't adjuncts' years of service merit the same respect? Stukel and TP give us the answer: The longer we "willingly" work as adjuncts, the more pathetically we seem to enable our own exploitation. Each year tenure-track faculty work should bring them rewards; each year adjuncts work should bring us shame.

Although my playfully alliterative description of tenure-track profs as "privileged, pampered, and paid off" was deliberately provocative, my point that the full-time faculty act as a buffer between the administration and the adjuncts is accurate. We are invisible, even though we are the majority of the faculty. In fact, according to the BCTC *2019–2020 Factbook*, part-time instructors were 66.3 percent of the faculty in fall 2018 (Office of Institutional Planning 79). The full-time faculty have regular meetings and elected leaders and representatives at every level of the system. They have offices in suites where they can discuss the employment issues that affect them. They have visibility and a voice. I imagine they often forget adjuncts exist.

In fact, the chair of the faculty council at BCTC once emailed everyone to explain that a new proposal would result in benefits equality for all faculty. He had to be reminded that adjuncts are also faculty members and that we receive no benefits. Adjuncts rarely meet each other, so we have little opportunity to discuss our common interests and act as one. Those few who speak up often face the ire of the full-time faculty who wash their hands of the exploitation of adjuncts.

Despite TP's insistence that my discontent was a personal failing not shared by other adjuncts, every time I made some public stand, I got private emails from other adjuncts thanking me for speaking out. They said that they felt alone until I said publicly what they were feeling privately. Hoping to build some sort of alliance, I always asked if the emailer would be willing to join a group. The response was always along the lines of "Are you kidding?!? I need this job" or "Only if my identity can remain a secret." They are not silent because they accept that their exploitation is their own fault, as TP assumes; they are silent because they are afraid of not being rehired.

We have no job security. Regardless of how long we have taught at a college, the college is under no obligation to offer us classes the next semester. And who decides which adjuncts get classes and how many classes they get? The regents? The president? The academic dean? No. Our bosses are full-time faculty members. The adjuncts who are afraid of speaking out are afraid of the full-time faculty.

This is not to say that tenure-track faculty members try to instill fear or that they are bad people. I have found many sympathetic tenured professors at BCTC, including some who do what they can to change the system of exploitation. One full-time professor published my previous essays in newspapers he edited. Another wrote an essay to accompany one of mine because he worried about me sticking my neck out alone. It's the system that is wrong, not the individuals in it. However, we all have a responsibility to try and change that system. Because they have an organization and a voice, full-time faculty members have more power to effect change than the isolated and invisible adjuncts do.

Stukel's letter prompted some full-time faculty members to push their fellows to join the fight. Amy Lynch-Biniek, a then-associate professor at Kutztown University, posted an open letter to other full-time professors. In it, she takes pride in the hard work that earned her a tenure-track position but acknowledges that her "adjunct colleagues have worked just as hard" without the same rewards. Lynch-Biniek concludes:

> The only way I am able to reconcile working in a field that systematically abuses the majority of its workers is to dedicate my service and scholarship to addressing the problem of labor in higher ed. Too many lucky tenured, though, believe as [Stukel] does, that they are special snowflakes. Or, they turn their eyes away, saying "I can't change it," or "I need to focus on my students." I call bullshit. We *can* change it, and improving the working conditions of all teachers *is* focusing on your students. The time for silence is over. In fact, there never was a time for silence. Become allies to your adjunct colleagues. Do something. Say something. Retweeting isn't enough.

In other words, change can only happen when everyone with a voice in higher education makes that change a priority.

Lynch-Biniek's point that the adjunct crisis affects students is important. The quality of education suffers if a professor doesn't have an office, a computer, institutional support, or healthcare coverage. Adjunct professors' health (and, therefore, their work) suffers not only from lack of medical care but also from exhaustion. Without even cost-of-living wage increases, adjuncts constantly must teach more classes at more schools to race inflation. Seven classes in the fall and six in the spring was my norm for several years. That's about the maximum a freshman comp teacher can do, but I've heard of adjuncts in other disciplines teaching ten classes or more.

To be fair to my full-time friends and colleagues, the system is unfair to them as well. Tenure-track faculty members must jump through endless hoops to be hired, tenured, and promoted. By contrast, at every adjunct job I've had, I've been offered the job *before* meeting with my boss. At that first meeting, I received my textbooks and was pointed toward my first class. Then I just stayed there year after year until the college ran out of classes for me. Garry Trudeau's 1996 depiction of adjunct professors as migrant day laborers only slightly exaggerated the truth. In a brief *Doonesbury* storyline, a guy standing on a flatbed truck said he needed two romantic lit profs, then he pointed to two random people holding up their hands (Trudeau). On the other hand, an assistant professor passes through a long vetting process to teach the same classes I teach after barely a critical glance. The system makes no sense for anyone.

As a profession, we need to rethink how professors are hired, retained, and supported. We need to do it as soon as possible, because our profession is being whittled away by regents, trustees, and state governments that see automated online courses combined with call center support as the best model for higher education. Regents and trustees are often corporate executives, and they see classrooms as the factory floor. Just as they turned manufacturing over to robots, with distribution and retail to follow, they will rid campuses of all full-time professors. The overdependence on adjuncts degrades our profession. Adjuncts are disposable, so the professoriate is disposable. Anyone who values higher education knows the value of having a living person with an active, engaged mind and a storehouse of subject knowledge standing at the front of a classroom. However, those who see colleges as factories will be attracted to the efficiency and homogeneity of automated online courses. The current system is unsustainable, perhaps by design. Why would anyone obtain a master's or doctoral degree with the intention of teaching in college when an adjunct position is the likely result?

So, what do we do?

1. **Unify the faculty.** The caste system breeds statusism that poisons the relationship between full-time and part-time faculty. To defend the professoriate, we must strengthen our profession. If the majority of professors are considered non-essential, how essential are the others? There must be one faculty.
2. **Guarantee adjuncts an equal voice.** As part of faculty unification, the role of faculty in governance must include proportional representation of adjunct faculty.
3. **Protect adjuncts from arbitrary dismissal.** An ombuds for adjunct faculty should be appointed to protect the rights of adjuncts, particularly those who voice adjunct concerns.
4. **Pay adjuncts equally for equal work.** Tenure-track professors estimate the percentage of time they spend teaching as opposed to other duties like committee work and advising. Therefore, it is an easy matter to arrive at the per-credit-hour rate full-time professors are paid at various levels of seniority. As the work of teaching is the same, the pay should be the same. Not recognizing that cheapens our profession. As teaching experience

should be valued regardless of the status of the teacher, adjuncts' years of service should be reflected in their rate of pay.
5. **Lengthen the appointments of established adjuncts.** It's ludicrous that some professors who have been teaching several years at a school are granted jobs for life while others who have been teaching a comparable number of years at the same school have to beg for classes each semester. Once adjuncts have proven their mettle, they should receive longer appointments. They should also be preferred candidates for full-time jobs.

I am writing this in late 2021, but a glance at my works cited will reveal that most of the material came from 2014, which is also when I crossed swords with TP. At that time, I considered myself an adjunct activist and was determined to engage daily in a national conversation about our issues. On February 25, 2015, I participated in National Adjunct Walkout Day by attending a meeting in Louisville and becoming part of a group that adjuncts there were forming. I assumed there would be a Walkout Day every year, but 2015 saw the first and last. The other adjuncts in the group we formed all left academia. My enthusiasm for constant struggle waned.

I sought contentment and, in many ways, have found it. While I hate my job, I love my work. Teaching is an art form, and I am passionate about it. I get to design my classes, and that keeps me from getting bored. More than anything else, I feel like I am doing something worthwhile. I sometimes shed a tear that "there are songs in me that won't be sung," as an old Roy Clark song says ("Yesterday, When I Was Young"). I'll never chair a committee, serve in faculty leadership, or coordinate a subject area. I think I'd excel at those things. However, I remind myself of the songs I've sung. I've introduced students to film noir and been asked what other black-and-white movies they should see. I've lectured on great works of literature and encouraged students to explore their own creativity. I've challenged students to think critically about important issues. Former students have stopped me on the sidewalk to tell me how much they value what they learned in my class, and fellow adjuncts have thanked me for saying out loud what they suffer in silence.

Works Cited

DeSantis, Nick. "Adjuncts at College in Louisiana Get Paychecks After Extra Delay." *The Ticker: Breaking News from All Corners of Academe, The Chronicle of Higher Education*, 24 Sept. 2014, https://www.chronicle.com/blogs/ticker/adjuncts-in-louisiana-get-paychecks-after-complaints-of-delays.

Lynch-Biniek, Amy. "Dear Tenured Faculty: Retweeting Isn't Enough." *Ramblings After Too Much Coffee*, 3 Sept. 2014, https://www.compositionist.net/blog/dear-tenured-faculty-retweeting-isnt-enough.

Office of Institutional Planning, Research, and Effectiveness. *2019–2020 Factbook*, Bluegrass Community and Technical College. *Bluegrass Community and*

Technical College, https://ites.bluegrass.kctcs.edu/modules/ipre/files/2019-20-factbook.pdf.

Pyle, Christian L. "Adjuncts: The Invisible Majority." *North of Center*, 27 Apr. 2011, https://noclexington.com/adjuncts-the-invisible-majority/.

———. "Life in Adjunct America." *Bluegrass Courier*, 24 Mar. 2014.

Stukel, Catherine. "Is That Whining Adjunct Someone We Want Teaching Our Young?," *Letters: Correspondence from* Chronicle *readers, The Chronicle of Higher Education*, 25 Aug. 2014, https://www.chronicle.com/blogs/letters/is-that-whining-adjunct-someone-we-want-teaching-our-young/.

Trudeau, Garry. "Doonesbury," GoComics, 9 Sept. 1996, https://www.gocomics.com/doonesbury/1996/09/09.

"Yesterday, When I Was Young." *Songfacts*, 2022, https://www.songfacts.com/lyrics/roy-clark/yesterday-when-i-was-young.

Chapter 8. Between a Rock and a Hard Place on a Deserted Island: Negotiated Mental Health on College Campuses Through the Lens of a Rebellious Adjunct Professor

Belle H. Foster
INDEPENDENT SCHOLAR

The rock represents people in power, the hard place represents students struggling with their mental health, and the deserted island is where I exist as an adjunct professor—in absolute isolation from any sort of meaningful human contact, let alone a supportive community. I have repeatedly hit barriers whenever trying to advocate for students in a mental health crisis. I have also repeatedly hit my mental health breaking point with seemingly no one to turn to. In a last ditch effort to save my own mental health, I started finding the loopholes in education systems as a way to survive the system and—honestly—survive in general.

This chapter is a confession of all the academic "sins" I've made. In other words, it's a chapter about how I worked the system so the system didn't destroy me. I hope this will be eye-opening for anyone working within or at the mercy of an institution of higher education. (And a little content warning for you: The sarcasm, satire, and cynicism ahead are the only coping mechanisms I have left after working for ten years in higher education.)

The Mental Health Rollercoaster of an Adjunct Professor

I've discovered there are four parts to the mental health roller coaster of an adjunct professor. They are as follows: (1) the new adjunct honeymoon phase, (2) the denial and disillusionment stage, (3) the forget* it milestone (* forget may be replaced with other "f" words), and (4) panic. I will share my regular journey on this rollercoaster to provide some context for why the mental health of adjuncts is not ok.

The new adjunct honeymoon phase is this incredible period of time post-grad school where you feel like you've made it—I miss this phase so much! The honeymoon phase goes something like this: feeling a euphoric sense of gratitude for having a contract (or eight); absolutely loving being in the classroom; being energized by working with so, so, so, so many students (probably serving more students than tenured faculty); and transforming a mediocre curriculum that was handed to you three days before having to teach it into a thing of beauty in front of students' eyes (and the students had no idea!). In the honeymoon phase, you're on fire—look at you displaying those skills (that no one taught you in grad school) and feeling like you have an unbelievable amount of agency because no one ever checks on you (like, ever)—and you get a taste of that glorious academic freedom we all yearn for! You have energy, you reply to emails in seconds, you are a fresh young educator multitasking as you haul your highly caffeinated self from campus to campus five days a week, you listen to pedagogy podcast episodes in your car as you cruise to your next class, and you even arrive early ready to implement whatever innovative strategy you soaked up on the car ride over.

This phase is a high. Your confidence and self-esteem are through the roof. This is your dream. You set a goal and achieved it. This phase can last up to six weeks of each semester. But the longer you teach, the shorter this phase becomes. It's called burnout. After teaching consistently for two years, you no longer have the ability to experience this phase because you can't feel positive feelings, so enjoy the honeymoon phase while it lasts.

The second part of the adjunct mental health roller coaster is the denial and disillusionment stage. (Reminder: This is the stage you start on after you've completed two years of teaching). This stage creeps in, sneaks up on you when you least expect it. Its signature is rationalization (i.e., the justification of unacceptable behavior). It starts with little things like being left off an email—we all make mistakes, no big deal. It starts to escalate to not being informed of a required department-wide meeting (the reminder was sent out before you were officially hired, but you somehow should have known about it). It escalates more to not being properly assigned to your course in the system (oops, administrative error). Therefore, you can't access materials, attendance records, or even be paid in a timely manner. This is where subtle denial and self-gaslighting starts to show up.

Our internal voice says, "It's not that big of a deal in the grand scheme of things," "I should have followed up on this earlier, it's my fault," "it was a mistake, they didn't mean to do this, I shouldn't be so upset," which can lead to thoughts such as "I should stop being so demanding," "I must be exaggerating," "I'm being dramatic," and "is this all in my head?" And eventually through this rationalization, denial, and self-gaslighting, you arrive at accepting how disillusioned you were about adjuncting. (And, for the record, we are spoon-fed this illusion from the moment we are taught the "only" thing to do after high school is to go to college. That's where the knowledge keepers and creators live, and we must join them in their ivory tower. And it's not until the gatekeepers allow us in that we see how dirty that facade is.) This phase can last for some or all of your time as an adjunct professor.

Next is the forget it milestone, which can be unbelievably liberating if you just surrender to it. See, you become a bitter old professor who probably should retire, but you're in your early thirties and haven't even had an interview for a tenure-track position. Probably because you don't have time to look for jobs let alone apply since you're teaching 18 credits in seven different departments while also working any other gigs you can get on the weekends to pay your bills.

So, you resolve to screw the system a little bit (not enough to get fired... but it might be pretty close in some cases, and it's quite an adrenaline rush). For example, since canceling classes is taboo (even if you're physically ill, let alone if you need a mental health day), you replace "class canceled" with "day for independent research with digital check in." You get a quasi day off and students get their work done—it's a win-win. You can get really creative in this part of the mental health rollercoaster, so have fun with it. You may also notice new behaviors emerge, such as not preparing for class, showing up barely on time, always dismissing class at least five minutes early, and increasing your grading speed—because your once carefully followed rubric has now been replaced with more gut-level, intuitive grading with statements like "Meh, I guess it's a B," and "Sure, let's call it an A," and "Ehhhhh, C... minus... or does a D still let them pass?"

And if anyone challenges you on any of this, let them know you're simply working to dismantle a system of oppression, which, according to the antiracist statement the old, White, straight, able-bodied, neurotypical administrators drafted out of guilt in the summer of 2020, is what we all should be striving for anyway. (And for what it's worth, adjuncts are the most marginalized, oppressed group in the academic world.) This part of the rollercoaster usually shows near the end of the semester; however, depending on how long you've been teaching, it could pop in before mid-terms... or day one of the semester.

Once you survive the forget it milestone with minimal liver damage, you reach the final part of the rollercoaster: panic. The panic sets in once you realize you've been so focused on surviving the semester that you haven't secured any contracts for future semesters. Now you're unemployed after living paycheck to paycheck with really poor mental health and no way to afford the care you need to start the rollercoaster all over again or the professional development you need to change careers.

So, either out of habit or preferring to dance with the devil you know, you get back in line and wait to ride it again. And I should note, you must ride this rollercoaster alone. Your colleagues may be on the same rollercoaster, but you only see them in passing, never long enough to commiserate or build a supportive network with them. Anticipate this part of the rollercoaster at least twice a year.

Just a "Full-Time" Adjunct

Over the past several years, I've started calling myself a "full-time" adjunct—meaning I'm either in a classroom or in a car for at least 12 hours a day, five days a week each semester. I've been teaching in higher education for about ten years. There's a cycle you go through as a contingent educator. At first, you feel grateful for being given the obscene privilege of being allowed in a precious classroom. There's the honeymoon phase of telling your friends and family you teach at a college. They don't understand the nuances, so they consider you a full-time, tenured professor (and I gave up on seeing this as an educational moment a long time ago).

Most students also don't understand the nuances of higher education, and they even call you Dr. because they just assume all professors have Ph.D. degrees. I prefer to dodge this educational moment because it's one of the few times in adjucting when you finally feel respected. So, let's talk about where all the disrespect comes from. The decision makers—the rocks—know how to crush you slowly. It's the continuous small comments, the pathetic attempts at empathy, and borderline microagressions that start to wear you down.

The Rocks

When I began sharing with other professionals in the field that I was an adjunct, I was repeatedly told by those in tenured positions that the only way to survive as an adjunct is to get a rich husband (i.e., perpetuate the heteronormative patriarchy, lean into toxic masculinity, engorge in capitalism, and maintain all the systemic oppression that got us here in the first place.) In hindsight, this should have been the warning sign to turn around and reconsider my career choices. But I was in the honeymoon phase, and no one was going to stop me.

I've been on the receiving end of my fair share of passive-aggressive comments from colleagues saying that being childless reduces my value and worth within a department—being childless also seems to green light extra exploitation because I couldn't possibly have any other responsibilities or want time away from working. This is where a lot of the denial and disillusionment showed up for me. I thought we were a faculty, a team, but I learned quickly where I was in the hierarchy of adjuncts.

I also witnessed one faculty member fat-shame a student, then reward her when she lost weight—the department chair said nothing. That same department chair sometimes turned to me in awe and say, "I don't know how you [adjuncts] do it." Because we have bills to pay and need to eat is how we do it. And we don't need your sympathy; we need you to change the system.

I've been told by a supervisor that I'm nothing more than a teacher who should only focus on teaching. That is, of course, unless there is the slightest suspicion that a student's mental health is plummeting. Then, we must submit early alerts and wellness check warnings immediately, only to be gaslit by the department heads who had not witnessed the same behavior, so the head of the department must be right and poor little ol' me is clearly out of touch with how the system of education is expertly [insert eye roll] set up to support students.

The Hard Places

Student mental health is not ok. We've all seen the news stories since COVID-19 hit, but I noticed student mental health deteriorating a few years prior, and schools were not adapting well then—or now—to this crisis. I think about the times student mental health directly changed my teaching: the student who was on her phone repeatedly in class because her mother had been admitted to the ER, the student who witnessed his mother flatline and be brought back to life, the student who failed out of school because the disability resource center didn't support him in time to pass his classes, the students navigating immigration and deportation with family members, the student with awful attendance whose abusive boyfriend wouldn't let her go to class, the student who was suddenly homeless when the dorms shut down for COVID-19, the student who's on the phone with a crisis counselor instead of logging into zoom, the student who won't turn their camera on because they can't stop crying, and my list could go on.

When you know what stress and trauma students are bringing into the classroom, it's really hard to just teach. It's hard to be a "good" teacher who holds students to policies and protocols that are so insignificant when you know students are dealing with actual life-and-death situations. So, what are we adjuncts supposed to do? Re-traumatize the students by having no empathy and failing them when they don't comply with the system? Get fired for allowing our students too much grace, which might be jeopardizing accreditation? Having to constantly toggle between these two pretty significant questions is exhausting. I need my poverty-wage job so I can survive. But always I am in a position of service where I hope everyone else survives the semester, too.

For me, risking getting fired is worth it to be able to sleep at night with my integrity intact. I choose to bend the rules as much as I can so that the system won't break any of us within it. And, yes, there are options for student to take an incomplete or withdraw due to extenuating circumstances. But the schools I've worked in have denied students those options because I'm an adjunct. What message does that send to students? Do you think they feel supported by the administration? Do you think their perception of me as their teacher changes? It sure does. And I also internalize it.

The Deserted Island

For me, the academic freedom that I felt in the honeymoon phase eventually morphed into a feeling of complete and utter isolation. My community consists of me and my students. That's it. Students are my community. I am connected on social media with more students than colleagues because I actually know my students. I could not pick my colleagues out of a lineup unless their email was taped to their forehead, and even then, 50/50 guess. The colleagues I do know are functional acquaintances at best, not people I can trust or turn to in times of struggle.

I see supervisors only under stressful situations (department-wide meetings and events and when something goes wrong). If I am one of the randomly selected adjuncts to have a teacher evaluation, then I might get some more interaction, but again, this occurs under an umbrella of stress. (Also, I have not received a teacher evaluation in over three years). Everyone around me operates under the "no news is good news" belief, so as long as I keep students happy enough not to complain, I don't have to see anyone. It starts as an odd blessing but eventually becomes very disheartening.

A Perfect Storm

While riding the mental health rollercoaster between a rock and a hard place on a deserted island, it's inevitable that the mental health of adjunct faculty members suffers. And we know the mind and body are connected, so when mental health suffers, so does physical health. And since some of us haven't found that rich husband yet, we must rely on mediocre health insurance to help put us back together long enough to teach a few more classes. But taking care of mental and physical health is expensive (even if insurance helps out), so we pick up another class or two in order to have the money to see a professional regularly. But that's more stress with more department demands and more students wanting access to you, plus more time in the car driving to and from counseling that could be used grading or eating or sleeping.

So, what can we give up? The contracts that give us at least a little bit of income? The therapist and doctor's appointments that make sure we can function somewhat properly? Deciding this while also navigating the system of education hiring processes, which is different at each school and in each department, while also between contracts navigating the unemployment system, which is not set up to support gig workers, while also navigating the healthcare system, all so we can work and get our basic needs met? Similar to why students don't abide by deadlines when they have a family crisis, as an adjunct, I could care less if I respond to emails fast enough because I'm also in crisis. The adjunct crisis is becoming a perfect storm. Give me one reason why it's worth staying.

Conclusion/Disclaimer Out of Extreme Guilt

Despite all that I've said here, I know somewhere out there positive things are happening in higher education. I would not be where I am and who I am today without my years in higher education (for better or worse). I have met classmates and colleagues who have become like family to me because of the opportunities I've had in higher education as a student and an employee. However, those positives are few and far between. The negatives do not *outweigh* the positives, but negatives do *outnumber* the positives by a landslide. It seems the longer I stay in higher education, the fewer positives I experience. Teaching through a pandemic has left me with few if any positives.

Call it burnout, call it trauma, call it whatever you want. There is not enough resiliency in the world to withstand the demands higher education is placing on adjuncts. With three-quarters of the faculty being contingent, decision makers need to address this crisis or the ivory towers will crumble. And, I will say, shout-out to those who are full time with secure contracts and benefits. I understand it's not easy, and you are also overworked and underpaid (or at least maybe half of you are). Being in education is not easy, but you have job security and a job that pays for your healthcare coverage during a pandemic. Your basic needs are met.

I was lucky enough to have my primary care physician write a note saying I couldn't teach in a classroom during the COVID-19 pandemic due to an ongoing, undiagnosed health condition. Without that note, I would have been required to be in unsafe work environments or forced to quit. Higher education is abusive to those who donate the greatest number of hours and need their jobs the most. My hope is that there are no rocks, no hard places, and no deserted islands in the future of higher education. But that can only happen sustainably with massive changes from the top down.

Chapter 9. Unheard Voices and Unseen Faces: The Experience of Adjuncts

Nooshan Ashtari and Pamela Minet-Lucid
INDEPENDENT SCHOLARS

Let's think about universities and colleges in the US and the world. What are these bastions of knowledge? How are these resources marketed, produced, and expressed? According to Junct Rebellion, in the United States, "state universities used to be free, or very low-cost; they used to employ full-time faculty," but today, "80% of faculty across the country are hired on 'adjunct' contracts, usually lasting one semester at a time. Classes are designed and overseen by administrators who have never taught. Administrators outnumber both faculty and students on most campuses across the U.S. In short, our academic system has been hijacked by for-profit business models . . . " ("About junctrebellion").

In this system, much of the teaching is accomplished by adjunct professors, also referred to as part-time or contingent faculty. Data supports this, and according to New Faculty Majority, "75.5 percent of U.S. college faculty are now off the tenure track...1.3 out of 1.8 million faculty members." Furthermore, of that contingent faculty, "just over 50% are . . . 'adjunct,'" which includes minimal wages, no health benefits, and no 403(b) contributions from their employer ("Facts about Adjuncts"). This presents a clear injustice and inequality between the full-time faculty and the adjunct faculty.

In "The Professional Identity of Adjunct Faculty: Exploratory Study at a Private University in the UAE," Taghreed Ibrahim Masri found through his qualitative study that adjunct faculty are in conflict about their professional selves because of "being perceived differently by their students, colleagues, administrators and themselves. Results also showed that adjuncts are vulnerable, insecure, and embarrassed to declare their identity to their students" (16). This is part of the adjunct dilemma: maintaining a professional role while feeling like a member of the underclass.

In this chapter, we will walk you through some of these adjuncts' stories. Scholars who wanted to be academics their whole lives, some of whom moved to other countries to do so and succeeded extraordinarily well, find that being an adjunct absolutely rips them to the soul. It is the insecurity of this job, which depends on semester-by-semester hiring, that renders adjuncts disposable in a department and causes them to feel like they are unseen.

Always being treated as disposable pieces in the system is extremely stressful and affects mental health, as in the case of the participants in this study. Often adjuncts operate completely on their own and do not have an office or much contact with full-time faculty; consequently, they are literally unseen in their departments, although in the classroom they are fully engaged with a passion for teaching and a commitment to the field in which they specialize.

The adjuncts' stories that we weave in this article tell of a desire to participate fully, of their love for teaching, of their grit and persistence within the unfortunate insecurity of life in a subtle but persistent class system made up of full-time and part-time faculty, and of the decision-making power of administrators. Most of the time, the voices of adjunct faculty are not heard, and their faces and problems are not seen nor addressed. Therefore, our hope is that we provide them, even if only minimally, with an opportunity to share their concerns and experiences.

Hearing their Voices, Seeing their Faces

The conditions we have described illustrate why we decided to investigate more closely the professional lives and work experiences of seven adjunct professors. Andy, David, Francesca, Jesse, Ken, Sylvia, and Zoe are pseudonyms chosen to protect the identities of the participants. Collectively, the participants have been adjunct professors at various colleges and universities for 10–18 years, and their ages range from their 30s to their 70s.

We chose narrative inquiry as the basis of this qualitative research to examine through their own voices and stories these adjuncts' lived experiences (Connelly and Clandinin 277; Merriam and Tisdell). We triangulated the data by using semi-structured interviews, journal entries, and focus groups. We then analyzed the collected, recorded, and transcribed data to lead us to the main themes that emerged, which we will explore further in the following sections.

Exploitation and Unjust Systems

One of the main themes that emerged from the data was exploitation and unjust systems in higher education. Without exception, all the participants expressed an incredible amount of passion when talking about teaching and sharing their knowledge, even though the work circumstances created for them have been far from ideal. Jesse, for instance, discussed the politics that take place behind the scenes each semester: "The politics of it all is hard to stomach sometimes because these are the people who decide if they have a course for you to teach, these are the people who decide if you get a promotion, and these are people who decide if you get to be on committees. This is part of the toxic culture of academia, the huge conflict of interest."

While discussing the exploitation experienced by adjuncts, Sylvia mentioned that after more than a decade of working as an adjunct faculty, she feels "like a shell—over time the system has made me feel like a shell." Zoe touched upon this subject further, adding, "I don't get paid equally. I don't know my future, my job could disappear any moment, but I still want to do it. There is no end. It is control based on your passion. A system that is progressively getting worse."

Similar sentiments were shared by Andy: "It used to be all I cared about, my true passion and goal in life, but after more than ten years of not having any kind of job security, stability, and having debilitating student loans that keep adding interest, I think that pursuing an academic career was one of the worst decisions of my life." This sentiment reveals the unending exploitation of deeply passionate and highly qualified experts by unfair treatment in higher education.

Identity Loss and Gains

Identity was also a significant topic when the participants explored their experiences as adjuncts. Francesca talked about the dual nature of her identity that comes with the respect and status of being called a professor but ironically being paid less than a construction worker. Sylvia examined her identity, expressing that she has lost touch with her true self as a teacher: "I feel like a puppet sometimes. I feel like being an adjunct for so many years has stolen my enthusiasm and identity."

Jesse compared being an adjunct with being in a codependent relationship:

> There's a lot of stress as an adjunct faculty member, and we do a lot, and that's kind of like a codependent relationship, where we let certain things happen to us because we have to, and we're at the same time part of that relationship, agreeing and consenting to things, but we know it's not in our best interest. So, you stay in this kind of yucky relationship, and we're just completely codependent on each other. It would be nice at some point to just erase the codependency and be like, "Hey, you're a valuable part of our community, and we're going to give you stability, and security, and benefits."

Authenticity and Autonomy

Mass standardization, inflexible curricula, and strict regulations are phenomena that have caused the authenticity and autonomy of adjunct faculty members to be threatened. Andy likened working as a contingent faculty member to "following the rules of the jungle" because of the huge power differences between adjuncts and full-time faculty:

> Every now and then, they throw us a bone by inviting us to some things, but we never get paid and are not treated equally, or as if we matter anyway. In a way, sometimes I feel some of the full-time faculty like it this way because the less secure adjuncts are in their positions, the more secure and powerful they are in their full-time positions. They have less competition and more control and power over everything that happens in the department.

This control and power also translates to what can or cannot be taught during class time. With many universities offering multiple sections of the same courses each semester, the full power and control over choosing the course content and assignments go to the full-time faculty while the part-time faculty are asked to follow the materials in detail. Zoe discussed how she tries to be authentic in her instruction despite having to use materials and assignments that she would not necessarily have chosen herself; she explained she does this by not pretending to be somebody else while teaching and by telling students "anecdotes that are relevant and enable transfer through metaphor." Sylvia also explored her difficulties with maintaining her authenticity and autonomy, saying:

> I see how following syllabi that I truly don't feel passionate about affects my teaching negatively and how it affects my students' learning negatively. It is also a huge disrespect to the mind and soul of a scholar and expert because it technically strips away any kind of professionality and individuality of a professor and researcher who has spent decades of their lives studying the field and working in all aspects of it.

Life Quality and Mental Health

Perhaps the most devastating aspects of being an adjunct faculty member are the negative effects of these uncertain jobs on life quality and mental health. Francesca talked about the stressful nature of not having consistent paychecks even though she is a highly qualified expert in her field, saying, "Being in a low income [bracket], you just live day by day. Every time you have a bill coming in, it's like, okay, how am I gonna pay it?" Jessie also highlighted this issue by discussing his constant stress, his financial uncertainties, and the fact that as a part-time faculty member, there is never a guarantee that courses will be available the following semester and, thus, the job can disappear overnight.

For some, such as Andy, the cut goes even deeper: "It has affected me in so many ways. I am in my 40s with no job security and no reliable paycheck and a mountain of debt and student loans I will never be able to pay back for the rest of my life. The way schools treat adjuncts is criminal. I hated every day of it for ten years." David also mentioned that he has not been able to make any concrete life plans, such as pursuing marriage and building a family, due to the unsettled nature of his part-time teaching jobs.

Furthermore, Sylvia discussed that the way she has been treated by full-time faculty members and administrators over the years has had long-term effects on her mental health by contributing to her anxiety and depression. When recalling an incident that involved having her fully enrolled courses abruptly taken away a few days before the beginning of a new semester because of low enrollment in the full-time faculty's sections, she elaborated:

When I complained, the first thing they told me was, "You were never going to become full-time anyway," which was the most condescending and irrelevant response they could possibly give. My complaint wasn't anything about becoming full-time. It was about not putting another fellow human in such a horrible situation with no warning, when now they are jobless with no possibility to look for other courses by that time of the semester. Even more than being professionals, which they weren't, for me it was about being decent humans, and the whole experience affected me to the extent that now even years later I can't trust any of my colleagues.

Future Possibilities or Lack Thereof

Some areas of study and expertise, such as engineering, law, and medicine, might have other options for adjunct faculty to pursue; however, other fields are not as fortunate. Andy highlighted this point by saying, "In my field of humanities, there are not that many options with a Ph.D. There are very limited opportunities for us outside of academia." Sylvia also echoes similar concerns: "Most of the time I am overqualified for the jobs that I could have easily taken with a B.A. or M.A., and even if I take them, I would still not be able to pay the huge amount of debt that was accumulated getting a useless terminal degree."

For some others participants who have jobs with more security, the horizons are brighter. For Ken, who is a school administrator as his main career, being an adjunct is a way to keep in touch with university students. However, Ken still recognizes that if he did not have his full-time job, the adjunct position would not be sufficient to maintain his normal lifestyle. He explains, "For the amount of money you receive, it is not like my real work as a school administrator. Yet coming in contact with wonderful students that have varied backgrounds, who also want to make a difference in the lives of children, is rewarding in and of itself."

Zoe also emphasizes that the best way to hold an adjunct or part time position is if a person has another source of support: "If you have another source of income, if you have a partner who is willing to support or share in the financial responsibilities, yes. But if you are a person without a partner, and you might have other people to take care of, whether it's a child, whether it's an adult who can't work for themselves, whether it's an elderly person, being an adjunct is absolutely impossible."

Overall, none of the participants could have survived in today's economy by solely relying on adjunct positions. The lack of possibilities, hope, and motivation that the limitations of the adjunct system impose in turn lowers the quality of educational systems, with more professors and true educators leaving the field because of the broken system that does not support its own members.

Discussion and Possible Solutions

Throughout this chapter, we aimed to pull the curtains so the faces and stories of adjunct professors, some of whom have devoted decades of their lives to their professional careers, could be seen and their voices could be heard: faces and voices that unfortunately the unjust systems of exploitation in higher education have chosen to ignore, silence, and hide by their lack of actions, care, and support. The common thread among all the stories was a narration of lives and work done out of passion and devotion, which have gone unappreciated and underpaid by those in charge of making decisions.

As documented in this chapter, the situation for adjuncts is grim not only financially but also in terms of identity and agency. Primarily, what can be seen in this systemic relationship is a lack of agency on the part of adjuncts. Why is this important? Because as Albert Bandura attests, "the capacity to exercise control over the nature and quality of one's life is the essence of humanness" (1), and having this capacity is having agency. Lacking this agency is de facto reducing the humanness of an adjunct professor. Bandura refers to the "nature and quality" of life. In the stories told by the participants, one can feel the lack of control over their own agency in their teaching, in their choices of syllabi, in their teaching materials, in their very plans for their daily or weekly classes.

Additionally, all the adjuncts interviewed for this study felt a lack of agency in terms of being able to advocate for themselves, being able to fully participate in departments, and being able to have a sense of control over their own futures. In the interviews with the participants, an extreme tension was exhibited between the desire to teach and the actual situation of teaching as a part-time faculty member in a university or college setting. This tension can be seen as a type of exploitation based on desire, where the desire to teach is manipulated by sovereign power, to use Foucault's term (Fendler 43), a hierarchical power that has control over the lives of the participants, in this case, adjunct faculty.

The hope of this chapter is that by bringing these stories to light, more doors will open for communication and transparency among the administrators and the full-time faculty in higher education to address the discrepancies that exist in hiring and treating the part-time faculty. Administrators and full-time faculty members need to see and acknowledge the selfless efforts, dedicated time, and shared personal resources adjuncts put on the line day in and day out of their professional lives with no expectations other than the hope to one day be treated fairly and equally.

The foundation of equality, community, knowledge, and justice that higher education was once built upon and promised to offer its members is absent for adjuncts, who now do the majority of teaching in higher education. Unfortunately, higher education seems to have moved into a business model, which puts cost above human treatment.

Is there a solution? Is there an end to this inequity? We'd like to provide some suggestions to administrators and other stakeholders in the university/college system on priorities for fixing this situation. The first suggestion has to do with the financial insecurity—a living wage with security is essential, and its lack was one of the major causes of stress for the participants. Course pay and payment for preparation time for adjuncts should be equal with what is provided for the full-time faculty, and if there is curriculum work, there should be remuneration for serving on committees or attending meetings. We advocate for equal remuneration for equal load. Administrators also need to have empathy and understanding in order for them to initiate some change.

One way to get to this point could be through workshops and by providing information to increase the emotional intelligence (Goleman) of the administrators and faculty who affect the lives of adjuncts. Increased valuing and development of emotional intelligence would lead to increased empathy towards the adjuncts' experience and the stress that they face.

A comprehensive review of the adjunct faculty situation should also be accomplished across structural, political, human resource, and symbolic frames (Bolman and Deal 236) of the organization. As Lee G. Bolman and Terrence E. Deal explain, in the symbolic frame, "myth and symbols help humans make sense of the chaotic, ambiguous world in which they live" (354). In the symbolic theater piece of adjunct life, adjuncts perform perfectly in their classrooms where they pretend to be fully integrated and valued members of the community in which they teach. To illustrate, one of the participants spoke of being a "puppet." To develop identity, there should be greater inclusion of adjunct faculty members in retreats, committees, and projects. Yet, this inclusion needs to be equal and remunerated, not the typical situation of the adjunct being unpaid and powerless to say no in order to keep their job.

Furthermore, on the systemic level, more full-time positions should be opened. Adjunct faculty members should be able to fill them, or if additional classes become available, the existing adjunct faculty members should fill them. A system overhaul is needed wherein the reliance on disposable contingent faculty is replaced by equitable hiring practices. In "There is No Such Thing as an Adjunct Professor," Junct Rebellion explores the language used around adjuncts:

> The label "adjunct" was applied to us by those who sought to deprofessionalize the role of the scholar, both on the campus and in the country.... The word means "supplemental, not essential." ... There is nothing "adjunct" about the role we play, and nothing supplemental to our responsibilities and role in fulfilling any mission dedicated to the pursuit of higher learning.... There is no such thing as an "adjunct" professor. We are essential.

Our hope is that by revealing the faces and unmuting the voices of the adjunct participants who shared with us, an increased awareness of their exploitation, stress, and identity, will lead to a ripple of change in the system. Telling the participants' personal stories can influence movement toward emergent strategies for change, "co-creating in the future more options for working with each other and embodying the things we fight for—dignity, collective power, love, generative conflict, and community" (Brown 9). This movement is fed by the deepened knowledge provided by narrative inquiry. We hope that these stories will contribute to a change in the treatment of adjunct faculty.

Works Cited

Bandura, Albert. "Social Cognitive Theory: An Agentic Perspective." *Annual Review of Psychology*, vol. 52, no. 1, 2001, pp. 1–26. *Annual Reviews*, https://doi.org/10.1146/annurev.psych.52.1.1.

Bolman, Lee G. and Terrence E. Deal. *Reframing Organizations: Artistry, Choice, and Leadership*. 6th ed., Jossey-Bass, 2017. *Wiley Online Library*, https://doi.org/10.1002/9781119281856.

Brown, Adrienne Maree *Emergent Strategy: Shaping Change, Changing Worlds*. AK Press, 2017.

Connelly, F. Michael, and D. Jean Clandinin. "Stories of Experience and Narrative Inquiry." *Educational Researcher*, vol. 19, no. 5, 1990, pp. 2–14. *SAGE Journals*, https://doi.org/10.3102%2F0013189X019005002.

"Facts about Adjuncts." *New Faculty Majority*, https://www.newfacultymajority.info/facts-about-adjuncts/.

Fendler, Lynn. *Michel Foucault*. Continuum, 2010.

Goleman, Daniel. "What Makes a Leader?" *Harvard Business Review*, Jan. 2004, https://hbr.org/2004/01/what-makes-a-leader.

Junct Rebellion. "About junctrebellion." *The Homeless Adjunct*, https://junctrebellion.wordpress.com/author/junctrebellion/.

———. "There is No Such Thing as an Adjunct Professor." *The Homeless Adjunct*, 18 Apr. 2020, https://junctrebellion.wordpress.com/2020/04/18/there-is-no-such-thing-as-an-adjunct-professor/.

Masri, Taghreed Ibrahim. "The Professional Identity of Adjunct Faculty: Exploratory Study at a Private University in the UAE." *English Language Teaching*, vol. 11, no. 10, 2018, pp. 16–29. *CCSE: Canadian Center of Science and Education*, https://doi.org/10.5539/elt.v11n10p16.

Merriam, Sharan B., and Elizabeth J. Tisdell. *Qualitative Research: A Guide to Design and Implementation*. 4th ed., Jossey-Bass, 2016.

Chapter 10. Ignorance Is Bliss

Ann Wiley
INDEPENDENT SCHOLAR

Let me preface this by saying, I could lose my *jobs* for writing this chapter.

– Ann Wiley

When an institution silences the voices of almost 50 percent of its faculty, even well-intentioned individuals will unknowingly create an uncomfortable work environment. There is a danger in dehumanizing and excluding adjuncts from conversations that ultimately affect the quality and integrity of higher education. This chapter explores the seemingly blissful ignorance in higher education decision-making that results from an absence of adjunct perspectives, and it explores this tendency from three different, yet overlapping, views: students, full-time faculty, and administration.

View 1: Student Awareness

What do college students really know about the differences between the full-time and part-time faculty, and how does it ultimately affect their course selection and cost of education? The secret has been out for a while now: "Both two-year and four-year colleges are particularly heavily reliant on short-term non-tenure instructors, which comprise 75 percent of all faculty in two-year colleges and 39 percent of all faculty in four-year colleges" (Ran and Xu 42). This decades-long trend in higher education has led to a rise in adjunct unionization across the country, drawing more attention to the poor working conditions and making more students aware of the volatile nature of many of their professors' employment. With this knowledge, many students now have leverage over their own mentors.

With over 13 years of experience as an adjunct instructor, I was curious about undergraduate students' perceptions and understandings of their part-time professors. In a recent casual interview, an undergraduate student currently attending the University of Pittsburgh who prefers to remain anonymous told me, "Across the various departments, students will typically take elective courses, which are often taught by adjunct professors. Students usually suspect these classes to be easier, but they are frequently surprised when they realize the courses require just as much work as any non-elective course."[1]

---

1. Interview. Conducted by Ann Wiley, 26 Sept 2021.

After hearing this comment, I asked another student, unaffiliated with the first, who currently attends a private four-year college in another state about the perceptions of adjuncts at their school, and to my surprise and disappointment, their response was quite similar. My head was reeling with questions and concerns for the future of higher education. When students lose respect for their professors and try to cheat the system, doesn't this pose a major risk to the quality of higher education?

According to a study conducted in 2017 by the Center for Analysis of Postsecondary Education and Employment,

> students on average received higher grades when taking courses with short-term non-tenure faculty, lower grades when taking courses with long-term non-tenure faculty, and even lower grades when taking courses with tenure faculty. In contrast to the positive results associated with contemporaneous course performance, however, both types of non-tenure instructors are negatively associated with students' subsequent course enrollment and performance, and taking courses taught by short-term non-tenure faculty is associated with the largest negative effects. (Ran and Xu 5)

Much to my dismay, the student rumors are often true about taking easier courses taught by adjuncts. As an adjunct myself who takes pride in my student outcomes, this is disheartening. According to this study, if students take introductory courses with adjuncts, they are more likely to get a better grade; however, they may not realize that they are also more likely to do worse in subsequent courses.

The strain and lack of support for contingent faculty who are employed on a temporary basis and have little to no job security may cause the reduction in the difficulty of course content or the relaxing of grading criteria to achieve better student evaluations. Whether an adjunct's semester-to-semester contract is renewed is often linked to the results of their student evaluations. In addition, adjuncts often are paid only for their time in the classroom, so any additional workload of course preparation and grading is unpaid labor. When part-time professors take on multiple classes at multiple institutions to make a living wage, the logistics of hours spent on classroom preparation must be divided up among multiple places of employment. There are only so many hours in the day.

Often adjuncts are hired for courses the same week that classes start with little to no paid preparation time. I was hired only a few days before the start of classes to teach two sections of a course I had never taught before. The full-time professor who normally taught the course was reluctant to share their instruction materials even though I was doing them a favor. I was expected to teach each section for $1,800 total, before taxes, for the entire semester—at the drop of a hat. Pregnant at the time and commuting between two different schools, I put 10,000 miles on my car that semester. I even took an extra change of clothes to shower in between classes at one of the school gyms.

Fortunately, I was able to time both of my pregnancies for the end of the spring semester, so I didn't miss out on much pay, could recover over the summer, and could return to teach in the fall without losing my jobs. There is currently no job protection, let alone maternity leave, for female adjuncts who get pregnant at any of the schools where I have taught. To top it all off, my husband and I at the time were both contract workers and could not afford insurance, so we were also preparing to go into debt for the cost of childbirth. This type of treatment doesn't seem to match the new equity initiatives that my places of employment are touting.

With these working conditions stacked against me, how fair is it to compare my quality of teaching to that of a full-time professor? I rarely shared this story out of pride and for fear that I could lose my job if my truths showed up in a student evaluation. I have always felt that revealing to students how little I am respected will only lead to an even larger amount of exploitation. When students know how little their school values many of their adjunct professors, then they have leverage over many of their professors. Students may feel they have the upper hand in these situations, but the system is also cheating many of them in the long run.

Adjunct professors often have qualifications equal to or sometimes higher than full-time professors, and many adjunct professors work at multiple institutions in the same region at the same time. In 2010, the Affordable Care Act provided an opportunity for many adjuncts along with other Americans who were not provided access to insurance through their employers to obtain a healthcare plan. In this way, it was helpful, but in other ways, it made the life of many adjuncts even more challenging because it ended up dispersing their labor among campuses. Schools placed a limit on the workload of part-time instructors to avoid the mandate to provide healthcare benefits (Bachinger).

With this change, adjuncts who taught five courses at one school were now only able to teach two or three and therefore had to pick up classes at other campuses. Postsecondary schools in the same region share from the same pool of adjuncts. There is nothing stopping an undergraduate student from taking an identical course taught by the same professor at a community college for a fraction of the cost of the nearby four-year private university. Of course, the credits would have to transfer, but many neighboring schools often have articulation agreements to ensure an easy transfer. With a little research, students could save themselves a lot of money while still completing their degree at a preferred institution.

View 2: Full-Time Allies with Strings Attached

> With these adjuncts, it's like hiring a pulse.
> – *Anonymous Full-Time Professor*

Full-time faculty members are often unintentionally insensitive to the situation of adjuncts due to the exclusion of adjunct representation in higher education. When adjuncts are not compensated for attending and therefore excluded from department meetings and the decisions made in them, full-time professors are more inclined to pile on more workload for them, pass stressors onto them, and dehumanize their experience. Even more disturbingly, the higher education system encourages adjunct faculty members to remain silent for fear that speaking up, even when it is critical to do so, may cause retribution. This section includes specific examples from a variety of adjunct experiences of full-time faculty members inflicting microaggressions, scheduling conflicts, workload-exceeding contracts, and pedagogical research thefts, all of which create an unprofessional work environment for adjunct faculty.

Decisions made by the full-time faculty that directly impact the working conditions of adjuncts often intentionally dismiss or unintentionally exclude the adjunct perspective. Adjuncts are rarely invited or compensated to attend department meetings in which they have little to no governance power anyway. In the rare event part-time faculty members are asked for their input, they often remain silent or gloss over their true opinions to prevent any form of discontent among their employers.

For example, at one institution, I was asked to attend a meeting led by two full-time faculty members on how the methods and content of the course I was teaching were to be changed. Of the five people in the meeting, the two full-time professors, who had never taught the course, were instructing the three adjuncts, who had decades of combined experience, on how to teach the course. Although on the surface the full-time faculty members appeared to be asking for candid feedback, it was obvious they just wanted reinforcement of a decision they had already made. What should have been collaborative research among colleagues resulted in an uncomfortable, disconnected, dismissive work environment. Extreme power differences between the full-time faculty and contractual professors can disturb and inhibit work relationships and, consequently, undermine organizational effectiveness.

Even in these unfavorable conditions, adjuncts are expected to continue their own research to stay relevant in their field with little to no support to do so. A colleague of mine, who wants to remain anonymous for fear of retaliation, was given the "opportunity" to develop an online course. They had been an adjunct for several years and jumped on this practically unpaid opportunity in hopes that it would lead to something more (as many adjuncts do in hopes that hard work will lead to a full-time position that rarely comes to fruition). At this school, there was little to no compensation for building online courses and no guarantee of teaching the very course you invested time to develop.

After a summer of unpaid workshops and hundreds of hours spent designing and redesigning the course, my colleague was instructed over private texts to send the full-time professor the new and improved course for review. The adjunct complied to their superior's request only to discover later that the full-time professor directly copied the course materials into their own section's online portal to teach that semester. It turns out that the full-time professor was supposed to develop their own course over the summer but instead decided to steal my colleague's homework because they were too busy to do their own. Personal images from the adjunct's family had even remained in the copied stolen course! As if that weren't enough, the full-time professor went on to accept an award for the class based on their adaptable teaching skills moving content to an online platform.

My colleague filed an official complaint with the dean, which ultimately resulted in no punishment for the abuse of power and plagiarized material. My fellow adjunct was expected to continue to teach and just forget about this irreparable event. Even when adjunct voices are heard, they can be buried and threatened into submission. Voices that are silenced are no different than voices that were never heard.

When adjunct voices are nonexistent in scheduling changes that will directly impact their working conditions, the logistics of their experience often get lost on paper. The basic needs of adjuncts at a school where I teach were not considered when making a major course scheduling change. To accommodate enrollment increases, the department added more sections of courses by decreasing the times between sections down to merely ten minutes. On paper, this solved the enrollment problem by allowing another section of studio classes to take place in the room while also providing students with more enrollment options. Nobody thought or cared to ask how this would affect the adjuncts who would be teaching these back-to-back, 2-hour-40-minute courses with only a ten-minute break between them.

In ten whole minutes, I answer questions after class, use the restroom, go to my car (because during the pandemic we cannot eat in the building unless we have an office), remove my mask, sanitize my hands, eat lunch, put on my mask, rush to the room, and prepare for my next class to begin. Let me mention that I do not have keys to the room, so each day while sitting in my car, I have anxiety about leaving my personal laptop and other equipment in the unlocked, unattended room.

When I started working at this university, there was a designated adjunct office that required ID access that could be used to meet with students, eat lunch, or just store personal items. It contained a desktop computer that could be used to check email and shelves each adjunct could label with their name; on mine I kept my reference textbooks, copies of handouts, a mug for tea or coffee, and a reusable plate and fork for lunch. With each passing year, the room filled up with the department's supplies, and eventually the computer was removed. Then one fall, I returned to discover the room had been turned into a storage closet, and my teaching materials and personal items were gone.

When I asked for my books, I was told that they would be replaced if I needed them. I searched and found them on the bottom of a cart waiting to be thrown away. This seemingly simple act of reorganizing the workspace for the full-time faculty had inadvertently taken away the one small space that provided me security for my belongings and made me feel included as a faculty member. Nobody even gave it a thought. Why would they? How can you be aware of issues that may arise with adjuncts if there is no platform where they can share such issues prior to changes?

I love teaching and have applied to the *two* full-time positions that have opened in my region over the past 13 years without success. Full-time positions have become rare, as universities replace full-time openings with multiple part-time positions to save money, thus perpetuating this vicious cycle of mistreatment. Most of my highly skilled adjunct professor colleagues have left higher education to teach at high schools or to take jobs in completely unrelated fields. I have a close friend who held the chair position in her department and just left to teach high school part time to escape the stressors of how unethical her higher ed job had become. Prior to her leaving, her department had been pared down to the bare minimum of only two full-time faculty members, including herself, to run the entire department comprised mostly of underpaid, overworked adjuncts.

Many full-time professors are allies to adjuncts, but that doesn't take away the imbalance of governance in the workplace. As Fernando Bartolomé and André Laurent explain, "Managers who worry excessively about offending their bosses are much less likely to defend subordinates when higher-ups deal unfairly with them." In turn, they note, "When subordinates sense that the boss won't defend them against unfairness, their morale will plummet, and they will withdraw commitment to the job." This lack of representation for adjuncts in higher education can cause ripple effects to job performance, morale, and devotion to one's workplace.

I want to believe that the full-time faculty don't realize what they are doing when they make these decisions, but the reality is that intentions don't matter when the outcome is the same. If adjuncts only have ten minutes between classes to talk to their full-time colleagues, there is even less time to hear any issues that may arise. There is no time to put a human experience to their name. It can be easier for the full-time faculty to ignore the enrollment caps on courses and not fight for equity when adjuncts aren't seen as colleagues but as "work horses," which is how a fellow adjunct once overheard a full-time professor refer to their part-time faculty colleagues.

View 3: Ivory Tower Syndrome

Administrators often rely on information supplied to them through the chain of command. When the bottom of the chain stops at the full-time faculty, then adjunct faculty feedback is nonexistent in the eyes of administrators. When a large percentage of adjunct faculty remain silent or gloss over their experience for fear of losing their job, the full-time faculty relay biases and skewed or missing information about adjunct positions. "In the business world," notes Mark Graybill, Ivory Tower Syndrome "means less-competitive products that cost too much to produce and ultimately risking company survival." Higher education appears to be participating in this same self-destructive behavior—possibly without even realizing it. This section addresses situations that could be damaging for schools due to the missing link at the end of the chain of command.

The 2014 documentary *Ivory Tower* "reveals how colleges in the United States, long regarded as leaders in higher education, came to embrace a business model that often promotes expansion over quality learning" (Rossi). This semester, my union representative informed me that an adjunct from another school was teaching 20 courses in one semester. To put that in perspective, a full course load in a semester is typically three to five courses. How is it possible to dedicate the time needed to provide excellent instruction when stretched so thin?

When one is hired as an adjunct, there is no official connection between the employer and the other schools of employment. There is nothing stopping adjuncts from teaching unlimited online courses at as many different schools as desired. Due to lack of communication among employers, the fear of getting caught diminishes because loss of one job will not affect employment at another. Misconduct could be running rampant in higher education, but nobody would know. Employees working in such a disconnected system have started to exploit the system in which they are being exploited. When part-time faculty members are given little respect or connection to their places of employment, then the same may be reciprocated.

According to Andrew J. Magda, Russell Poulin, and David L. Clinefelter, authors of a report on the 2015 surveys jointly conducted by The Learning House, Inc. and the Western Interstate Commission for Higher Education Cooperative for Educational Technologies (WCET), "one out of 11 institutions do not require any essential training for online faculty" (18), including adjunct faculty. In addition, Magda and his coauthors found there is little consistency in the hiring process of online adjuncts; some schools used decentralized systems, some centralized, and some a combination of the two (11), making some departments completely disconnected from hiring the faculty who will teach online program courses. In addition, they noted "approximately half of the institutions . . . surveyed [did] not have written requirements regarding adjunct faculty members' responsiveness to student communication and grading" (22).

At one place of employment, I developed an online course that eventually would come to be taught by other instructors. These instructors were hired by the online learning department, which had no background in the field of study and no ties to the department in which I taught the course originally. How could the online learning department ensure proficiency in teaching course content or in achieving outcomes when evaluating these instructors? There was little oversight of teaching except for student evaluations. Many students do not complain when passing with high grades. If institutions hire just anyone with a pulse who can facilitate a course and have no connection between employers, then how can adjuncts prevent themselves from being exploited by this type of system with such a large percentage of faculty as underpaid and disconnected to their place of employment? When schools take on more of a business model, then they are more concerned with money than the quality of product.

For many institutions across the country, unionization is providing representation and some improved working conditions for adjuncts. However, many schools pay top lawyers to prevent union effectiveness. Unions do not appear to be a permanent solution. I am currently on the bargaining committee for the new contract at one of my places of employment. We are fighting for compensation for required training and online course development, both of which currently require unpaid labor.

The truth of how little we can accomplish with maximum effort is demoralizing and exhausting. The truth of the matter is that compensation for part-time instructors should be comparable in hourly earnings to that of similarly experienced full-time faculty members. Innovative contracts for part-time faculty members could benefit the schools and the students by providing the support and collegial community so greatly desired by many part-time adjuncts. The current system appears to be unsustainable. Students deserve better, especially with how expensive post-secondary education has become.

How did higher education get to this place of manipulation and disrespect for over 50 percent of the professionals who are providing the product that post-secondary schools are selling? Wouldn't it make sense for schools to hire more full-time faculty members to provide a secure work environment for all faculty to thrive and for students to be able to connect with their mentors on a sustained basis? When faculty members feel they easily could be replaced, it is much harder for them to remain committed and take pride in their place(s) of employment. If colleges want to approach education like a business, then they should implement long-term business strategies for success from the bottom up.

Works Cited

Bachinger, Mary. "Affordable Care Act: Final Rules on Coverage for Adjuncts and Students." *National Association of College and University Business Officers*, 18 Feb. 2014, https://www.nacubo.org/News/2014/2/Affordable-Care-Act-Final-Rules-on-Coverage-for-Adjuncts-and-Students.

Bartolomé, Fernando, and André Laurent. "The Manager: Master and Servant of Power." *Harvard Business Review*, Nov. 1986, https://hbr.org/1986/11/the-manager-master-and-servant-of-power.

Graybill, Mark. "How Leaders Can Overcome Ivory Tower Syndrome." *AboutLeaders*, https://aboutleaders.com/ivory-tower-syndrome/.

Ivory Tower. Directed by Andrew Rossi, Samuel Goldwyn Company, 2014.

Magda, Andrew J., et al. *Recruiting, Orienting, and Supporting Online Adjunct Faculty: A Survey of Practices*. The Learning House, Inc. and WICHE Cooperative for Educational Technologies, Nov. 2015. *WCET*, https://wcet.wiche.edu/wp-content/uploads/sites/11/2021/04/OnlineAdjunctFacultySurveyReport.pdf.

Ran, Florence Xiaotao, and Di Xu. *How and Why Do Adjunct Instructors Affect Students' Academic Outcomes? Evidence from Two-Year and Four-Year Colleges: A CAPSEE Working Paper*, Center for Analysis of Postsecondary Education and Employment, Jan. 2017. *Center for Analysis of Postsecondary Education and Employment*, 2017, https://ccrc.tc.columbia.edu/media/k2/attachments/how-and-why-do-adjunct-instructors-affect-students-academic-outcomes.pdf.

Part III. Knee-Deep in the Trenches/What Now?

Part III is for those in the thick of it. Advice comes in from variety of sources (part-time faculty members, full-time faculty members, administrators, and chairs) from various institutions and locales across the United States. But they all have one question in common: What do we do now? The answer, obviously, varies from school to school and also location to location. It's one thing to gather up the pitchforks and strike at a unionized institution in the North, but what about those toiling in private colleges in the South? If anything is clear, it is that the present-day hiring trend is not sustainable.

- In "This Is What Solidarity Looks Like: A Model of Thick Solidarity at the University of Illinois," Andrew Bowman, A. Kay Emmert, Shawn Gilmore, and Bruce Kovanen detail their successful efforts to improve the lives of contingent faculty members on their campus, the University of Illinois Urbana-Champaign (UIUC), with the help of the Graduate Employees' Organization (GEO) and the Non-Tenure Faculty Coalition (NTFC).
- Likewise, Katie Rieger and Sarah Lonelodge share the struggles many young academics face when wading through the glutted job market ("food and housing insecurities, . . . [going] without medicines and treatments, or . . . [creating] online fundraisers to make ends meet—all while working for top-tier universities with multimillion dollar budgets and all while engaging in the same teaching load as full-time faculty members"). Their activist agenda presents possibilities for change.
- Anne Balay, author of *Steel Closets: Voices of Gay, Lesbian, and Transgender Steelworkers* (2014) and *Semi Queer: Inside the World of Gay, Trans, and Black Truck Drivers* (2018), earned her Ph.D. in English, but she never found stable academic work. As a lifetime adjunct and now an organizer, her chapter discusses how she advocates for and organizes adjunct faculty members for SEIU Local 1 in St. Louis, Missouri. She notes that she once worked as an automobile mechanic and that the sense of camaraderie she experienced in that role is missing in work of an adjunct.
- In "Alternative to Nothing: Rejecting 'Alt-Ac' Success Stories and Acknowledging Failure," Daniel S. Brown decries the current system of academics earning doctoral degrees when there are not enough (good) positions in the field, a phenomenon that runs rampant in the liberal arts and humanities. He advocates accepting fewer graduate students, ceasing the exploitation of contingent faculty, and forgiving existing student loan debt.

- Jennifer K. Johnson and Nicole Warwick, full-time lecturers in the writing program at the University of California, Santa Barbara, stress the importance of cultivating sustainable faculty lines with no end date associated with them. They see this development as necessary in order to retain and support faculty for the long haul.
- In "From Being One to Hiring One: Both Sides of the Adjunct Phenomenon in Higher Education," Kimberly M. Miller and Joanna Whetstone detail their journeys from adjuncts to their positions as chairs of their respective English departments. They highlight the dos and don'ts they would have liked to follow as administrators, given the chance to choose this path all over again, and they share advice with contingent employees looking for options.
- Finally, Devan Bissonette, who once taught as many as 13 classes at a time to make ends meet, discusses ways contingent faculty can empower themselves within a system that eats its young, including exploring everything from asynchronous learning and pre-packaged courses to strikes and walkouts. He contends that when adjuncts know their worth and power in numbers, they are a force of nature to be reckoned with in academia.

Individually and collectively, these narratives show that while the horizon is not so cheery at the moment, the contingent faculty are now the new faculty majority. Power in numbers is a noted value here, but one must never forget the precarious nature of not being protected. Therefore, it is imperative that those in positions of so-called power (tenured faculty members, chairs, and administrators) become allies and advocate right alongside the adjuncts.

Chapter 11. This is What Solidarity Looks Like: A Model of Thick Solidarity at the University of Illinois

Andrew Bowman, A. Kay Emmert,
Shawn Gilmore, and Bruce Kovanen
UNIVERSITY OF ILLINOIS URBANA-CHAMPAIGN

In "Intergroup Solidarity and Collaboration in Higher Education Organizing and Bargaining in the United States," Daniel Scott and Adrianna J. Kezar argue for the importance of intergroup solidarity and collaboration between academic labor unions to resist neoliberal market logics. They call on academic worker unions to "identify, document, and make visible these common interests—increasing job insecurity, outsourcing, reduction or stagnation in wages, eradication of benefits," to build "intergroup solidarity and collaboration," and to "devise more complex strategies involving members from multiple different positions" in order to take control from administrators who "are transforming higher education into an unrecognizable enterprise focused on generating profit rather than ensuring the public good" (Scott and Kezar 120).

On our campus, the University of Illinois Urbana-Champaign (UIUC), the Graduate Employees' Organization (GEO) and the Non-Tenure Faculty Coalition (NTFC) have worked over several years to build and maintain solidarity across our unions while challenging the corporatization of higher education, fighting the rampant abuse of academic labor, and building a university worthy of us, our work, and our students.

Following are stories of how GEO and NTFC worked together on our campus and, in so doing, further developed capacities for what Roseann Liu and Savannah Shange call "thick solidarity," which is "based on a radical belief in the inherent value of each other's lives despite not being able to fully understand or fully share in the experience of those lives" (190). As our stories demonstrate, working together isn't always an easy process. Our unions have different goals and different resources. Thick solidarity is a messy process, but potential complications should not scare off potential academic employees from organizing widely on their campuses.

In fact, these complications foster "a thickness that can withstand the tension of critique, the pulling back and forth between that which we owe and that which we share" (Liu and Shange 196). By acknowledging—rather than pasting over—our differences, GEO and NTFC have built a strong collaborative connection that has led to power on our campus.

Disruption is Loud—And Silent

A video was taken of the interior of the UIUC English Building during the NTFC strike of 2016. It was taken at 8:30 in the morning on a Wednesday in April. In the video, you walk down a double-wide hallway with white industrial tiles. The camera pans right and left, revealing classroom doors swung wide open. No one is inside. No students, no instructors, no administrators. Not even you. You float disembodied through the four-story building where the only sound is the echoing footsteps of the unseen person recording this video. As non-tenure-track faculty members cancel their classes, graduate employees cancel or move their own off site.

Figure 1. NTFC Poster.

As you draw near the double doors that lead to the outside, a sound emerges. You hear them. The chanting of hundreds of voices grows louder as you step out of the red brick and white stone building topped with twin low-rising domes and pineapple spires that is the English Building on the UIUC campus. The call of "NT" and response of "FC" can be heard from blocks away all day. The silence of the empty classrooms and offices behind you will be heard for years into a future through halls permanently affected by labor actions. These are the dual sounds of disruption that would not have been possible without the solidarity of other groups on campus like GEO.

NTFC went on strike twice in April 2016, an action that followed state educational labor board certification in 2014, more than a year of negotiations toward the union's first collective-bargaining agreement, and various forms of escalation in the months preceding.[1] Leading up to and during the strike days, a key form NTFC's activity took was occupation of the chancellor's, provost's, and president's offices. Staging a few protestors in administrative spaces forces administrators and those with business in the building to walk past evidence of unrest on their way to their administrative tasks.

Injecting these issues into spaces often devoid of them thus serves both the direct purpose of agitation while also troubling the easy separation of union concerns and "official" business. NTFC has extended this practice, targeting key phone lines and email accounts. In a single afternoon, the provost's phone lines became unavailable as NTFC members and their supporters flooded the system with a high volume of calls in a short time span. These strategies have been employed by both NTFC and GEO successfully. The goal was not to break the system but to inject union priorities into the ordinary flow of the administration's

---

1. For an account of NTFC's formation, see Shawn Gilmore's "Forming a Union: The Non-Tenure Faculty Coalition, Local 6546 at the University of Illinois, Urbana-Champaign."

day, keeping them from shunting union issues to a far-flung corner of campus or to a windowless conference room buried within human resources.

Always Be Sharing

So much of the work necessary to win labor disputes is mostly invisible, the quiet sharing of resources, knowledge, and strategy behind the more explosive displays. At UIUC, both NTFC and GEO have high turnover rates, and with contract negotiations spaced out over three, four, or five years, many of the people who had developed a healthy rapport with administrators, even in an adversarial setting, had moved on, taking with them much of the knowledge about what works and doesn't in negotiations and in collective action. By the time GEO was ready to strike in 2018, there was no one left in the organization with institutional knowledge of the group's previous strike strategies. GEO had not been on strike since 2009, and almost all the members from that time had graduated and left the union.

Figure 2. Christina De Angelo speaks into a microphone with a raised fist.

Fortunately, GEO could rely on the experience of its union family members in NTFC. Two GEO members who had participated in the 2009 strike had graduated, been hired as contingent faculty members, helped form NTFC, and brought with them many of the strategies that were then used in NTFC's 2016 strike. Christina De Angelo, NTFC strike captain, developed a strike manual based on advice from affiliate organizations like AFT and IFT, months of assessing the best locations for action, and lessons learned as a GEO member while on strike in 2009.

With membership at 37 percent and only 40 days to plan a strike that normally takes months to prepare for, GEO gained a swift understanding from NTFC of both *where* and *how* to picket, protest, and occupy. For example, while NTFC focused on shutting down the English Building during their strike, because of GEO's larger size, they were able to build on NTFC's plan for picketing the English department by shutting down buildings across the *entire* main quad. When it came time for the GEO strike, NTFC donated to the GEO strike fund, which reimbursed GEO members for their lost wages, and supported the GEO by moving classes out of picketed buildings and joining picket lines just as GEO members had done in 2016 for NTFC. What NTFC brought to this collaboration in the 2016 and 2018 strikes was the institutional knowledge of strategy and planning that is necessary when organizing a group of employees who may be slow to awaken but sturdy in the face of adversity.

Not only were some of NTFC's officers former GEO members, but the unions held offices in the same non-university building, an easy walk from the west side of the UIUC quadrangle and the main sites of the pickets. The physical proximity of the offices, as well as the easy access to each groups' people, materials, and planning spaces, meant that neither NTFC nor GEO had to go it alone but instead could rely on a variety of interlinked support mechanisms between the unions, which, in turn, helped NTFC and GEO coordinate with other labor groups. In practical terms, this interlinking involved sharing the effort of physically attaching signs to sticks and sharing space for the storage for signs, water-cooler drums, megaphones, rain gear, and the like, and it also meant sharing a central location to hold sensitive information and the numerous meetings necessary for every next step of escalation to and through strike days. The union members shared meals together, shared in the aches of mobilizing in the rain and snow, and processed the successes and failures together.

Since both unions negotiated against the same employer, and often the same individuals, the unions were able to compare notes not only on strategies but also on inconsistencies. Sometimes employers will use an excuse against one group, then completely reverse course against another. NTFC's lead negotiator, A. Kay Emmert, one of the authors of this chapter, had recently spent two years bargaining with the same employer representatives that GEO would be facing in 2018. The unions were able to share bargaining strategies, information about what did and didn't work to get the other side to move on their position, and personality assessments of the exact people they would be bargaining against.

The unions knew what would push administrators' buttons, what would catch them off guard, or put them at ease. NTFC and GEO were able to share advice about clarity of message and the building of your negotiator's reputation so that when the administration was given an out before escalation, they would believe the negotiator, and when the administration was delivered with an intention to strike, they believed that, too. The unions shared strategies over the theatrics of bargaining on the record, the advisability of alternative side-bar approaches that would allow both sides to talk more candidly, and how to respond when the other side tried to take advantage of being off the record. In comparing notes, the unions were able to identify how UIUC treated the two groups differently and how the power dynamic changed based on how the members of the two unions were perceived.

Respect Difference

Every group is going to have weaknesses and challenges, and that's where collaborating and solidarity are most necessary. While NTFC has longer institutional knowledge through longer-employed members, GEO as an organization has a much longer history of activism. GEO has always been able to turn out people quickly. NTFC benefited from this in 2016 when GEO was able to call day-of actions to support the negotiations, packing halls and flooding streets in emergency calls-to-action.

With NTFC representing just over 500 non-tenure-track faculty members on campus compared to the thousands of graduate employees in GEO, GEO showed up in numbers to fill out picket lines, marches, and rallies during NTFC's 2016 strike. Its members' performative outrage and willingness to make noise despite being in some of the most precarious positions on campus became an inspiration. As the longer-standing union made up of mostly younger activists, GEO's consistent presence protesting inequality and unfairness in many forms, the energy and spirit of rightness embodied in GEO, showed NTFC the true strength of collective action.

Figure 3. Striking graduate workers walk through campus.

This spirit of challenging institutional oppression created quite a reputation for GEO of being made up of rabble-rousers, and UIUC often treated its members that way. In 2018, when GEO employed the same occupy actions that NTFC had used two years earlier, the first response graduate employees received came from the campus security department. Campus police ordered GEO members to vacate the president's office. The confrontation looked likely to lead to arrests. That is, until GEO called on its allies in NTFC. Shawn Gilmore, another author of this chapter who was then NTFC's president, along with many other faculty members both on and off the tenure track, showed up quickly to provide support, not so much in numbers but in political complication. The policy on evicting faculty from office buildings was not as clear as the policies on student demonstrations.

Shortly after this show of solidarity by faculty members, campus police returned, and there was a noticeable change in demeanor. The message was no longer, "get out or else," but was instead that the demonstrators could stay so long as they maintained certain restrictions, restrictions that GEO had already planned to abide by, such as not blocking the flow of traffic and not entering offices. NTFC helped GEO be taken more seriously within the very institutional power structures that rely on its members' marginalized labor. Just as NTFC could not have won in 2016 without the rowdy, disruptive power of allies, it was the occupation and other non-traditional actions that eventually won GEO's contract in 2018, and the success of these occupations relied on the political power of faculty members and graduate students working in solidarity.

One piece of advice that stems from this experience is to lean into the unique attributes of your group—don't hegemonize and try to make yourselves fit another's model if it doesn't fit. According to every metric in the field of organized labor, NTFC and GEO shouldn't have won in 2016 and 2018, but the unions capitalized on what each group was good at, and that embracing of difference made the unions unstoppable.

Addressing COVID-19 in the Classroom

Strikes might be the most exciting part of these unions' shared story, but for both GEO and NTFC, solidarity is iterative—not isolated. The unions' partnership is maintained in shared workspaces and through everyday interaction to address common problems. The two unions' work together in the English department to influence COVID-19-related policies is a good example of the durability of the coalition and of the methods used to ensure continued communication and support.

Figure 4. Graduate workers rally before a bargaining session.

At the beginning of fall 2021, COVID-19 had already upended instruction at UIUC. While many instructors (and *every* administrator) hoped for a smooth transition back to pre-pandemic normalcy, the COVID-19 Delta variant shattered those plans. GEO and NTFC members returned to classrooms with locked doors, broken technology, and no personal protective equipment. While everyone in the English department agreed that these issues were a problem, the administration's response to addressing them was inadequate.

The English department at UIUC operates on a hierarchical model. The department is organized under the direction of a head who is appointed by the dean, instead of a chair elected by the department faculty. This structure gives the department head *wide latitude* to manage the department without consulting their workers. To be heard, department members would have to fight. This fight took several forms. It began with a demand letter that was drafted by graduate workers in the department and presented at the first department meeting of the semester. NTFC members immediately expressed their support in the meeting, not allowing the tenured faculty members to dismiss the concerns addressed in the letter. NTFC members also circulated a statement of support for the graduate student demands.

Other types of support were less overt. Historically, the English department has struggled with ensuring their instructors are informed about what's happening on campus. GEO and NTFC members have countered this dangerous and disempowering dynamic by creating informal networks through which to share information. This helps members of both unions to see the wider structural causes of issues they both have had. For example, both unions recently filed a grievance with university administration because of late payments and missing paychecks. The back-channel communication between NTFC and GEO allowed both unions to ascertain the extent of the payment delays and identify the cause of the problem before the administration ever reached out.

Conclusion

As providers of contingent labor, both graduate employees and non-tenure-track faculty members at UIUC had been trained to two conditions: first, that the avenues of shared governance were closed to them, and second, that if there's work to do in the trenches, they're the ones to do it. These workers were already used to getting their hands dirty; picking up a picket sign didn't feel so strange.

As Scott and Kezar point out, different types of academic workers are often siloed from each other. GEO and NTFC joining each other on their respective picket lines was an example of how "existing unions can play a crucial part in breaking down these silos by creating spaces of conversation across historically separated groups" (Scott and Kezar 101).

Figure 5. Non-tenure track faculty walking picket lines.

During the strikes at UIUC, at the end of each day, the picket lines would come together to hear the news from the bargaining table. Every day, until the last day of each of the strikes, the news was the same: the unions either had to continue to accept nothing or wake up tomorrow and keep fighting. To do nothing meant betraying so many of the principles the members hoped to model to their students. To do nothing was to admit the unions had no power, their members' work wasn't valued, and that change was really just a theory after all. The unions chose to fight. They won.

Academics bemoan the fall of academia to corporatization and to dwindling state funding. Many have studied the theory of democracy and grassroots efforts, but it was these unions' willingness to put the theory into practice that created change. They came together not to make all their concerns the same but to take turns standing behind one another and to lend voices and the sound of stomping feet to amplify each other's unique struggles. Through these narratives, we've described our enactment of thick solidarity, which "layers interpersonal empathy *with* historical analysis, political acumen, and a willingness to be led by those most directly impacted" (Liu and Shange 196). At its heart, "thick solidarity" is about showing up, and it pushes us to acknowledge and work with the "specificity, irreducibility, and incommensurability" of experiences of difference (Liu and Shange 190). In the case of our collaboration at UIUC, nothing was expected in return except the greater strengthening of collective action that contributes to the ever forward march toward better working conditions for all. That's what solidarity looks like.

Works Cited

Gilmore, Shawn. "Forming a Union: The Non-Tenure Faculty Coalition, Local 6546 at the University of Illinois, Urbana-Champaign." *Professors in the Gig Economy: Unionizing Adjunct Faculty in America*, edited by Kim Tolley, Johns Hopkins University Press, 2018, pp. 39–52. https://doi.org/10.1353/book.57938.

Liu, Roseann, and Savannah Shange. "Toward Thick Solidarity: Theorizing Empathy in Social Justice Movements." *Radical History Review*, vol. 2018, no. 131, 2018, pp. 189–98. *Duke University Press*, https://doi.org/10.1215/01636545-4355341.

Scottt, Daniel, and Adrianna J. Kezar. "Intergroup Solidarity and Collaboration in Higher Education Organizing and Bargaining in the United States. "*Academic Labor: Research and Artistry*, vol. 3, no. 1, 2019, pp. 100–24. *Cal Poly Humboldt Digital Commons*, https://digitalcommons.humboldt.edu/alra/vol3/iss1/10/.

Figure 6. Chapter authors standing outside GEO office.

Chapter 12. Where to Start? An Overview of the (Ab)use of Contingent/NTT Laborers and a Call for Radical Transparency to Assist the New Faculty Majority

Katie Rieger and Sarah Lonelodge
UNIVERSITY OF MISSOURI AND EASTERN NEW MEXICO UNIVERSITY

The (ab)use of contingent and non-tenure-track (contingent/NTT) individuals in higher education has been an ongoing conversation. For the past two decades, universities have hired more contingent labor in lieu of full-time, tenure-track (FTT) positions ("Background Facts"). While these positions are "on the fringes" (Schreyer 83) when it comes to full involvement in university culture, contingent laborers make up the majority (more than 60 percent) of instructors at the collegiate level ("Background Facts") and account for about 1.5 million instructors in the United States alone ("Characteristics of Postsecondary Faculty"). In other words, contingent/NTT are the new faculty majority.

Contingent/NTT individuals often do not have stability in their roles. A devastating example of the precarious nature of these roles is the life and tragic death of Margaret Mary Vojtko. She worked for 25 years as a per course instructor at Duquesne University, made roughly $10,000 a year, was not offered health insurance, was left in a destitute situation in which she was unable to afford heat and often rent, and died due to health complications (Dorfeld A8).

Considering this and other situations, we offer an overview of some of the present data regarding contingent/NTT labor to better illustrate such ab(use). For general higher education, many contingent individuals

- teach the equivalent of a full-time course load ("Background Facts"),
- have contracts at multiple institutions to make ends meet ("Background Facts"; Colby and Shultz Colby 61),
- are provided little recognition for their scholarship (which would assist many in career aspirations) as well as "virtually no time to carry it out" even though many are actively engaged in research (Doe et al. 444),
- may also be graduate students who are told that teaching is an "apprenticeship" that will enhance their graduate studies when, in reality, this

work "distracts from, rather than complementing, graduate studies" ("Background Facts"),
- have dwindling chances of obtaining FTT positions due to limited availability ("Background Facts") and the collapse of the humanities job market (Micciche 434),
- are at institutions that use differential workload distribution, "which reinforces hierarchies, marginalizes teaching, and makes success difficult to achieve, even for those contingent faculty with a research component as part of their workload" (Doe et al. 438),
- lack access to resources such as "offices, computer support, and photocopying services" ("Background Facts") as well as research databases, and office phones (Doe et al. 444),
- have their working hours kept below "the thirty-hour per week threshold established by the 2010 Affordable Care Act that would trigger access to employer healthcare benefits" (Goldstene qtd. in Kahn et al., "Introduction" 6), and
- "receive food stamps" (Goldstene qtd. in Kahn et al., "Introduction" 6).

Narrowing the scope to the English/writing field, most of the previous information is similar, with the following added specifics:

- Adjuncts are the instructors of "more than 70% of general education writing courses" (Kahn, "Anyone Can Teach" 363).
- In some institutions, "part-time faculty [teach] more than 95 percent of the first-year writing courses" (McBeth and McCormack 43), which leads to "burnout and intellectual stagnation" (Colby and Schultz Colby 65) due to the high paper count, grading, and mental load.
- Eighty-three percent of techincal and professional communication service courses are taught by contingent/NTT individuals (Melonçon and England 399).
- Research shows many adjuncts lack access to teaching support (Colby and Shultz Colby 57).
- Contingent/NTT instructors suffer from professional disrespect (Kahn 592) and the "de-professionalization of teaching" (Melonçon et al. 130).
- At some institutions, pay raises are based not only on performance reviews and student evaluations but also on D/F/W rates, placing primacy on student retention instead labor conditions (Nardo and Heifferon 39), and many institutions lack structured pay increases that come with promotions for contingent/NTT faculty members (Colby and Shultz Colby 62).

We argue, like Anna K. Nardo and Barbara Heifferon, that pushing past a rhetoric of despair mentality is necessary when approaching the current labor issue

(27) and suggest that a deeper understanding of contingent labor(ers) is necessary, for as James Rushing Daniel suggests, such an understanding may encourage solidarity among faculty of all ranks (65) to better support the larger goal of creating and enacting equitable labor practices. In this chapter, we offer our snapshots of the experiences of contingent faculty members to humanize some of the data, and we suggest tangible calls to action at the local and system level.

Katie

During 2015 and through most of 2020, I served in a plethora of contingent roles including graduate research assistant, writing center consultant, assistant director, graduate teaching instructor, adjunct, and three-fourths-time NTT assistant professor. This past year, I found myself in a fortunate position where my three-fourths-time NTT position transitioned to an FTT position. I want to share that I acknowledge my experience is an exception to the norm that contingent laborers face.

In my master's program and my Ph.D. program, I was fortunate to have graduate assistantships that paid for my courses and provided a monthly stipend. While earning my master's degree, I was paid a pre-tax amount of roughly $956 a month (for nine months) with no health insurance, and during my Ph.D., I earned roughly $1,500 (for nine months). The cost of most of my health insurance was included, but I had to pay for activity fees, which were usually around $1,000–$2,000 a semester. With this stipend, I could pay for housing (with contributions from roommates and then a spouse) and food, but I found myself struggling financially (to pay for undergraduate debt, gas for my car, and other utilities).

To help pay for my studies, I contracted myself out as contingent labor elsewhere. During my Ph.D. studies, I worked 20 hours per week in my English department, four hours per week in a secondary writing center, and taught two to five additional courses as an adjunct elsewhere. With these additional sources of income, I found myself able to make ends meet, but I also found myself extremely stressed and disappointed in myself due to the lack of attention I was able to give to my doctoral studies. During my third year in my program (2019), I started looking for full-time jobs and was lucky to find a contingent, three-fourths-time position that would pay more than my current contingent labor combined. For comparison, and to offer transparency, this position came with a $46,000 salary.

In this position, I taught a 4/3 load and had service requirements, such as serving on two committees and starting a writing center. During this time, I also taught two to three overload courses (depending on the semester). I, like many other contingent laborers, tried to root myself in the system in hopes that I would be offered an FTT position. While in this three-fourths-time position, I found that (even with the unpaid service and paid overload work) I had more time to dedicate to my dissertation work and research, and I also quickly started developing my research activist agenda based on my experiences as a contingent laborer.

I would like to note that at times I did feel overworked, but for most of that time I felt overwhelmingly thankful for having a position with a sense of security.

I was offered an FTT position the following year (2021). As part of this new position, I would teach one more class and direct and further develop the writing center. However, the institution shared they would not be able to pay me a full-time wage immediately. Rather, I would get small bonuses, over a period of several years, to get me to a full-time salary. Out of excitement and chasing a sense of security, I accepted this position. However, I have since left teaching.

Sarah

My career in academia began in the fall of 2011. My experiences in the decade since have illuminated several issues that affect contingent laborers and that reveal the extent to which these individuals are used and abused.

Two weeks before my first semester as a master's degree student, I was offered a graduate teaching assistantship. I was grateful and immediately accepted. I found out later that the position paid $955 per month for teaching two courses and did not include medical or any other kind of insurance. While I did receive a tuition waiver, I was responsible for paying for fees, books, transportation, and other necessities. Rent was over half of my monthly income even in the small town I lived in, which was nearly an hour commute to the university, and moving closer was impossible due to higher rents. In other words, I was not paid enough to live near my place of work.

Therefore, instead of completely leaving the full-time employment I had before graduate school, I moved into a part-time position. This meant that I worked in an office for four hours each weekday morning, drove an hour, taught two courses, attended my graduate courses, held office hours, and commuted home another hour. During my "off" time, I created lesson plans, gave feedback on student writing, conferenced with students, and completed additional teaching-related work. For all this, I was paid $955 per month.

However, I felt that my hard work and lack of resources would be worth it. I worked almost constantly to finish my master's degree in two years and was ready to begin my career. I was told—and I believed—that I would easily find a position and that it would certainly be full time, with benefits, and in a place that fit my needs.

I quickly realized, however, that most permanent, full-time positions required or preferred a Ph.D. degree. What was available to me were mostly adjunct positions or full-time, non-permanent positions in different states that would require me to uproot my husband and our children. This option seemed impossible since we had little to no savings after two years of graduate school.

I, therefore, applied for and was offered an adjunct position at the university where I received my M.A. I was paid $700 per credit hour, which, for four classes, was about $1,900 per month. I had no insurance, and I still could not afford to live near the university. Although my income was higher, I was essentially teaching a 4/4 load and being paid about 50 percent less than FTT faculty members teaching the same load. Eventually, expenses, including payments on student loans, accumulated, and I took on an additional adjunct position at a community college. This position paid $660 per credit hour and added three courses each semester to the four I was already teaching. It also required more commuting, more grading, and additional planning due to differing program requirements.

After two years of adjuncting at two schools and, because adjuncts are not paid in the summer, eventually adding a third institution where I could work in the summer, increasingly I began to feel symptoms of burnout, so I applied and was accepted to a Ph.D. program. It offered a stipend of about $1700 per month, included health insurance and a tuition waiver, and offered a scholarship for the first semester. Although the pay was low, I was able to publish and get needed experience in teaching upper-division courses and in administrative work as an assistant director of first-year composition.

Upon completion of my Ph.D. program, I secured a full-time teaching assistant professor position that includes adequate pay and benefits. Although it is a one-year renewable contract, the stability and income are a significant step up from my previous adjunct and graduate student work.

Taking Action

We offer our experiences to bring increased awareness to the precarious nature of contingent/NTT work in higher education. Low pay, a lack of benefits, high workloads, and increasing burnout are real issues that are important to tackle. We know several adjunct instructors and graduate students personally who have faced food and housing insecurities, who have had to go without medicines and treatments, or who have had to create online fundraisers to make ends meet—all while working for top-tier universities with multimillion dollar budgets and all while engaging in the same teaching load as full-time faculty members. In an effort not to just discuss and highlight these issues but to take action on them, we have developed an activist agenda that presents possibilities for change.

To create real change, we must recognize the "wicked problem" (Murray 235) of contingent/NTT labor issues. This work should start locally and should stem from listening to contingent/NTT individuals. We follow the efforts of Kahn et al. to provide "concrete steps to fight . . . exploitation of contingent faculty" ("Introduction" 7). Many scholars have argued that equitable pay, a seat on governance boards (both departmentally and institutionally), and compensated professional development opportunities are needed (Bartholomae; Kezar and Sam; Mazurek; Melonçon). We add to this discussion a call to start locally at individual program, department, and/or institution levels. Then, larger transdisciplinary, cross-institutional collaborations can begin to address the larger, systemic issues.

First, we suggest that *radical transparency* is necessary. In business fields, transparency is the idea of an open-door policy where employees can share frustrations with the organization. Radical transparency goes a step further to involve sharing information to prevent informational silos and to present feedback, frustrations, innovations, and ideas to all levels in the organization (Reid and Rout; Scott). For the field of English/writing studies, radical transparency applies to sharing experiences, data, instruments, and resources and to housing this information in centralized, accessible locations. We suggest that local work within one's own institution, department, or program is a first step to better understanding the community within that institution/department/program—the individuals within that community and the division of labor, tools, and activities.

One way to create radical transparency is through institutional ethnography (IE). IE draws on data from interviews, case studies, focus groups, textual analysis, discourse analysis, autoethnography, participant observation, and archival research. Michelle LaFrance and Melissa Nicolas explore ways that IE can be used to uncover the activities performed by an individual in an organization and what factors shape these activities (130). We extend their work to contingent laborers and their experiences. Marjorie L. DeVault suggests IE typically involves three stages:

1. Identify an experience.
2. Identify some of the institutional processes shaping that experience.
3. Investigate those processes to describe analytically how they operate as the ground of experience. (20)

Because material conditions within departments and programs can differ (Kahn et al., "Introduction" 10), IE creates an opportunity to better understand each individuals' experiences, thoughts, frustrations, and ideas for solutions. Rather than TT scholars offering blanket solutions, hearing directly from contingent/NTT laborers about the tensions and aspects of labor that aren't addressed in literature is fundamental to developing real, impactful solutions.

To identify some of the institutional processes shaping contingent laborers' experiences, those who wish to take action could collect survey responses, job descriptions, and interviews from contingent laborers in their departments. By hearing directly from those impacted, researchers and activists may begin to see potential for support. Khan et al., for example, suggest that many times there are a variety of solutions we can turn to support our colleagues ("Introduction," 10), some of which may be non-monetary. These may include creating helpful onboarding documents, ensuring release time for professional development, hosting social events, and more. However, though non-monetary aids are beneficial, we do not wish to detract from the fight for equitable wages.

Second, sharing experiences and findings with the field is necessary. Possibilities for sharing may include publishing articles that include datasets and providing access to narratives, implementation descriptions, models of policies and procedures, and other resources. By sharing these materials openly, our field can achieve three goals:

1. Create a richer understanding of the English/writing studies workforce;
2. Invite more collaboration and innovation on a cross-institutional basis for tackling this issue; and
3. Draw upon more data to conduct replicability studies, create research-based sustainable solutions, and/or share information with administrators to support contingent/NTT laborers.

Working toward achieving all of these goals can better the English/writing studies field by providing more sustainable and impactful research (Melonçon and St. Amant 129). Sharing data, instruments, and solutions is part of the process toward creating radical transparency. Our field tends to be supportive in its sharing of information—especially on listservs like nextGEN and WCENTER. However, it can be very difficult to find information, even when using the archival services these listservs provide. Having a centralized location where resources, data, and instruments are shared can benefit the field by making more information easier to access. Rather than creating silos, let's create a centralized location for support.

In addition to these larger goals, the local level is an important first step. Katie, for example, has worked closely with two new adjuncts to help improve their experiences. She is working on an onboarding document to situate new faculty members to new hiring requirements, grading/teaching dates, and campus resources, and she hopes to organize events where all faculty members can mingle (post-COVID-19).

As a new contingent/NTT faculty member, Sarah has been well supported by her department. She received funding that provides support for professional development during the first semester. In addition, the department holds asset-mapping meetings that are attended only by contingent/NTT faculty members (to allow for confidential, open dialogue) in which individuals can discuss benefits of the position as well as present ideas for bettering their experiences. Contingent/NTT faculty members also have opportunities to participate in committee work and governance that positions them to have a voice within the department and program.

While these efforts and experiences are moving in the right direction, we also recognize that systemic changes require radical transparency at higher levels, so we are also collecting data from contingent/NTT laborers through a grant funded by the Council for Programs in Technical and Scientific Communication (CPTSC). We hope to use this data to accurately document experiences and conditions from our field and share this information in a centralized location.

Conclusion

Contingent/NTT laborers' work is "essential, meaningful, and even central to the function of colleges and universities" (Doe et al. 432). As Chris Anson says, it is time to "stop reflecting ... and do something" (qtd. in Reed 135). To start paving the way, we must listen to these laborers to learn about their activities, needs, requests, and experiences. Small, local work that studies labor and activities is an important first step. Then, sharing information in transdisciplinary and cross-institutional settings will create solidarity and alliances that are helpful against divisive forces (Daniel 65).

Works Cited

"Background Facts on Contingent Faculty Positions." *AAUP: American Association of University Professors*, https://www.aaup.org/issues/contingency/background-facts.

Bartholomae, David. "Teaching On and Off the Tenure Track: Highlights from the ADE Survey of Staffing Patterns in English." *Pedagogy: Critical Approaches to Teaching Literature, Language, Composition, and Culture*, vol. 11, no. 1, 2011, pp. 7–32. *Duke University Press*, https://doi.org/10.1215/15314200-2010-012.

"Characteristics of Postsecondary Faculty." *National Center for Education Statistics (NCES)*, May 2020, https://nces.ed.gov/programs/coe/indicator_csc.asp.

"Contingent Appointments and the Academic Profession." *American Association of University Professors (AAUP)*, 2020, https://www.aaup.org/report/contingent-appointments-and-academic-profession.

Colby, Richard, and Rebekah Shultz Colby. "Real Faculty but Not: The Full-Time, Non-Tenure-Track Position as Contingent Labor." Seth Kahn et al., pp. 57–70. *WAC Clearinghouse*, https://doi.org/10.37514/PER-B.2017.0858.2.04.

Daniel, James Rushing. "Freshman Composition as a Precariat Enterprise." *College English*, vol. 80, no. 1, 2017, pp. 63–85.

DeVault, Marjorie L. "Introduction: What is Institutional Ethnography." *Social Problems*, vol. 53, no. 3, 2006, pp. 294–98. *Oxford Academic*, https://doi.org/10.1525/sp.2006.53.3.294.

Doe, Sue, et al. "Discourse of the Firetenders: Considering Contingent Faculty through the Lens of Activity Theory." *College English*, vol. 73, no. 4, 2011, pp. 428–49.

Dorfeld, Natalie. M. "National Adjunct Walkout: Now What?" *Forum: Issues about Part-Time and Contingent Faculty*, vol. 19, no. 1, 2015, pp. A8–A13. *NCTE: National Council of Teachers of English*, https://library.ncte.org/journals/CCC/issues/v67-1/27445.

Kahn, Seth. "Anyone Can Teach Writing." *Bad Ideas about Writing*, edited by Cheryl E. Ball and Drew M. Loewe, Digital Publishing Institute, 2017, pp. 363–68. *West Virginia University Libraries*, https://textbooks.lib.wvu.edu/badideas/badideasaboutwriting-book.pdf.

———. "We Value Teaching Too Much to Keep Devaluing It." *College English,* vol. 82, no. 6, 2020, p. 591–611. *NCTE: National Council of Teachers of English,* https://library.ncte.org/journals/ce/issues/v82-6/30805.

——— et al. "Introduction: Paths Toward Solidarity." Kahn et al., pp. 3–11. *WAC Clearinghouse,* https://doi.org/10.37514/PER-B.2017.0858.1.3.

——— et al., editors. *Contingency, Exploitation, and Solidarity: Labor and Action in English Composition.* The WAC Clearinghouse/University Press of Colorado, 2017. *WAC Clearinghouse,* https://doi.org/10.37514/PER-B.2017.0858.

Kezar, Adrianna and Cecile Sam. "Understanding the New Majority of Non-Tenure-Track Faculty in Higher Education: Demographics, Experiences, and Plans of Action." *ASHE Higher Education Report,* vol. 36, no. 4, 2010, pp. 1–133. *Wiley Online Library,* https://doi.org/10.1002/aehe.3604.

LaFrance, Michelle, and Melissa Nicolas. "Institutional Ethnography as Materialist Framework for Writing Program Research and the Faculty-Staff Work Standpoints Project." *College Composition and Communication,* vol. 64, no. 1, 2012, pp. 130–50.

Mazurek, Raymond A. "Academic Labor is a Class Issue: Professional Organizations Confront the Exploitation of Contingent Faculty." *Journal of Workplace Rights,* vol. 16 no. 3, 2012, pp. 353–66. *CLOCKSS Archive,* https://doi.org/10.2190/WR.16.3-4.f.

McBeth, Mark, and Tim McCormack. "An Apologia and a Way Forward: In Defense of the Lecturer Line in Writing Programs." Seth Kahn et al., pp. 41–56. *WAC Clearinghouse,* https://doi.org/10.37514/PER-B.2017.0858.2.03.

Melonçon, Lisa. "Contingent Faculty, Online Writing Instruction, and Professional Development in Technical and Professional Communication." *Technical Communication Quarterly,* vol. 26., no. 3, 2017, pp. 256–72. *Taylor and Francis Online,* https://doi.org/10.1080/10572252.2017.1339489.

——— and Kirk St. Amant. "Empirical Research in Technical and Professional Communication: A 5-Year Examination of Research Methods and a Call for Research Sustainability." *Journal of Technical Writing and Communication,* vol. 49, no. 2, 2019, pp. 128–55. *SAGE Journals,* https://doi.org/10.1177%2F0047281618764611.

——— and Peter England. "The Current Status of Contingent Faculty in Technical and Professional Communication." *College English,* vol. 73, no. 4, 2011, pp. 396–408.

——— et al. "Looking Forward: Considering Next Steps for Contingent Labor Material Work Conditions." *Academic Labor: Research and Artistry,* vol. 4, no. 1, 2020, pp. 127–151. *Cal Poly Humboldt Digital Commons,* https://digitalcommons.humboldt.edu/alra/vol4/iss1/8/.

Micciche, Laura R. "More than a Feeling: Disappointment and WPA Work." *College English,* vol. 64, no. 4, 2002, pp. 432–58.

Murray, Darrin S. "The Precarious New Faculty Majority: Communication and Instruction Research and Contingent Labor in Higher Education." *Communication Education,* vol. 68, no. 2, 2019, pp. 235–45. *Taylor and Francis Online,* https://doi.org/10.1080/03634523.2019.1568512.

Nardo, Anna K., and Barbara Heifferon. "Despair Is Not a Strategy." Seth Kahn et al., pp. 27–40. *WAC Clearinghouse,* https://doi.org/10.37514/PER-B.2017.0858.2.02.

Reed, Meridith. "Review Essay: Rewriting Labor in Composition." *WPA: Writing Program Administration,* vol. 42, no. 1, 2018, pp. 130–35. *WPA Journal Archives,* https://wpacouncil.org/aws/CWPA/asset_manager/get_file/381955.

Reid, John, and Matthew Rout. "Developing Sustainability Indicators—The Need for Radical Transparency." *Ecological Indicators,* vol. 110, March 2020. *ScienceDirect,* https://doi.org/10.1016/j.ecolind.2019.105941.

Schreyer, Jessica. "Inviting the 'Outsiders' In: Local Efforts to Improve Adjunct Working Conditions." *Journal of Basic Writing,* vol. 31, no. 2, 2012, pp. 83–102. *WAC Clearinghouse,* https://10.37514/JBW-J.2012.31.2.05.

Scott, Susan. "The Case for Radical Transparency." *YouTube,* uploaded by TedX Talks, 1 July 2011, https://www.youtube.com/watch?v=0VKaXUB4EFg.

Smith, Dorothy E. "Institutional Ethnography: A Sociology for People." AltaMira Press, 2005.

Chapter 13. "Ten... Toil Where One Reposes": Stories of an Adjunct Faculty Organizer

Anne Balay
SEIU Local 1

One of my bargaining units, a Jesuit university in a small Midwestern city, decided to welcome new members at a Halloween-themed event. Thirty new adjuncts had been added to the school's roster this second pandemic fall semester, and 23 of these had joined the union. As a lifetime adjunct and now an organizer, I appreciated the campiness of their plan.

Adjuncts are low-wage workers who pretend to be professors. Since we have no job security and no academic freedom, we get to keep pretending this only if we do it well—if our act convinces our full-time colleagues, our administrators, and our students. If we allow gaps to show—let slip that we are not allowed to use the copy machine or reveal that we're holding office hours in the coffee shop, not because we're too cool for the office, but because we don't have one—the department may not be able to "find" classes for us in future.

By camping up the masquerade that our professional life requires, adjuncts demonstrate that full-timers are faking it as much as we are—that "professor" is a narrative we tell ourselves. Walking into a classroom is what makes it feel real. So, when a handful of adjuncts sit at a table in front of the library and self-consciously, deliberately, exaggeratedly occupy their professional role, tenure-track faculty members and administrators might feel uncomfortable. Is a professor something you do, or is it someone you are?

You can't identify adjuncts by looking at them, by visiting their classes, or by asking students who they are. We imitate the originals so well that we become indistinguishable from them. This serves management well because we can't find each other; adjuncts feel isolated and stigmatized. Teaching provides few opportunities to create the community that might counteract that.

Still, adjuncts *are* different from the tenure-track faculty members with whom they share education, job description, and culture: we get maybe one-tenth of their pay and live in permanent, destabilizing uncertainty. Though I work for a union that tries to deliver "more pay and more say" to these and other workers, we can offer little material relief. Even a reasonable raise does little to close the gap with full-timers, and job security is never even bargained for. What we do offer is community and a chance to share stories with other workers.

A Voice from the Field

"Angela" has a Ph.D., has published in her field's prestigious journals, and is beloved by her students. She had a tenure-track job in another state, but both her parents got sick. Her dad (a retired union carpenter) was caring for her mom, who was sliding precipitously into Alzheimer's, and this was a huge drain on his health. Then, her husband got a job offer here, so they decided to leave her full-time professor gig and move back home. It was too late to relieve her dad from his care burden, but at least she was here when he died. And still here, adjuncting, when her husband and his full-time income left. Without health insurance or job stability, she is now putting two kids through college. Though she gets five or six classes per semester across two schools, I think she will probably lose the house.

Her dad's union experience encourages "Angela" to believe that our union can make this better. She remembers walking the picket line with strikers and her family getting support from the union to survive those lean months. More, she remembers the parties and picnics and the sense that co-workers are family: they argue, but they stick together. But carpenters work side by side on the job and form social bonds. "Angela" says they went to each other's BBQs and held their wedding receptions at the union hall. That comradery is just not automatic with adjuncts, who rarely have offices or other places to congregate on campus and are usually rushing off to teach another class at another campus.

All academics are isolated. I worked as a car mechanic before teaching, and that job (like carpentry) forces workers together in a small place, solving problems, sharing tools, eating, and shooting the shit together. After eight years, I knew everything about the men I worked with. In contrast, faculty members do their jobs in isolation, interacting more with students than with other faculty members. What brings them together is committee work, departmental meetings, and the shared stress of promotion and tenure preparations. None of that social grease is available to adjuncts.

This isolation is not accidental. Low-wage workers are ships passing in the night so that we won't meet, compare notes, and organize. Turnover is high, and morale is low. The pandemic has further increased this isolation—milling around in hallways or chatting at the printer are even less likely than before.

For "Angela," once her dad died and her husband left, she was panicky and overwhelmed. As the pandemic unfolded, she was teaching in-person because those were the only classes her college offered her. An email went out to the faculty saying that during these difficult times, students, staff, and faculty were encouraged to reach out to the counseling center for support. As "Angela" informed her students of this policy, it occurred to her that she might benefit from it herself. However, when she called, she was informed that these free services were available only to full-time employees and students.

My challenge as an organizer is to shift from this personal story of injustice and abuse to a collective movement for change. Anyone who takes the time to listen to adjuncts will hear similar stories of trauma. Part-time faculty members were pushed to the razor's edge of tolerance even before the pandemic took everything up a notch. Most gig workers in the US and globally are under similar pressures. Stories of individual hardship animate organized resistance and thus change. But to activate these stories, we need to theorize links between them and a shared, social movement.

Sharing Stories

The steward and I were setting up an information table at a university during the early stages of contract bargaining preparations. We had cookies, coffee, and copies of the old contract, and we had contacted the list of new adjunct hires who we hoped would stop by for a chat. One goal was to identify potential leaders for the contract campaign. Another was to get adjuncts talking to each other since stories are the best way to combat isolation and apathy.

And that all worked. People who said they could stay for only ten minutes wound up staying longer while they exchanged stories and laughed and worried with other adjuncts. This university has been doing some restructuring and has rolled out new requirements and policies. Among these is one that states students will no longer need to take one year of language instruction. As is common, adjuncts dominate the world language department, and they assume that enrollments will now drop precipitously and that within a few years, most will have lost their jobs. They're not wrong, and it sucks. One adjunct who has taught at the university for many years relies on three classes plus a lab each semester, which makes him eligible (post ACA) to buy the employer's health insurance. He and his husband depend on these benefits. As we stand there listening, we are witness. And we are helpless.

Later, a different adjunct in the same department remarks, "I'm lucky—they've asked me to teach Spanish for medical students. It's like first- and second-year Spanish compressed into one year with medical terminology added. And they're really pushing it with their pre-med students, so I should still get classes."

This prompts another adjunct, new this semester, to add that he has three sections of introductory sociology, all over-enrolled, chiefly with premed freshman who signed up because the MCAT has added a sociology section. He, in turn, feels lucky because a national corporate giant is motivating students to enroll in his classes.

When each describes their circumstance as "lucky," I cringe. Each is offered an unusually challenging pedagogical ask, and since the alternative is no work at all, they tell themselves that they are favored by fate. Because we are together, sharing stories collectively, I can ask them to step back and think critically about the story they are telling themselves. When several people take subservience to an oppressive regime and reinterpret it as individual good fortune, it's easier to notice than when we stay isolated and tell these stories only to ourselves. That is the task and the possibility of labor organizing: to tell individual stories collectively so that the workers notice trends and systems and begin to seek change.

It helps to realize that this pressure to "think positive" shapes low-wage gig work generally, just as it shapes U.S. neoliberal culture. I recently asked a friend who drives a semi-truck to explain the backlog of container ships in the ports, a situation which had suddenly gotten media attention in the fall of 2021. She told me the situation wasn't new but that COVID-19 has worsened it in ways I hadn't imagined, ways that are not making their way to the mainstream media. What struck me in her explanation, though, was her claim that "me, personally, I'm fortunate," because she is able to use indoor bathrooms with hot water for hand washing near the ports during her 14-hour workdays. Sounds familiar, no?

Finding themselves lucky is a strategy workers use to distance themselves from their crappy working conditions by giving them some control. It's a source of self-esteem within a context with few others, but it thwarts organizing by personalizing conditions that are structural. However, even to make that distinction (to entrench a binary opposition between structural and personal effects) reifies and hardens what I hope instead to change. People's stories—how we understand and narrate our experiences—can fuel change when they find collective, shared, and public expression. Management knows this, which is why it makes it hard for adjuncts and other low-wage gig workers to meet.

Ride-sharing drivers, for example, are always in their own cars. Though they are everywhere, there isn't a central location where they gather to get work—or to discuss it amongst themselves—until they use the app that divides them against themselves.[1] Often it's easier to identify other workers' oppression than our own, especially given the working-class injunction against whining and the general culture's insistence on staying positive. But adjuncts can't see other adjuncts at work because we look like any other professors.

Unlike various other status markers, class is not necessarily visible—its marks can be hidden, at least temporarily. In the U.S. context, this potential invisibility contributes to the erasure of class as meaningful. It's because class stratification can be invisible that it perpetuates and reproduces itself inescapably.

Conclusion

Organizing adjunct faculty into labor unions resists this invisibility process. Once adjuncts have been to a union meeting, they can identify each other in the halls and parking lots. And seeing other adjuncts makes visible the covert class structure of academia since it lets us see the tenure-track faculty also. Any divide between the full-time and part-time faculty relies on their invisibility. As with any binary, once the sorting process is noticed, its arbitrary rules

---

1. One such story is well told in Callum Cant's Riding for Deliveroo: Resistance in the New Economy.

are exposed and, though it reconstitutes and justifies itself continuously, the gig is up.

When adjuncts stage their own orientation events as costume parties, sending up their own ability to walk the walk and talk the talk, they're using camp to critique higher education's hierarchical structures. Parody is a mobile strategy that can resist hegemony's inexorable march. People in higher education aren't entrenching an oppressive labor hierarchy in which "ten . . . toil where one reposes" (Oppenheim)—it's more like a game of pretend that everyone participates in. By laughing at ourselves, at full-timers, and at the silly distinctions between us, we can imagine new ways to act and teach and think and engage.

What does it mean to be a professor? To teach? People complain about teaching in a mask during the COVID-19 pandemic and about not seeing the majority of students' faces in the classroom, whether behind a mask or on a Zoom call with their cameras muted. But maybe this opens up a change in higher education hierarchies by emphasizing the imaginary nature of classroom authority, of leadership, and of learning.

Works Cited

Cant, Callum. *Riding for Deliveroo: Resistance in the New Economy*. Polity Press, 2020.

Oppenheim, James. "Bread and Roses." *The American Magazine*, Dec. 1911. *Jewish Women's Archive*, 2022, https://jwa.org/media/bread-and-roses-poem.

Chapter 14. Alternative to Nothing: Rejecting "Alt-Ac" Success Stories and Acknowledging Failure

Daniel S. Brown
LINCOLN MEMORIAL UNIVERSITY

I've made a huge mistake.

*– Recurring catchphrase uttered by several
Arrested Development characters*

I must preface this essay by stating that I am quite happy with my current line of work—in fact, much happier than I was with any of the positions I obtained in the years following my completion of a Ph.D. in English. After many years, I have mostly made my peace with the path my career has taken, and if it weren't for the massive debt that I have been saddled with, I might have nothing left to complain about. But what a debt it is—taken on in the naïve hope that it would be liberating, but instead proving much the opposite. No one should be saddled with that.

In short, the problem is that there are simply more people earning doctoral degrees than there are positions that require these degrees. This is especially the case with the liberal arts and humanities. For many of these degrees, the only jobs for which they are truly required are professorships, and there simply aren't enough of those positions for the number of those credentialed. Of course, people with doctoral degrees in all sorts of fields find employment. These success stories often are held up as examples of the type of work available in an "alternative academic" or "alt-ac" job market. Yet, the supposed success of the "alt-ac" market leaves unaddressed whether doctoral degrees were needed for these jobs in the first place, and, more importantly, whether they were worth the investment of time, effort, and money.

My current work as an academic librarian is, by all definitions, an "alt-ac" position, even though my doctoral degree was in no way necessary for entry. In fact, as I will discuss in this essay, getting onto this career path meant "giving up" and "starting over" after several years of trying and failing to get into a tenure-track professorship. Moreover, this original goal was one that I honestly believed would suit me, and not—as some "alt-ac" proponents such as Rebeca Schuman argue—one imposed on me by hidebound faculty mentors ("Alt-Ac Talk"). Thus, I would be loath for anyone to associate my professional success with the "alt-ac" market, as such a move would only serve to perpetuate deep-seated problems with the academic system.

My Story

I was raised with a very grim approach to work. It was simply a necessity for life, and, despite high academic achievements, I was not to set high goals for myself or view myself as too good for any occupation. My mother frequently advised me—apparently without irony—that I could always resort to ditch digging if necessary. Work meant an endless tedium, a soul-crushing obligation to keep oneself afloat no matter what else. Even after completing an undergraduate degree, some part of me accepted that I could get by with the dish washing that I had been doing as a source of pocket money.

However, my father, after changing careers several times, was a librarian, and, having spent much time with him at his job, I thought this might be something I also could do. So, I applied for graduate programs in library science, and I was accepted into a good program, although my performance in that program was admittedly not very good. I finished that program and obtained a job at a small, local liberal arts college. I decided I might like academic librarianship and, realizing that would require a second graduate degree, enrolled in a broad-based master's degree in liberal arts.

A number of factors then conspired to lead me into seeking a doctoral degree in English. Some of it was the result of therapy, in which I was encouraged to seek out better opportunities for myself and to embrace my interests more enthusiastically. Some of it was also the influence of a professor who saw potential in me and encouraged me to go farther with my studies. I had hoped this would be a path that might liberate me from an otherwise bleak perception of the future and the working world. My pursuit of a doctoral degree thus came in earnest, with a genuine belief—supported by people whose opinions I trusted and valued—that it would be a good move not just professionally but also for my overall wellbeing.

Although it came with its frustrations, particularly towards the end, graduate school proved to be a respite. Being young and intellectually curious, I could spend time reading, writing, and reflecting on abstract concepts, which I thoroughly enjoyed. I liked the community of intellectuals and the exchange of ideas. I imagined the possibility of a career in which I might continue to enjoy this lifestyle.

My first academic job after graduation was as a visiting instructor, a three-year, contracted gig teaching technical writing to business and engineering students. This was a long way from Victorian literature, which had been the focus of my dissertation, but I had some experience teaching this subject as a graduate assistant, and the job at least kept me in the academic pipeline. The salary was not especially good, and I didn't much care for the teaching, but I figured I was paying my dues.

While working this gig, I spent considerable time on professional development. I worked on converting my dissertation into a book, which I hoped would confer an advantage on the job market. I attended conferences, workshops and even a month-long NEH symposium. And I applied for jobs—literally hundreds of them. I applied, of course, to tenure-track positions in my specialty, but also to generalist positions and positions teaching composition and technical writing, no matter how poor the pay or the workload. I was raised, after all, to be not very selective when it came to work, and I figured my malleability would put me in good stead. Unfortunately, this would be the highest-paying, most secure position I would ever hold in any sort of professorial capacity.

When that gig ended, I moved into my parents' two-bedroom apartment and stitched together a meager living from several part-time jobs. Some, such as scoring SAT English tests, I could work remotely from their apartment. Others required two- to three-hour round-trip drives to community colleges spread out across two states to teach English composition and technical writing courses for around $2,000 for an entire semester. Some nights I would book a hotel room so that I didn't have to commute back to my parents' place.

While I did all of this temporary work, I continued to apply for academic jobs and develop myself professionally. I even completed the book and got it published. Sadly, none of this helped me in getting tenure-track employment. I had one interview at an MLA convention, and that was it. Eventually, I decided this would not work and started to ask myself what else I might do.

Thus began the process of surrender and rebuilding. I had the library science degree to fall back on but hadn't worked in a library for over a decade. I applied for a few library jobs, but no one responded. I needed to find a way, no matter how small, to get back into the industry. So, I applied for and received a part-time job through a temp agency doing what was essentially data entry for a company that created library products. Much of my time was spent reviewing transcripts of Holocaust survivor testimonies—fascinating but bleak. For a while, I worked this job and also taught several English courses as an adjunct, continuing on as a "freeway warrior."

However, when the company offered me a full-time position in a different department, I quit the adjunct teaching positions altogether. I was given an annual salary of $44,000, which was the most I had ever received in my life. I was part of a team of five new hires—two of us had doctoral degrees in humanities subjects, and two of us had master's degrees in library science. None of us needed these degrees to do the work we did, which was trolling the internet for content to supply to a database. After a year, two of the team members quit, and I quit shortly after they did. In all, I worked nearly three years for this company, doing the sort of monotonous, data-entry work from which I had hoped a doctoral degree would spare me.

When I left, it was for a librarian position at an academic library in a developing nation. Because of my experience with this company, the staff at my new job put me in charge of electronic resources. This was an aspect of library work that I had not considered before—in fact, I had not even really heard of it before. Yet, I found that I enjoyed it. It suited my analytic, introverted nature. After several years there, and with the help of a professional resume-writing company, I applied for similar jobs in the US. The results have been surprising. When applying for academic jobs previously, I would get three or four interview requests out of 100 applications. Now, I was getting interview requests for about three out of every four jobs that I applied for. I seemed to have finally found a line of work that I was suited for.

I am currently in a good position as head of a technical services department at a university library in the US. I can't complain about that at all. But the path to get there has been a long one, filled with uncertainty and emotional hardship. And the Ph.D. in English, with all of its resulting career moves, was a long diversion on the way to get here. What I did to get here was what most people do to advance in a line of work—I began at an entry-level position and worked my way up by demonstrating a good work ethic and taking advantage of opportunities when they arose. No Ph.D. required.

What I am doing now is not an alternative to anything other than being unemployed, and I refuse to use my career path to celebrate the success of an "alt-ac" marketplace. It is a job that I came to after years of struggle and failures. "Alt-ac" is a term that only serves to protect a sector of the academy that over-produces doctoral degrees. It needs to stop being used.

What Is Meant by the Term "Alt-Ac"?

The term "alt-ac" has been criticized as a buzzword both too capacious to have any concrete meaning and yet still somehow not inclusive enough. Nonetheless, although its use may have declined some in the past few years, it remains familiar enough that most understand it roughly to mean jobs for Ph.D. holders other than a tenure-track professorship. As Bethany Nowviskie explains, she first coined the term in a Twitter post in 2010 ("#alt-ac"). From what I can gather, its uses generally fall into two categories: as career advice, and as a form of "face saving." The two are not necessarily mutually exclusive, although proponents of the latter occasionally characterize the former as overly narrow and mercenary. Perhaps because it was a term born digitally, most of the discourse surrounding it appears online.

The career advice strand of "alt-ac" discourse is relatively innocuous, focusing mainly on practical advice for the holder of a Ph.D. who is struggling to find work. Brenda Bethman and Shaun Longstreet's "Defining Terms" is the quintessential career advice essay, suggesting Ph.D. holders go into other academic fields, such as advising, libraries, grant writing, administration, etc. Some readers might notice that the piece is dated; however, Maria LaMonaca Wisdom's 2020 "Getting past 'Alt-Ac'" fits into the same line of thought. Although Wisdom begins with a caveat that the nebulous term makes her "cringe," she nonetheless uses it to launch into a piece on career advice for Ph.D. holders. Such advice usually falls into the lines of identifying one's skills and passions, networking, and using other general job search strategies. Oftentimes, career advice continues a line of argument used to defend undergraduate degrees in the humanities, presenting the Ph.D. as a sort of super-sized helping of "soft skills" or as evidence of the graduate's intelligence and work ethic. The goal of these essays seems to be to help their audiences make the best of bad situations rather than aim to reform a system that has produced Ph.D. holders without any discernable plan for employing them.

What I call the "face saving" essays tend to reject the idea of "alt-ac" as practical advice, focusing instead on redeeming the image of those who find employment outside of tenure-track professorships. To Nowviskie's 2010 blog post in which she explains the origin of the term, she appended a statement in 2013 emphasizing her original use of the term as a "pushback" against the prevailing discourse, which she "felt . . . diminished humanities scholars who continued to use their skills in and around the academy." In a post that this update links to, she clarifies that, "by 'alt-ac,' a growing community speaks not of 'alternatives to academic employment,' but rather of 'alternative academics'" ("Lunaticks"). She is also disparaging towards those who have "co-opted" the movement, "selling 'coaching' services to under-employed academics . . . and a brain-dead brand of jobs-crisis 'solutionism'" ("#alt-ac").

Another good example of a face-saving use of "alt-ac" comes from Rebecca Schuman's 2014 *Slate* essay, "'Alt-Ac' to the Rescue?" in which she pushes against "the shame that is drilled into many doctoral candidates at the very notion of working outside the academy." Schuman is similarly dismissive of "alt-ac" as career advice, boiling hers down to "serendipitous encounters, making fortuitous connections, or taking on small, part-time contract work and proving yourself—like a normal person." For both Nowviskie and Schuman, "alt-ac" is much more about recovering one's dignity than about finding work.

In contrast to the banality of "alt-ac" career advice, "alt-ac" face-saving is more rhetorically sophisticated but also more seductive in maintaining the status quo. Celebrating accomplishments might soothe wounded egos —as Schuman encourages us to think, "Not 'I got a doctorate *but* all I do is teach high school.' 'I got a doctorate *and* I teach high school'" ("Alt-Ac Talk")—but it leaves unanswered the question of whether the investment into the Ph.D. was in any way equal to the rewards. In attempting to save face, "alt-ac" champions may be refusing to examine whether the investment into the Ph.D. was, in fact, a mistake.

If earning a Ph.D. was a mistake, it is important to face that fact without being burdened by a sense of shame or failure. Schuman speaks of the pursuer of a Ph.D. as a person somehow incapable of grasping the concept of finding "normal" work in the "real" world ("'Alt-Ac' to the Rescue"), but this doesn't ring true for me. I understood how to find work, but professorship sounded like something I would enjoy. I never was motivated by fears that I would disappoint my faculty advisor or be shunned in the eyes of the academy. Any sense of failure came from the dashing of my own hopes and expectations. I can view the whole experience as a growth opportunity, but that doesn't get me out of financial debt. Ph.D.

overproduction is a broader social problem that needs to be rectified regardless of how we feel about what we did with our degrees.

What's to be Done?

I can imagine a number of solutions to this problem—most of which seem fairly obvious yet still somehow fail to be implemented. University departments could accept fewer graduate students. Universities could stop hiring contingent faculty. Or the cost of graduate education simply could be made affordable, with existing student loan debt more easily forgiven. I lack the ability to address the feasibility of any of these solutions but would like to offer a few thoughts on what each might do to rectify the situation.

University departments could accept fewer graduate students. Everyone hears the horror stories about job prospects post-graduation, but that does not seem to stop students from applying to graduate school. It didn't stop me. I applied to maybe ten graduate programs, many of which only accepted one or two candidates in a cohort. The best program that accepted me had cohorts of 12 or more. I cannot speculate on why this department saw fit to accept so many graduate students, but it seems unethical to allow so many to invest in a program that only prepares them for jobs that do not exist. Admitting fewer students into graduate programs could save many from making grave mistakes. It would also, unfortunately, bar many from intellectual exploration and restrict Ph.D. holders to an even narrower pool of elite, over-represented groups.

Universities could stop hiring contingent faculty. University administrators will likely argue that hiring contingent faculty is the only affordable option, but universities are notorious enough for wage inequalities and financial waste to make such an argument incredible.[1] However, this solution would also likely require compromise on the part of graduate programs. Much has been written already about offering secure contracts that offer living wages to academic instructors who are expected to teach overwhelming loads of introductory courses. But reducing the number of contingent faculty might also require shrinking the size of graduate school admissions or reducing the number of courses offered. At the very least, it would require a reform of graduate school curricula, with more focus on developing skills in classroom instruction and less emphasis on specialized research so that graduates could be hired into full-time positions that involve enough teaching to cover the load of current contingent faculty members. Although more practical, this could undermine the appeal of graduate school to those—myself included—who were more interested in research than teaching.

Finally, the cost of graduate education could be made affordable, with existing student loan debt more easily forgiven. This is the option that I favor the

---

1. One excellent work that explores this is Benjamin Ginsberg's *The Fall of the Faculty: The Rise of the All-Administrative University and Why It Matters.*

most, even if it is also the least likely to occur. Affordable higher education would encourage more people to engage in intellectual inquiry and exploration without the fear of crippling debt. It would also allow the pursuit of a doctoral degrees to be an experience of personal growth without needing to be a gateway into the professoriate. Unfortunately, this possibility seems unlikely to gain much traction beyond that of talking points and wishful thinking.

While many potential solutions to the problem exist, the current scene appears to be one of gridlock. Those who could make decisions to change or reform the current system seem unwilling to make any compromises. In the meantime, the holders of doctoral degrees suffer, having spent a considerable portion of their lives in pursuit of something that has left them with little other than crippling debt. A doctoral degree undoubtedly offers personal enrichment, but $150,000 is a steep price to pay for personal growth. For that kind of money, one might have easily travelled the world several times over, which sounds like more fun to me.

Conclusion

Whether the problem stems from a glut of doctoral degrees or the stinginess of university administrations, what does not help is celebrating any instance of a Ph.D. holder finding work as a sign of success for an "alternative" market. Most people find work. Whether that work is enjoyable or personally rewarding is another matter, and, unfortunately, not something everyone can afford to consider. Many of us, however, sought something more rewarding through the pursuit of higher education. Sadly, under the current climate, to follow such a pursuit is to make a costly mistake. It should not be this way, but if celebrating an "alternative" market causes us to gloss over this harsh reality, then doing so creates a barrier to reform.

If we acknowledge our doctoral degrees as failures, we can view the credentialing system as one that sets up its participants to fail. I can think of no reason why anyone would voluntarily, rationally participate in such a system. Don't go into a graduate program that offers more long-term burdens than advantages. Don't accept ridiculously underpaid teaching positions. And if you have done either of these, quit now. If we do not contribute to the system, we do not feed the system. And starving the system—depriving it of graduate students and instructors—may well be the only way to force it into the shock that will necessitate some sort of change.

Works Cited

Arrested Development, created by Mitchell Hurwitz, Fox Broadcasting/Netflix, 2003–2006/2013–2019.

Bethman, Brenda, and Shaun Longstreet. "Defining Terms." *Inside Higher Ed*, 22 May 2013, https://www.insidehighered.com/advice/2013/05/22/essay-defining-alt-ac-new-phd-job-searches.

Ginsberg, Benjamin. *The Fall of the Faculty: The Rise of the All-Administrative University and Why It Matters*. Oxford UP, 2013.
Nowviskie, Bethany. "#alt-ac: alternate academic careers for humanities scholars." *Bethany Nowiskie*, 3 Jan. 2010, http://nowviskie.org/2010/alt-ac/.
———. "two and a half cheers for the lunaticks." *Bethany Nowiskie*, 8 Jan. 2012, http://nowviskie.org/2012/lunaticks/.
Schuman, Rebecca. "Alt-Ac Talk." *Pan Kisses Kafka*, 19 Sept. 2014. *Pan Kisses Kafka*, 2014, https://pankisseskafka.files.wordpress.com/2014/09/alt-ac-talk-final.pdf.
———. "'Alt-Ac' to the Rescue?" *Slate*, 18 Sept. 2014, https://slate.com/human-interest/2014/09/a-changing-view-of-alt-ac-jobs-in-which-ph-d-s-work-outside-of-academia.html.
Wisdom, Maria LaMonaca. "Getting past 'Alt-Ac.'" *Blog*, Duke Versatile Humanists, 12 Oct. 2020, https://versatilehumanists.duke.edu/2020/10/12/getting-past-alt-ac/.

Chapter 15. Reconsidering the Status of Contingency: Are These Really the Trenches?

Jennifer K. Johnson and Nicole Warwick
University of California, Santa Barbara

Lecturer. Assistant Professor. To those outside of academia, there is little to no recognition of the distinction between these academic ranks. But within U.S. academic circles, there is a huge disparity between them in terms of what they convey about job security, salary, privileges, and respect.

As continuing lecturers[1] in the University of California, Santa Barbara (UCSB) writing program, we'd like to share our experiences with building our careers as non-tenure-track, full-time university faculty members who enjoy significant job security, a livable wage, and access to a plethora of teaching, research, and service opportunities, both within and beyond our department and campus. And while technically our positions are considered contingent because they rely on programmatic need, our continuing lecturer status means that our contracts do not have an end date associated with them.

In this chapter, we hope to discuss the benefits of roles like ours and disrupt the commonly held perception that non-tenure-track positions are always and by definition inferior to tenure-track positions. As Eileen E. Schell points out in Seth Khan et al.'s edited collection *Contingency, Exploitation, and Solidarity: Labor and Action in English Composition*, "While the term contingent describes positions in which faculty members teach on short term contracts with low pay and little or no job security, inadequate office space, and challenging curricular and professional conditions, the idea of contingency fails to capture the true complexity of positions located off the tenure track" ("Foreword" x). Our story highlights an additional path for graduate students and early career professionals to consider, particularly because these positions are overlooked so often.

We begin by sharing our respective stories of how we came to be continuing lecturers and subsequently embraced that role—albeit with some initial trepidation. We then consider the many benefits our positions offer, despite the stigmatization of our rank. We close by discussing how these lectureships originated and

---

1. The continuing lecturer title is used in the UC system to denote a lecturer who has passed a sixth-year excellence review and whose contract therefore does not have an ending date. We agree with Seth Kahn et al., who make the point that "names matter" and that titles "help identify local conditions and contexts" ("Introduction" 7); thus, we are using this localized title throughout our chapter.

arguing for the importance of a strong union and ethical administrators who are committed to maintaining them.

The Future Looks Bright, So Long as It's on the Tenure Track

Our story begins in the fall of 2001. We met when we were both pursuing M.A. degrees in English at California State University, Northridge (CSUN), where we also served as TAs and adjunct instructors. Later, we both attended Indiana University of Pennsylvania (IUP), where we earned our doctorates in the composition and TESOL program. Now we work together in UCSB's independent writing program, where we both teach first-year and upper-division writing courses, and where we also mentor and train composition TAs.

Because the two of us have shared so many experiences in our academic lives as both graduate students and professionals, we have a collective story as well as respective ones. Our stories chronicle our individual paths to becoming continuing lecturers and consider the ways in which we had to overcome some deeply entrenched ideas about what our careers should look like. Ironically, these ideas led us both perilously close to missing out on what we were actually seeking in our professional lives.

Jennifer's Story

After earning my M.A. in English at CSUN, I spent a year cobbling together an income as an adjunct at two different institutions within four different departments. I had been told as a TA that the life of the adjunct "freeway flyer" (an instructor who works at multiple schools) was not an easy one, and at this point I was discovering this for myself. Not only was it complicated to teach four to five completely different courses each semester, but the compensation was abysmal. Moreover, the only way to maintain health insurance was to secure at least three courses per semester at one institution.

I knew I needed to find a way out. My M.A. program had ingrained in me the idea that the solution was to get a Ph.D. and a tenure-track job, so that fall I applied to IUP's low-residency summer program in composition and TESOL. This program felt like a godsend, as it would allow me to continue teaching and living in California (where my extended family was) while still moving toward my goal of becoming an assistant professor somewhere.

A few months later, an assistant professor position opened up at the community college where I was teaching. Something like 140 people applied for this position, which entailed a 4/4 teaching load, significant committee work, and service and publication requirements in order to reach tenure. While it felt like somewhat of a long shot, given that I had not yet started my Ph.D. work, I applied, and I was pleased to be invited for an interview and teaching demonstration.

Around this same time, then-director of the UCSB writing program, Susan McLeod, posted an ad for a lecturer position on the WPA listserv. The ad said something about how some people used these lectureships as postdocs while others fell in love with the students and the campus culture and stayed forever. Having been thoroughly acculturated to see the tenure-track as the holy grail of academic life, I could not imagine how someone could settle for a lectureship over a tenure-track gig. After all, I was pursuing a Ph.D., which seemed to me a sure precursor to landing a tenure-track job. I imagined that if I could get this lectureship, I would keep it for a few years before going on the job market and pursuing what I envisioned would be my "real" job.

I applied to the UCSB job, and soon after having a brief telephone interview, I received an offer from the program for a two-year, renewable contract that could lead to a series of one- and two-year contracts prior to a sixth-year excellence review, which if passed would result in a permanent contract. I appreciated the fact that the contract was ostensibly renewable, and after asking how often these contracts were in fact renewed and gaining assurance that they generally were, I figured this was a pretty safe bet. I was also intrigued by the idea of working in an independent writing program, separate from the English department, as this meant I would be joining a group of 30-some full-time faculty members who were dedicated to teaching first-year and developmental composition along with a whole host of interesting upper-division writing courses.

At this point, I was fifth on the list at the community college, and that department was not ready to make any offers. Even so, a part of me really wanted to hold out for the possibility of being offered the community college job. This may sound crazy, as the lectureship offer was a sure thing and a definite step up from my then-status as an adjunct. On the other hand, the community college job was tenure-track. The starting salary was about $20,000 higher than what the lectureship offered.

Moreover, because the community college job was at the college where I had earned my A.A. degree and where my parents had met some 30 years prior when they worked on the school newspaper together, it was a safe and comfortable place to imagine my future. All this aside, given that there were four applicants ahead of me, it was far from a sure thing.

Despite this little detail, I agonized over what to do. My friends and family outside of academia were, like me, enamored by the idea of the significantly higher salary the community college job offered. They also were not super keen on the idea of me accepting a job 100 miles away from the community in which I had been born and raised and where they all still lived, which the UCSB job was. Still, they were impressed by the fact that I had received the offer from UCSB, as they understood that a university teaching position carried with it a measure of respect, although they had no clue about the differences between a lectureship and an assistant professorship.

But three people in particular understood all of these nuances. The first was my thesis advisor, who was delighted and somewhat floored that I had received the UCSB offer, particularly as I was just beginning my Ph.D. work.[2]

The second was my best friend, who had recently earned tenure at a Cal State university and was pleased to see me pursuing a career in academia. She let me know in no uncertain terms that she regarded the lectureship as a far more illustrious opportunity than the community college position—despite the lower salary it offered—because it was at a University of California campus versus a community college (suggesting yet another hierarchical structure in addition to the tenure-track/non-tenure track divide). All these years later, she wryly admits to having been a little envious that I had managed to finagle an offer from a University of California institution.

The third person who encouraged me to jump at the UCSB lectureship was a full professor at CSUN who was nearing retirement. I had served as a TA for her the previous year, and at this point I was working with her as an adjunct. She sat me down one evening after class and talked me through the relative benefits and drawbacks of each job, pointing out that while the community college position offered both security and a higher salary, it would likely lock me in to a five-day-a-week schedule teaching the same few classes over and over to first- and second-year students forever, whereas the lectureship would open up all sorts of opportunities in terms of research, teaching, and service, something the community college simply could not offer.

While she made a compelling case, I had no way of knowing just how right she was. But her words—coupled with the increasingly inescapable fact that I did in fact have only one offer on the table—resonated with me and helped me make my decision. Within a few days of my conversation with her, I accepted the lectureship offer, perceiving this move as both a wonderful opportunity and a veritable stepping-stone to bigger and better things down the road.

Nicole's Story

After earning my M.A. in the English department at CSUN, I was hired into the composition adjunct pool, and I ended up teaching composition as an adjunct faculty member there for 13 years. I decided not to go on for a Ph.D. right away. In that time, I began to grow professionally and to improve my teaching as I read scholarship about teaching writing in response to questions and problems that arose in my classes.

I was also asked by tenure-track faculty members to fill different leadership positions in the English department and related programs. I was hired as the

---

2. Since the time I was hired in 2005, the job requirements have become more stringent. Applicants must now have completed all requirements for a Ph.D. except the dissertation, OR have a terminal degree (M.F.A., M.B.A, Ph.D.) when they apply.

assistant coordinator for the campus' writing exit exam. This was a paid position that helped me supplement my income as an adjunct faculty member. I was also asked to be the coordinator for the composition program's portfolio readings.

Being in these positions helped me see that I was capable of leadership within the field and that I perhaps wanted more from my career, which to me meant pursuing a Ph.D. and eventually a tenure-track position. After teaching writing at CSUN for five years, I applied and was accepted to IUP's doctoral program in composition and TESOL. Because of IUP's limited residency model, I could work on my Ph.D. during the summers and stay at CSUN and teach writing during the academic year; however, I decided to give up my administrative position.

Though I expected to go on the academic job market once I earned my Ph.D., I also started entertaining a dream of being hired into a tenure-track position in the composition program at CSUN. I believe some of the tenured composition faculty members also saw the potential because I was earning a Ph.D. and because I effectively fulfilled my duties in serving on committees and taking on leadership roles. Plus, two of the tenured faculty members in the program at the time had been hired as tenure-track faculty from adjunct positions. I felt like I had a chance of securing a tenure-track position in composition there if one ever came up.

I was about a year out from finishing my doctorate when a full-time lectureship position was advertised at UCSB. I applied and was hired for the 2013–2014 academic year. Much like Jennifer, I saw this as a stepping-stone for my dream job as a tenure-track faculty member. One step it achieved on the path to a tenure-track job was that it was a full-time position. Another was that I would be able to take on more responsibilities, such as more committee work and teaching a variety of writing classes. In other words, I would gain valuable experience that would make me a more eligible candidate if a tenure-track position opened up at CSUN. When I talked to my colleagues at CSUN about leaving, I said, "Sometimes you have to leave to come back." But it didn't work out that way. I left for UCSB but then never went back.

A tenure-track position at CSUN was advertised the fall that I began teaching at USCB. I applied for the position and was invited to interview in January 2014, but I didn't make it past the interview stage. I was so disappointed for all kinds of reasons, but mainly because it was the end of a dream I had really started believing in. For a long time after that, everything just felt wrong. At the same time, though, I was grateful to have the UCSB position. But still at this point, I considered it a "fallback" position and not necessarily a dream job. I figured I could stay and teach there and regroup to figure out what I wanted to do next.

Eventually, I came to feel relieved about not having gotten the tenure-track position at CSUN, as I began to see more clearly what I wanted out of my career, which turned out to be a teaching-focused position with less pressure to publish. But coming to terms with not getting the job at CSUN and starting to see the position at UCSB as more than a stepping-stone was a process—a process that lasted a year or more.

At this point, Jennifer and my stories come back together, and now here we are, solidly into our careers as continuing lecturers in the UCSB writing program. We have been teaching in this program for 25 collective years, and we both have embraced these positions as our "dream jobs." In the next section, we want to take a moment to highlight the benefits and opportunities that these positions afford, thereby answering the question that Schell poses in her contribution to *Moving a Mountain: Transforming the Role of Contingent Faculty in Composition Studies and Higher Education*: "What are the benefits incurred in programs that employ a steady, professionally active group of part-time or full-time non-tenure track faculty?" (327).

Not Looking Back—Embracing a Rich Academic Life off the Tenure Track

At first, both of us felt ambivalent about our positions in the UCSB writing program. However, after our first years in these positions, we realized they were fulfilling roles, rich with opportunities to teach new classes, to collaborate with colleagues on a variety of engaging research projects, and to engage in interesting and worthwhile service activities. As that job ad so many years ago suggested, we fell in love with the campus and students and are now committed to staying forever.

"But," those of you who see tenure as the end-goal of the academic career hunt may be thinking, "how can you be satisfied with being just a lecturer?" Well, as Schell concludes,

> . . . many colleges and universities have successfully created non-tenure-track positions with salaries, benefits, and renewable or multiyear contracts. These institutions have come to realize that the quality of instruction across the institution is affected by the ways in which writing faculty are hired, contracted, paid, oriented (or not), mentored (or not), evaluated (or not), and/or offered professional development opportunities (or not). ("What's the Bottom Line" 333–34)

Much to our own surprise, we have indeed found this to be the case. For one thing, because we see ourselves as teachers first, we are very comfortable in these teaching-focused roles. Our teaching load is three courses per quarter for three quarters, but we get service credit for two courses, so we teach seven courses a year rather than nine. We are encouraged to choose from courses including developmental composition; first-year composition; and a slew of required upper-division, advanced writing courses focusing on writing for academic, professional, and civic contexts.[3] We also both work with graduate student TAs to whom we offer mentor-

---

3. Our program has a writing minor offering six different tracks: professional editing, writing and civic engagement, multimedia communication, business communication,

ship as they teach first-year writing.

As for professional development, we are encouraged to engage with the profession in whatever ways we find fulfilling. Our colleagues come from a variety of academic and professional backgrounds and continue to practice their writing crafts in a variety of genres, including business, journalism, creative nonfiction, and poetry. The two of us regularly collaborate on scholarly projects by presenting at national and regional conferences, conducting research projects, and writing articles and book chapters. We are supported in this work through travel and research funding and are also rewarded for it in the continuing lecturer merit review system that we participate in every three years. In addition, we are often invited by our colleagues to participate in various scholarly activities, and there is abundant mentoring available to us.

In terms of service, because our unit is self-governing, we are expected to sit on multiple departmental committees associated with curriculum and program initiatives. As continuing lecturers, we are permanent members of the personnel committee, and we have both served on the hiring committee, experiences that have provided us with a voice in the hiring and retention of our colleagues.

Finally, our benefits are generous, and our salaries are reasonable. We receive yearly cost of living increases, and merit increases result from a review process in which our colleagues evaluate our teaching, service, and scholarly activities. We evaluate theirs as well. All in all, it's a pretty great gig.

Disrupting the Vortex of Tenure as Ultimate Goal

In addition to highlighting what's good about these positions, we also want to focus on the powerful struggle we experienced in coming to terms with accepting a career trajectory that was different than what we had initially imagined for ourselves and that went against the grain of what is expected of newly minted (or close-to-being minted) Ph.D.s. Both of us having to undergo this process exposes some deeper issues at work. Indeed, both of our stories highlight a kind of myopic focus on the tenure track—specifically a focus on tenure-track positions in four-year universities.

One of the theories that has helped us think about this issue is Francois Lionnet and Shu-mei Shih's theory of minor transnationalism. In their theory, they use the metaphors of vertical and horizontal frameworks to discuss relationships between dominant and minority cultures, but we have found that their metaphors work well in discussing relationships between any dominant or minority group, such as those we find in the academy, like tenure-track and non-tenure-track faculty.

Lionnet and Shih describe a dominant culture as functioning like a vortex: At the center of the vortex, we find a value or "norm" from the dominant culture;

---

science communication, and journalism.

this vortex then sucks in other cultures' values and norms and measures them against the value or norm at the center, with other cultures ranked based on how well their values and norms measure up to those of the dominant group, creating a vertical, hierarchical structure (5). Furthermore, the constant direction and redirection of attention to the dominant values and norms creates a narrow frame that obscures other meaningful interactions that could be occurring beyond the scope of the dominant (1).

Lionnet and Shih describe how their theory of minor transnationalism emerged from insights they had about their respective subdiscipline-discipline relationships. They note that they both had careers in ethnic studies, but Lionnet's home discipline was French and Shih's home discipline was Chinese. They tell of meeting by chance at an international conference in Paris and explain that as they talked about their careers at the conference and then later at a cafe, they realized that their subdiscipline-discipline relationships were framed vertically. That is, by focusing all their attention on the disciplines of French or Chinese, they did not look to other ethnic studies programs for support or interaction. They did not look to other ethnic studies programs to see what they were doing. But for this chance encounter, they otherwise would be too caught up in the construct of relating to their disciplines vertically to have interacted across them (1).

While this limitation was a consequence of university systems, it was also a consequence of a habit of mind. Lionnet and Shih learned to see relationships vertically. They explain, " . . . our battles are always framed vertically, and we forget to look sideways to lateral networks that are not readily apparent" (1). Minor groups learn to see themselves in relation to dominant groups as opposed to being in relation to other minor groups or even just themselves, so focusing attention on the dominant group becomes naturalized.

In a way, the two of us see ourselves undergoing a similar process as Lionnet and Shih: We have realized that we were measuring our positions in the writing program against values that place tenure-track positions at the center and against which all other positions are measured. We were so focused on tenure-track positions, we missed seeing the richness the full-time UCSB continuing lectureship had to offer and missed seeing it as a career goal as opposed to a stepping-stone.

Lionnet and Shih also teach us to "look sideways to lateral networks" (1) because in doing so, we can look for the bigger picture. It is this process of reframing that helped the two of us come to value our positions in the UCSB writing program and embrace the continuing lecturer position as a career goal, just as others embrace tenure-track positions as career goals. Academia is a richer and more nuanced place than we often give it credit for, a view Mark McBeth and Tim McCormack encourage us to take:

> As Steve Street suggests in *Academe*, we need to move past this full-time/part-time divide to understand that we already have

a professoriate that has a multiplicity of tiers: adjunct faculty (recently hired one course), adjunct faculty (long time/more than one course), graduate teaching fellows, faculty emeritus who still teach, tenure-track faculty, tenured faculty, emeritus faculty who do not teach, faculty chairs, lecturers, instructors, and teaching assistants. All faculty positions would benefit from the explicitly defined and carefully guarded job descriptions we have delineated for our lecturer lines. (54)

And Yet...

We also want to point out that as much as our positions have going for them, they did not appear out of thin air. The story of how UCSB's writing program came to have the lecture lines the two of us occupy is clearly laid out in Nicholas Tingle and Judy Kirscht's "A Place to Stand: The Role of Unions in the Development of Writing Programs." Tingle and Kirscht explain that after years of negotiation, in 1986 the UC-AFT union finally succeeded in securing continuing lecturer status for those faculty who passed a sixth-year excellence review. They note that prior to this achievement, the university had a policy that dictated lecturers could only be given eight successive year-long contracts, after which they were automatically prevented from being rehired, a practice that was reduced in 1983 to a "four years and you are out" policy (221–22).

Due to the ongoing diligence of both the union and supportive administration and departmental leadership, the affordances for UCSB writing program continuing lecturers have improved from there. However, we also want to point out that advancements in working conditions have depended on careful strategy and deliberate action. As past program directors Madeleine Sorapure and Linda Adler-Kassner explain in "Context, Strategy, Identity: A History of Change in the UC Santa Barbara Writing Program," "To survive and thrive, independent writing programs must remain responsive to and proactive within ever shifting contexts" (110).

Sorapure and Adler-Kassner's piece exemplifies five strategies masterfully designed to respond to five distinct eras in the UCSB writing program's history. Similarly, in an interview conducted by Sorapure, Susan McLeod recalls some of the ways in which she strove to support continuing lecturers' professionalization and improve their working conditions by increasing salaries and improving hiring and retention practices when she directed the writing program from 2001–2006.

Tingle and Kirscht also point out that the UCSB writing program is a unique place, even within the UC system, and that "this success is not accidental" (230). They highlight four key events necessary to the program's success and survival:

> (1) collective action (the union won three-year contracts that provided a permanent faculty,); (2) separation from the English

> department, where its interests could never be primary; (3) development of a cross-disciplinary curriculum, including linked classes that took program faculty out of their isolated ghettoes and built relationships across campus; (4) membership on university-wide committees, giving program faculty increased visibility and therefore gradual acceptance as an integral part of the university community. (230)

As we have been outlining and as Tingle and Kirscht corroborate, our positions were hard won through strategic planning, union activism, and contextual forces, but the hard work did not and does not stop there. The advancements that were achieved need to be maintained and allowed to evolve, and the union and ethical administrators—which include committed program directors and attuned deans, chancellors, etc.—play key roles in this work.

For instance, as we have been writing this chapter, our union and the university have been engaged in protracted, contentious negotiations. Our current contract expired almost two years ago, and despite a succession of 55 bargaining meetings, the university and our union's bargaining team have found it challenging to come to an agreement. This week, in fact, a two-day strike was called and subsequently canceled just hours before it was to take place when the two sides finally came to a tentative agreement. At the time of this writing, it had not yet been ratified, but if it is, this agreement will result in the strongest improvements to the UC continuing lecturer contract in 20 years, as it will increase security for continuing lecturers in their first six years of employment, raise compensation for all continuing lecturers, and provide all continuing lecturers with paid time off for family care and child bonding. It has been hailed by the union president as "the best contract in UC-AFT history and among the best nationwide for contingent faculty" (Shalby and Watanabe). This achievement is both something to celebrate and a clear reminder that "helpless acceptance of an underclass role is suicidal; we must maintain the attitude that created the union and sustained it through its infancy" (Tingle and Kirscht 230).

In the End . . .

While we are aware that positions like ours are not a panacea to the many labor issues facing both contingent and tenured faculty in higher education, we believe these positions are far more worthy of consideration than dominant narratives suggest—dominant narratives we had uncritically accepted. As McBeth and McCormack have noted about their program, which provides many of the same benefits and affordances as ours does, "Our lecturer lines are not perfect by any means, but in terms of incrementally 'fairer and fairer' employment practice, we now have a point of departure upon which to improve" (54).

We sincerely hope that our chapter has served to challenge entrenched narratives about the stigma surrounding non-tenure-track faculty positions and to reframe the conversation surrounding these positions. We urge others to consider looking sideways and beyond the tenure-track, particularly in a time when tenure-track positions are becoming less available and non-tenure-track positions are becoming more common. We hope that our stories can help others know what's possible, which, in turn, can empower people to make more deliberate decisions and embrace opportunities like these more readily than we did. We'd like to prevent others from experiencing the cognitive dissonance that we underwent as we came to terms with our roles, and ultimately we hope to help others avoid missing out on fulfilling academic careers, just because they are off the tenure track.

Works Cited

Kahn, Seth, et al. "Introduction: Paths Toward Solidarity." Kahn et al., pp. 3–11. *WAC Clearinghouse*, https://doi.org/10.37514/PER-B.2017.0858.1.3.

———— et al., editors. *Contingency, Exploitation, and Solidarity: Labor and Action in English Composition*. The WAC Clearinghouse/University Press of Colorado, 2017. *WAC Clearinghouse*, https://doi.org/10.37514/PER-B.2017.0858.

Lionnet, Francoise and Shu-mei Shih. "Introduction: Thinking Through the Minor, Transnationally." *Minor Transnationalism*, edited by Francoise Lionnet and Shu-mei Shih, Duke UP, 2005, pp. 1–23. *Duke University Press Books*, https://doi.org/10.1215/9780822386643-001.

McBeth, Mark, and Tim McCormack. "An Apologia and a Way Forward: In Defense of the Lecturer Line in Writing Programs." Seth Kahn et al., pp. 41–55. *WAC Clearinghouse*, https://doi.org/10.37514/PER-B.2017.0858.2.03.

McLeod, Sue. Interview by Madeleine Sorapure. *SoundCloud*, 2017, https://soundcloud.com/user-403737189/sue-mcleod-online-audio-convertercom.

Schell, Eileeen E. "Foreword: The New Faculty Majority in Writing Programs: Organizing for Change." Seth Kahn et al., pp. ix-xx. *WAC Clearinghouse*, https://doi.org/10.37514/PER-B.2017.0858.1.2.

————. "What's the Bottom Line? Literacy and Quality Education in the Twenty-First Century." Eileen E. Schell and Patricia Lambert Stock, pp. 324–40. *ERIC*, http://files.eric.ed.gov/fulltext/ED447500.pdf.

———— and Patricia Lambert Stock, editors. *Moving a Mountain: Transforming the Role of Contingent Faculty in Composition Studies and Higher Education*, National Council of Teachers of English, 2001. *ERIC*, http://files.eric.ed.gov/fulltext/ED447500.pdf.

Shalby, Colleen, and Teresa Watanabe. "Critical Role of UC Lecturers Affirmed as Strike is Averted, Tentative Agreement Reached." *Los Angeles Times*, 17 November 2021, https://www.latimes.com/california/story/2021-11-17/uc-lecturer-strike-averted-tentative-agreement-reached.

Sorapure, Madeleine, and Linda Adler-Kassner. "Context, Strategy, Identity: A

History of Change in the UC Santa Barbara Writing Program." *Weathering the Storm: Independent Writing Programs in the Age of Fiscal Austerity*, edited by Richard N. Matzen, Jr., and Matthew Abraham, Utah State UP, 2019, pp. 110–17.

Tingle, Nicholas, and Judy Kirscht. "A Place to Stand: The Role of Unions in the Development of Writing Programs." Eileen E. Schell and Patricia Lambert Stock, pp. 218–32. *ERIC*, http://files.eric.ed.gov/fulltext/ED447500.pdf.

Chapter 16. From Being One to Hiring One: Both Sides of the Adjunct Phenomenon in Higher Education

Kimberly M. Miller and Joanna Whetstone
Grove City College and Lakeland Community College

Background (Kim)

When I accepted my first teaching position, I had no idea what being an adjunct instructor would mean or that others like me were part of a larger, national conversation about contingent faculty, a group that at the time made up half of all faculty appointments in higher education (Backlund 6). In more recent years, others have claimed that the numbers are much higher and in need of more examination (Murray 235).

People presumed when I got a degree in writing that I planned to teach, but the idea of standing in front of a classroom of disinterested students turned my stomach. I even took my required public speaking course in a summer two-week session because in my mind I would never need to know a thing about speaking in public. Maybe you should remember that as you consider my advice.

I accepted a part-time position teaching one film studies course at a small, private college in Pennsylvania when the chair of the communication department called me into service at the recommendation of some kind professors from my graduate school days who must have seen something in me that I didn't yet see in myself.

Unlike most other contingent faculty, I did eventually move into the ranks of full-time teaching at the same institution where I began as an adjunct after realizing this was, in fact, the path I wanted to follow.

Fast forwarding to today, I'm still at the same institution. I now have a Ph.D., am the chair of my department, and teach a full load each semester in addition to doing administrative work. Perhaps, as Murray notes, every story is unique (237). Given what I've heard and seen from others, I'm not sure every story is this encouraging, but honestly, it's the only story I have to tell.

Background (Joanna)

Unlike Kim's story of unexpected origins, my goal to become a teacher stems back to kindergarten, when I lined up my baby dolls on the basement couch and pulled out the green chalkboard that flipped to a black chalkboard where I would teach them the lessons I had learned at school. My early exposure to a pedagogy of care laid a framework for my later experiences as not only an instructor but also more specifically a female instructor in the collegiate environment.

Sara C. Motta and Anna Bennett remark that our education system is becoming increasingly neoliberal, emphasizing intellect over care and emotion. They also argued that for institutions to truly embrace diversity and inclusion, they must break the hold of careless "hegemonic masculinities" (631). Similar to what Motta and Bennett describe, I found in my educational experiences an emphasis on academic content rather than an emphasis on achieving a more emotional connection to students. It is perhaps my leaning toward this often feminized, unpraised, and under-preferred approach that made my journey more emotionally draining, challenging, and, I would argue, rewarding.

I continued my basement teaching ritual for many years, though increasingly less frequently, until sixth grade algebra when I worked out problems on the board trying to stop crying and start learning through teaching. Despite Mr. What's-His-Face making me come to hate those beautiful letters they shamefully mixed with numbers, he didn't squelch my passion for teaching. I earned a B.S. in writing and an M.A. in English before venturing out to the adjunct world.

Quite honestly, I did wander away from the teaching path for a bit, dreaming of becoming an editor at a publishing firm as I worked on my B.S. in writing, but after spending a year at home post-graduation being offered jobs as an editorial assistant in Boston and New York, along with contact numbers for other assistants who shared apartments with four others and were looking for a fifth, I realized it was a long, arduous journey of low-paying work with only a chance, albeit miniscule, that I would be able to make the big bucks. Instead, I decided I would teach at the college level.

In my media-induced fever, I dreamt of the floor-to-ceiling bookcases, the busts of Hemingway and Shakespeare sitting on a windowsill behind my enormous oak desk. That's where the job security and the comfortable living was, I thought. If you could all suppress your laughter for a moment, you know I'll soon get to the real story of my journey.

After earning my M.A. in English, I ventured out to the adjuncting world, looking for my impressive office anywhere I could find it.

Adjunct Life (Kim)

To say I had no idea what I was doing when I started as a part-time college professor would be an understatement. Those fourteen students in the advanced film theory course were about to face a stay-at-home mom who'd had no formal instruction or coursework in the field of education. And other than some basic technology instruction, I also had no formal training from the institution that hired me to handle the class either.

What I had was an advanced degree, though not a terminal one, and a willingness to jump into a situation for which I was woefully unprepared and given almost no guidelines. Luckily, my students were kind and accepting and shared my love of film. In the year that followed, I taught a basic film course and a few sections of journalism, too.

My student evaluations were good, and my department chair encouraged me to create and teach a special topics film course. For all that I could tell, things were going very well. And what I didn't know about teaching or being an adjunct never bothered me—because I didn't know enough to be bothered. Now, in hindsight, I've gained the experience to be capable of fairly assessing how the institution treated me in this role of part-time instructor.

In speaking to adjuncts at other institutions, I discovered the pay I received for my work was somewhere between the middle and higher end of the scale. And because our department had recently split from the English department, there weren't many full-time faculty members competing for classes, which meant I got some say in choosing class times, though the courses were given to me regardless of my preference and skill set.

As for participating in faculty meetings, having a say in departmental decisions, receiving employment benefits, or even getting taken advantage of as so many other adjuncts have endured, I didn't realize I should be concerned with any of it. As Jeremy C. Young and Robert B. Townsend note, every adjunct has their own reasons for accepting the position, and while many suffer for this decision, nearly three-fourths of those they surveyed were "satisfied with the position overall." Given that evidence abounds that adjuncts often live at or below the poverty level (Quart), it is possible that those surveyed by Young and Townsend had spouses or others to support them, making their salary and overall institutional treatment less of a factor in their job satisfaction ratings.

In my case, I was grateful to have a job and presumed in my naivete that however I was being treated in that situation was normal and fair, though as Young and Townsend also point out, "acknowledging that non-tenure-track instructors are a highly varied group does not in any way minimize the problem of contingent labor." Still, from my perspective as a part-time professor, I didn't expect to be included in departmental or college-wide decisions, and with two small children, I was happy to avoid the additional time meetings would have taken from being home with them. Teaching was enough. I truly appreciated the opportunity. It never crossed my mind to wonder if my work was "valued" by the institution.

While I suppose you're hoping I'll say I know better now, I'm not sure that I do. I even asked a colleague recently about his adjunct experience at our institution, and he agreed that while the college isn't perfect, it does treat adjuncts well. That said, now that I'm on the other side of being an adjunct, I can see many ways we could do better for the part-time faculty who work to support our mission, our students, and our individual departments, often without much thanks. I will elaborate on this in the next section.

The full-time position that I was covering stayed open until the provost called me to his office and asked me to apply for it. After a year and a half of adjunct work, I moved into a full-time position, and though I remained at the rank of "instructor" for several years, I did eventually become a full professor shortly after receiving my Ph.D. Then I assumed the role of interim department chair, and I officially took over as department chair a few years ago. And that means I can speak with some authority regarding my institution's treatment of adjuncts with a different level of insight than I've ever had before.

Adjunct Life (Joanna)

Unlike Kim's adjunct story, mine was more that of a dirty hippie's, traveling from school to school through the Pennsylvania winters in my less-than-reliable vehicle. I started my adjunct experience in the information systems department, actually, teaching people the parts of a computer—nothing fancy, more like "Hey, this is called a monitor," followed by pounding on the blackboard to demonstrate how to double-click a mouse. Informed by my many years working in our campus writing center that was adjacent to the computer lab, which, by geography, made all writing center tutors makeshift help desk employees, I wiggled my way into teaching the IT course that no self-respecting IT professor wanted.

After a semester of that, I began teaching English courses and, probably like many people reading this chapter, spent my semesters teaching for multiple institutions in multiple counties at all kinds of insane hours. One semester, I taught a 7:30 a.m. section in a high school before their regular school hours, traveled to a second county for two more classes, ate lunch, then traveled to a third school in a third county to teach another two sections, ending just shortly before 9:00 p.m.

In my life of a wandering adjunct, I lived out of my trunk. With materials for each class section in its own milk crate with hanging files, I attempted to keep my life organized and structured. Getting paid only to spend my salary on supplies and gas was never easy. I qualified for unemployment in the summers, though even teaching six sections a semester kept me under the poverty line. Apparently, this experience is not unique. In a 2020 report titled "An Army of Temps," the American Federation of Teachers notes, "One-third of respondents [to a survey of contingent faculty members] earn less than $25,000 annually, placing them below the federal poverty guideline for a family of four" (1).

In my case, teaching all these sections put me below the poverty level with no benefits. The experience made me humble, requiring me to learn to accept an undignified position for very hard academic efforts. Waiting tables on the weekends to make ends meet and pay my rent was demoralizing. How could I be working so hard for so little? Having to teach on so many campuses also meant no time to get to know people at any of the schools, really, which caused me to feel even more disconnected from my field and from life. Occasionally, I was able to attend a division meeting and feel like my face was being seen, but much of the time, I drove and drove and drove and graded and graded and graded. My one-bedroom ranch house had a makeshift office space, which was a fold-up table in front of the TV.

I guess I was naïve. I thought that being a college professor meant wearing cozy sweaters and sitting in my dark wood-paneled office with floor-to-ceiling bookshelves and a huge leather couch where students would come to visit me to talk about our latest reading from Foucault. In reality, if I had an office space at all, it was an empty metal desk shared by hundreds of others without even a key to the filing cabinet. We were mobile teachers without space, without a place, and without anything to call our own. It was definitely not how I imagined teaching college would be.

When I came to discover that I was actually in the majority, with about 60 percent of faculty members being adjunct at that time, I was even more floored. How was this possible? This lifestyle was beyond just challenging. It was a time in my life that made me question my goal to become a teacher. I often referred to this experience as academic hazing, waiting to earn the "letters" bestowed upon us as tenured professors.

However, I was lucky. My big break occurred two years later when I started a full-time adjunct position at a four-year university. I finally found out what it meant to be a college instructor. I shared an office with just one or two other people, which was magical. I attended weekly department meetings during which my voice was not only heard but also encouraged. I was able to join committees with others from different departments. I started to see the world on the other side of the tracks, so to speak. When I was treated as equally important in driving the department and campus, I felt important and listened to.

Quite honestly, many of the faculty members I worked with did not even realize I was adjunct. Once I had this position, with a salary and benefits, I was motivated to begin my Ph.D. program. I know, that sounds crazy, right? When I was continuing to live as an adjunct with a temporary contract and no guarantee of anything, why would I invest more time and energy into a degree I wasn't sure I could even use for a full-time job? As fellow adjuncts can attest, it is a calling, I suppose.

Working in one county, going to night classes in another, and living in a third made for a taxing two years of coursework, but I did it. I lived this routine through all my doctoral coursework. While ABD, I applied for tenure-track jobs and landed one! I quickly packed up and moved, feeling pretty lucky to be one of the chosen few, the 40 percent who made it out of the adjunct lifestyle. I have been at that job ever since, circa 2007.

Chair Experience (Kim)

Our department has consistently struggled with and been overburdened by the number of students we are trying to serve with only a few full-time faculty members. This means we rely on cross-departmental support from full-time faculty members as well as support from adjuncts who are professionals in another career field rather than part-timers looking for a full-time position. But I'd be lying if I said we don't also rely on adjuncts who teach for us and at other institutions part-time as well, sometimes covering more classes in a semester than some full-time faculty members teach in an entire year.

Because my story in administration has consisted almost solely of survival for most of my tenure as chair, I admit to not being sensitive or considerate to the adjunct situation until very recently when one of my part-timers noted how close to the start of the semester he received his contract. Murray states that this kind of "job insecurity" is only made worse by a host of other issues (238). In light of this conversation, I realized that I was seeing only a small glimpse of a much bigger and possibly more frustrating problem.

Many, or maybe all, adjuncts tend to be treated as a disrespected afterthought in the grand scheme of semester planning. In his analysis, Murray reveals concerning situations in which contingent faculty are "sometimes treated as virtually invisible by some departments that take contingent labor for granted" (238). While we may not mean to do so, the point is that we are not considering all faculty as equals.

I hope that by starting this conversation with adjuncts about what they need and then taking those needs to the administration, we can begin to change this pattern on my campus. After the conversation with my colleague, I set forth to write a document to pass along to the administration. This "work in progress" included several concerns, such as late contracts and the "onboarding" of new adjuncts in regard to parking, computer use, and other matters that, as a full-time faculty member for a number of years, I now take for granted.

As I wrote, I realized something about my own experience that should have taken place but never did. If only I'd been mentored and trained regarding what to expect as a new faculty member, where to find what I needed, and who to ask for help, I might have been able to avoid some of the awkward and even embarrassing moments early in my teaching career.

Sure, being mistaken for a student isn't necessarily a terrible thing, but at the same time, it's difficult to expect respect or inclusion from colleagues who don't know you exist. And further, it's impossible to feel valued. Sadly, as William Pannapacker states, many faculty members do not feel "adequately valued," a problem that left him wondering whether he should leave academia altogether, and this as a tenured faculty member. It's shocking to note that, while the problems considered in this chapter begin in the adjunct realm, they are pervasive across every level of "success" in academe. Perhaps creating a consistent system of onboarding adjuncts and making them part of the structure of the institution will not only change feelings of isolation and being undervalued, but it might also begin a trend for all faculty members to feel relevant in their departments and institutions.

And that is my next endeavor as a department chair, a tactic I hope will eliminate or at the very least minimize the challenges of being an adjunct faculty member or even a new full-time faculty member at our institution. Currently,

I've begun writing a document listing and explaining common onboarding procedures with the goal of creating a consistent system for not only our department but also the entire college.

As I indicated earlier, I don't see our system as being ineffective, but that doesn't mean there isn't room for improvement. And, as Jessica Schreyer notes, "If enough people are engaging in these conversations, progress can be made toward excellent working conditions for all faculty" (98). Finding the issues within our system and working to address and improve them for our contingent faculty members is the least I can do in my role as an administrator. I'm happy to report that my dean is supportive and excited about the ideas and would like to work with me on it so that we can pass them along to the administration.

Chair Experience (Joanna)

My school relies heavily on adjuncts to fill our schedule. The ratio is sadly like many schools, with about 40 sections taught by our full-time faculty members and the remaining 60 sections taught by our adjunct faculty members.

I work for a two-year community college and belong to a department with 11 full-time faculty members and 54 adjuncts. The role I am in is of co-chair, an advocate for our faculty but not an administrative role in the traditional sense. My co-chair and I do not see ourselves as "in charge" of the department but rather as advocates for our faculty. In our department, co-chairs rotate every three years on a staggered schedule, always having an experienced chair in place as the new one rotates in. This creates a sense of continuity but also serves as a reminder that we are only in that role for a short period of time.

Serving as an advocate for 54 temporary, part-time, non-tenure-track faculty members, I realized that forcing them to teach fewer than 12 credits to avoid the institution having to provide them with healthcare insurance is inhumane. I know what it is like wondering how to pay the heating bill and sitting under piles of blankets grading papers late at night after having taught six classes over the course of 12 hours in three counties. I have been there. I want to be a better advocate, but how? My adjuncts are worth more than $792 per credit hour, especially when faced with a pandemic.

As I noted earlier, one of the biggest pieces to feeling my worth when I was an adjunct was feeling like I mattered, like my voice and presence were recognized. As a result, as co-chair, I have invited our adjuncts to come to committee meetings about our course outlines and book adoptions and to department meetings. I want them to know we appreciate their contribution, which translates to teaching nearly 100 sections a semester, more than double what our full-time faculty members are teaching but without the same professional and financial support, geographical landing space of an office, and daily interactions with other faculty members about our pedagogy, a dynamic I find so incredibly invigorating as a teacher.

In its "An Army of Temps" report, the American Federation of Teachers points out the finding that "faculty in contingent positions are often cut out of department and institution-wide planning, though they may teach the majority of some types of courses, especially in community colleges and at the introductory and developmental levels in four-year institutions" (7). When most of the faculty members on a campus are adjunct, why are they left in the margins when it comes to decision making? With that said, involvement is incredibly challenging on the adjuncts' end while they do that traveling from school to school and prepping along the way. Finding the time to commit to these involvements is not easy. I know that. Sometimes being in my role of co-chair is overwhelming, always remembering how hard their job is, but I will keep fighting.

Seeing more and more full-time tenured faculty members at my institution retiring and not being replaced, our statistic of adjunct to full-time faculty members are growing increasingly disproportionate. We must rely on adjunct faculty members and, therefore, must treasure their desire for inclusion. How do we do that?

Solutions (Kim)

I am not about to pretend that the small, private college where I work is a perfect place or that it has the answers to the challenges that likely will continue to be there for adjuncts. I also can't, and won't, say that stepping into the world of academia as an adjunct faculty member, whether as one with the intention of pursuing a full-time teaching position or as one who is content to stay in an adjunct role while working full-time in another profession, is a wise plan. However, I can say that there are some things to keep in mind.

I hope my story illustrates that there is hope in academia, but at the same time, I truly understand that my experience is rare and not without its flaws. My institution does not offer tenure, but instead yearly contracts, which to some could be seen as problematic.

Most adjuncts struggle to attain full-time, or even stable, employment in academia, and many never succeed. Schreyer states that her attempts to support contingent faculty members and improve working conditions at her institution fell short of addressing "the most critical issues facing contingent faculty, including pay, stability, and promotion" (84). Even with the involvement of individuals with a sensitive eye toward adjunct faculty members, solutions require institutional support that can be hard to achieve.

I understand and acknowledge the rarity of being one of the few to make the leap from the precarious adjunct world to the more stable, full-time one. To pursue full-time employment in academia means a lot of thankless hard work with no guarantee there will be any reward in the end. Because I entered the profession out of necessity with no intention of staying, it is possible that I didn't set myself up for disappointment. Perhaps that is a takeaway. Perhaps not.

After all, my recent foray into administration as a department chair came in the same way my teaching career did—without applying or pursuing the opportunity. And from the start, being chair has been fraught with drama and challenges for which I was largely unprepared. I'm not necessarily on an easier road, and in all this analysis, I didn't even touch on the difficulties of being a woman in academia, not to mention one who was under 30 years old when she took that first adjunct position. Those will have to be issues for another, different chapter in the future.

Most of my colleagues who have made the leap from adjunct work to full-time employment successfully have done so with a foot firmly planted in another career—something to fall back on. It's possible this was out of necessity with their financial situations or life plans, and in some cases the "other" career was a passion and came easily. This also might have allowed them the flexibility and courage to take the leap to academia with an awareness of that "Plan B" as a place to go back to should their adjunct work fall through.

While I'm not sure I'd necessarily do anything differently in my path to becoming a full-time faculty member and then chair of the department, having more support in my early years as well as a set of expectations for what this career would entail might have been helpful. As Wes Anthony et al. note, "The structure of most institutional systems [does] not provide a platform for these part-time teaching professionals to have any real voice on matters concerning the classroom, their teaching practices, training or decisions that apply to the departments in which they teach" (3). In light of this, it's likely that my problem is one that transcends my institution, and yet the solution is one that must start at that very level.

Anthony et al. continues, "Full-time faculty, especially those who serve as Discipline Chairs and in other adjunct supervisory roles, must promote Professional Development opportunities that involve adjunct faculty" (5). Like Anthony et al. suggest, I'd certainly have appreciated a "big picture" plan and a helping hand to navigate through contracts, difficult colleagues, and effective classroom management when I was an adjunct. Now, as a department chair, it is my role to offer such support to my contingent faculty members.

Schreyer's work and analysis illustrates something all department chairs should address, which is that if we work to understand the nuances of the specific contingent faculty situation at our institutions, we can work locally at improving those conditions (83–100). Schreyer states that her goal, and I would argue the goal of all department chairs, should be to "help create positive change" (90), and she also notes that if we "truly want high-quality programs, we must discuss not only the needs of students in those programs, but the needs of the faculty as well" (91). Her implied and understood meaning is that administration must understand the needs of not only our students but of all of our faculty members—tenured, non-tenured, full-time, and contingent part-timers—as well.

I can't change the path I took as an adjunct faculty member all those years ago, but certainly I can learn from my experience and use my position now to ensure inclusion for part-time faculty members. By taking small, purposeful steps to discover, articulate, and solve the problems facing our adjunct faculty, I can become part of what will hopefully be a trend in higher education to improve working conditions for all.

Solutions (Joanna)

My story is quite unlike Kim's in that I have always wanted to teach, never imagining much outside of academe. I was one of the ones Kim references who set herself up for disappointments. There were many of them, including the incredible hours without fair compensation as an adjunct: working 70- or 80-hour work weeks as a tenure-track and eventually tenured full professor at least comes with much better compensation than adjuncts receive.

While I would like to see a world of unionized adjuncts or a profession wherein 80 percent of courses were taught by full-time faculty members who receive reliable, respectful salaries and benefits, that does not seem to be the reality of life for most of academia. Instead, full-time instructors and professors must advocate for and include adjunct faculty members. We must also recognize the increasing trend of full-time lines being replaced with even more adjunct positions as full-time faculty members retire, saving the institutions money but putting departments that employ a large number of adjuncts at risk of losing their voices. Adjuncts matter to all of us, despite their $792 dollar per credit-hour salary they earn at my college.

My position as co-chair has afforded me the opportunity to advocate for my department's adjuncts in order to curate a more positive experience for them, which, in turn, will improve student and institutional success. Richard L. Wagoner, citing Wood and Hilton, offers "five paradigms that can be considered in ethical decision-making" that I believe apply to my role at my community college: an "ethics of justice" that asks us to make decisions that focus on "the good of the majority, the most good for the most people"; an "ethics of critique" in which we "question decisions that can and do reinforce inequities even if those decisions benefit the largest number of people and are based on accepted laws, policies, and procedures"; an "ethics of profession" that "focuses on the norms, practices, and guidelines of particular professions"; and an "ethics of local community" through which "decisions should be made contemplating the greatest good to the local community" (91).

It is incredibly difficult to advocate for the over 50 people working as adjuncts in my department when I have no real power to help with compensation and when I can only wish I could provide them with the opportunity I have to work full time with benefits, but I apply these ethical considerations to my decisions as co-chair for my department, which is comprised significantly by adjuncts, so that I can reinvigorate my department. What does that mean logistically?

College department heads need to include their adjuncts in committee work, including work on issues of curriculum development, student success initiatives, and on-campus departmental promotion. Adjuncts should also be included in departmental decisions and meetings. Full-time faculty members need to actively mentor adjunct faculty members, helping them through their professional experiences. We need to advocate for inclusion of adjuncts in contract negotiations to improve their pay, benefits, and teaching schedules. These initiatives will improve adjuncts' sense of professional worth and self-worth. In turn, their attitudes, accessibility, and engagement with students on campus will improve.

Our departments will become thriving communities for students who will return to their studies so they can continue to see the adjunct faculty members who are their teachers. I would love to see the day when our department and division meetings are held in lecture halls instead of small conference spaces, filled with hundreds of adjuncts attending, talking, collaborating, and building relationships with our full-time faculty members. Building up adjunct faculty members emotionally, psychologically, and professionally is how we will begin to see their lives, our lives, our students' lives, and our institutions' lives all improve tenfold.

Rather than accepting the dystopian depictions of the future of adjunct life continuing like this or possibly getting worse, what can we do to make it a better world? As the burden of college enrollment turns on the shoulders of the taxpayers, as the dynamic of the college campus changes, and as the pandemic lingers on, driving more courses online, the cheaper adjunct workforce will always have work, but at what cost?

Works Cited

An Army of Temps: AFT 2020 Adjunct Faculty Quality of Work/Life Report, American Federation of Teachers, 2020. *American Federation of Teachers*, https://www.aft.org/sites/default/files/adjuncts_qualityworklife2020.pdf.

Anthony, Wes, et al. "The Plight of Adjuncts in Higher Education." *Practitioner to Practitioner*, Winter, 2020, pp. 3–10. *NOSS: National Organization for Student Success*, https://thenoss.org/resources/Documents/NOSS%20Practitioner/NOSS%20Practitioner%20to%20PractitioneUpdated%20version%20Feb%202020.pdf.

Backlund, Phil. "What Can Communication Departments Do to Support Adjunct Faculty?" *Spectra*, vol. 45, no. 5, May 2009, p. 6–11.

Motta, Sara C., and Anna Bennett. "Pedagogies of Care, Care-Full Epistemological Practice and 'Other' Caring Subjectivities in Enabling Education." *Teaching in Higher Education*, vol. 23, no. 5, 2018, pp. 631–46. *Taylor and Francis Online*, https://doi.org/10.1080/13562517.2018.1465911.

Murray, Darrin S. "The Precarious New Faculty Majority: Communication and Instruction Research and Contingent Labor in Higher Education." *Communication Education*, vol. 68, no. 2, 2019, pp. 235–45. *Taylor and Francis Online*, https://doi.org/10.1080/03634523.2019.1568512.

Pannapacker, William. "On Why I'm Leaving Academe." *The Chronicle of Higher Education*, 13 Sept. 2021, https://www.chronicle.com/article/on-why-im-leaving-academe.

Quart, Alissa. "Professor, Can You Spare a Dime?" *Pacific Standard*, 14 June 2017, https://psmag.com/social-justice/professor-can-you-spare-a-dime.

Schreyer, Jessica. "Inviting the 'Outsiders' In: Local Efforts to Improve Adjunct Working Conditions." *Journal of Basic Writing*, vol. 31, no. 2, 2012, pp. 83–102. *WAC Clearinghouse*, https://10.37514/JBW-J.2012.31.2.05.

Wagoner, Richard L. "Ethics of Employment: The New Adjunct Majority." *New Directions for Community Colleges*, vol. 2019, no. 185, 2019, pp. 89–96. *Wiley Online Library*, https://doi.org/10.1002/cc.20341.

Young, Jeremy C., and Robert B. Townsend. "The Adjunct Problem is a Data Problem." *The Chronicle of Higher Education*, 30 Aug. 2021, https://www.chronicle.com/article/the-adjunct-problem-is-a-data-problem.

Chapter 17. Adjuncting without Anguish: A 21st Century Roadmap to Success for Contingent Faculty

Devan Bissonette
NIAGARA UNIVERSITY

"If you're here and other places," a program coordinator recently told me, "it's easy to put it into autopilot and [cut] corners, overwhelmed a little bit in what you're doing." The solution, he explained, was mandating a term off each year for all adjunct (contingent) faculty. This admin-splaining, said without evidence or logic—telling adjuncts the problem is them, not the system, and the solution is less work (making the situation worse, not better)—is the type of approach that causes so much of the low morale among the adjunct population in the academic world today.

According to the American Association of University Professors (AAUP), more than 60 percent of faculty members are non-tenure track ("Background Facts"). Today, 40 percent of adjuncts struggle to pay their bills, and about 1/3 earn less than $25,000 a year, and since the average salary for a class hovers around $3,500 and can be as low as $2,000 (Flaherty, "Barely Getting By"), an adjunct has to teach as many as 13 classes a year to rise above the poverty line (Schlaerth 6–7), which the U.S. Department of Health and Human Services' Office of the Assistant Secretary of Planning and Evaluation defines as $26,500 for a family of four ("2021 Poverty Guidelines"). No wonder that as of 2014, about 90 percent of adjuncts were working at least one other job (Flaherty, "Congress").

Back in 2009, I was a full year into the academic job market search. As I was applying for yet another full-time job at an institution for which I didn't want to work in yet another place where I didn't want to live, I started to see academia in a different light, something more corporate, something less humane, something, at worst, soul-sucking. I knew I still wanted an academic career, but I wanted it on my terms, and that is when I started to consider adjuncting. While much of the focus on adjunct life understandably paints a pretty dim picture, there are ways to make a living and still get some satisfaction out of such a career path. In the following paragraphs, I hope to shine a light how one can make the adjunct life sustainable as well as reflect on how we as adjuncts can use our voice to help improve working conditions today and in the future.

Strategic Adjuncting

Originally, adjuncting gave professionals in non-teaching fields a way to share their knowledge and experience while still retaining their positions in their respective careers, and it also gave graduate students a way to get their feet wet as teachers (Schlaerth 6). Today, though, adjuncts—the most high-risk faculty members in terms of pay and status—often are tasked with instructing at-risk students, who inevitably demand extra time and attention, and those increased demands on adjuncts already stretched thin trying to make ends meet lead to poor outcomes for students and faculty alike (Kezar and DePaola 32–33; McNaughtan et al. 12). While the pressures on adjuncts are unquestionably vast, I have found three key areas, detailed in the following, where some of the worst negatives adjuncts face can be turned into positives to carve out a meaningful career as contingent faculty members.

Online, Asynchronous Teaching

Knowing that the cost alone of driving to multiple schools to teach wasn't sustainable on an adjunct's salary, I quickly found that asynchronous, online teaching allowed me far more flexibility to make my own schedule while managing other responsibilities. The growth of the for-profit sector has opened up plenty of such jobs (Proper 97-98), often with wages that outstrip those at more traditional colleges if one takes into account how much more frequently classes tend to run.

I have taught as many as 13 classes at a time to make ends meet, with children, older parents, and a myriad of other time pressures to balance simultaneously. Were it not for the flexibility of online, asynchronous teaching, there is simply no way adjuncting would be financially sustainable if I had to be in specific places at specific times.

Pre-packaged Courses

This is perhaps one of the dirtier phrases in academia right now, as it takes academic freedom away from instructors in lieu of a common curriculum into which faculty members can be easily placed. The general impetus to that strategy, as one dean put it, is to make programs "lean and very responsive" (Roscorla), yet the little financial data there is throws into question whether this adjunct-heavy model is either lean or responsive (Ginsberg 125–160; Hearn and Burns 351–353).

If universities are convinced that wasting the subject matter expertise of adjuncts through this type of course design is the way to go (Kezar and DePaola 37), this opens an opportunity for adjuncts to focus on building rapport with students to best achieve course outcomes. When I am expected to teach a course that is ready to go as soon as I'm hired, I immediately focus on making the course my own in discussion, feedback, and announcements. This not only helps me focus my prep work, but it also addresses what students demand most from online faculty, a clear sense of presence (Nye 120). In an age in which one student review can close the door to future employment, focusing on students helps me justify to employers my continued adjunct employment and has proven time and again to be a great way for me to show through positive student reviews in my application materials that I can make an employer's course designs work for students.

Another factor that makes pre-packaged classes look that much more attractive, aside from the constant fear of having a course you put a lot of work into designing canceled, is the idea that a class you design actually does you more harm than good. One university where I taught informed us that our classes, once designed, were its property and thus anyone could teach them (which later, in fact, happened to me).

At another school, when my class was shifted to a tenured faculty member— because full-timers couldn't fill up their own courses— I was told by this faculty member that she wouldn't be "teaching the course with the materials [I] had already loaded" and that her choice was "apart from whatever position the college is currently taking." Whether it's worth investing time and effort into designing a course that you might not end up teaching is worth considering.

Distance from a Department's Epicenter

"The full-timers are meeting this Friday" to discuss the new syllabus plan for the course I was scheduled to teach, I was told by a department chair while writing this very article. "I'd prefer to get their feedback" before putting the new course design into place, the chair said. This type of conversation, where the input of part-timers is flippantly ignored, is one that adjuncts know well. Adjuncts not only can be structurally separated from their full-time counterparts but also can be separated physically by placing their offices away from the department's hub, and their place within a department's structure no doubt relates to the struggles of the adjunct to make ends meet (Finley; Prosper 106–107; Schlaerth 5).

According to a recent study, over half of faculty surveyed (full- and part-time) report issues with burnout and cite decisions by their administrations as a key point of stress; not coincidently, about the same amount report that more supportive decisions by higher-ups would reduce their current stress levels ("Faculty Wellness"), levels that have doubled since 2019 "Fidelity Investments").

At the almost dozen schools where I have taught, department drama has never been in short supply. Taking sides, especially against a department chair, rarely bodes well for contingent faculty. So, not only can distance make the heart grow fonder, it also can allow for space from departmental squabbling, making it far easier to avoid taking sides that could affect one's future employment—and it helps reduce stress as well.

Finding Power in the Process

Finding ways around the realities of the profession to live sustainably are not just about adjuncts and their happiness, stability, and so forth. There is a huge trickle-down effect across academia. As one professor lamented, university administrators often forget the reality that to achieve student success, you need the faculty and staff to be in a good place, too (Lashuel). The recognition that adjuncts' well-being is damaged because of their unequal treatment is certainly nothing new. About two-thirds of college senates lack any means for adjunct participation, and about half report no meaningful power for adjuncts in faculty governance, even indirectly. Coupled with the loss of control over syllabi, adjuncts are swiftly losing power in this new world order of higher education, and as well-meaning as full-time faculty members may be, adjuncts understand their situation in a way others do not, so lacking representation in university governance does matter (Finkelstein et al. 460, 485; Finley; Schlaerth 11). Yet, since adjuncts teach a majority of classes, they retain a huge, latent power over how colleges operate.

So, what can adjuncts do to improve the situation? Individually, options are limited, but here I think it essential that adjuncts remember that there is power in numbers and that they have a huge advantage there. Adjunct strikes or walkouts are one way to get attention, as they can grind a campus to a halt. Especially as teaching in higher education is increasingly viewed as a service profession, more and more unions have been willing to support adjuncts and their rights. Such backing from otherwise strange bedfellows such as the United Auto Workers and others provide adjuncts a key platform to present their concerns (Schlaerth 7–8).

There were 42 faculty strikes between 2012 and 2018, and adjuncts and full-time faculty participated in almost all of them (Duncan 504; Flaherty, "New Data on Faculty Strikes"). However, in the case of Wright State University, ads for "long term" adjuncts were put out in an attempt to break the strike there (Pettit), showing how easily adjuncts can be cast as enemies of the full-time faculty. On the other hand, there have been some recent successes using this collective approach that give credence to it as a tool to spark change. For example, faculty protests in New Jersey recently produced a $230 per-credit-hour bump in adjunct pay (Carrera).

Strikes may seem a bit extreme, but after years of inaction and indifference from administrators, it often takes something extraordinary to start to effect change. However, the contingent faculty simply being recognized as a bargaining unit within their colleges has shown positive results. At both Elon University and Ithaca College, recent decisions by arbiters have affirmed that adjuncts are in fact employees under the National Labor Relations Act and thus have a right to organize (Salvatore et al.). This development is important for adjuncts, as collective bargaining is critical in giving them power to do more than just take-it-or-leave-it with respect to contracts (Duncan 576–84).

Representation, of course, is about more than just portraying adjuncts as some amorphous blob of faculty that share the same characteristics. Race, class, and other individualized elements do much to frame the adjunct experience (Flaherty, "Barely Getting By"; Hesli and Lee). With non-tenure-track jobs on the upswing, these positions have become the dominant means to usher in more traditionally under-represented groups into teaching at the college level, particularly at two-year colleges (Flaherty, "More Faculty Diversity"; McNaughtan et al. 22).

While the growth of adjunct faculty positions may not mean more power over administrative decision-making, this situation opens up a huge door for adjunct faculty members to educate students about the academic hiring system and the world they are playing a part in supporting. This is a good reminder of the power we adjuncts have to fuel generational change about issues far broader than education.

Reflection

"Adjuncts allow departments to provide the course offerings so our students can graduate on time," notes Kevin Guskiewicz, former interim chancellor at the University of North Carolina, "while allowing our tenure-track faculty to balance teaching, scholarship and service" (Douglas-Gabriel). This says it all—adjuncts exist so full-timers can research, write, and mentor and so students can move through college swiftly to make room for new students and new enrollment dollars. The scholarship and service of an adjunct is not valued. The lack of respect (financially or otherwise) we are accorded in practice in higher education shows that we are viewed by those in charge of the system as the necessary evil.

Since I began full-time adjuncting in 2009, I have taught for almost a dozen schools. I left the first after I found out it recruited students from homeless shelters. Yet even at that institution, adjuncts were given more of a voice and recognition than at other, more "reputable" colleges where I have worked. As adjuncts, we walk a fine line between making money, maintaining our personal ethics, supporting students, and ensuring our individual happiness. There is no hard-and-fast primer to determine the right balance, as these are intensely individual choices we all must make when navigating the adjunct world. Don't ignore these decisions, and do not be surprised that the more you adjunct, the more lines become blurred.

Being an adjunct means you'll see academia in a way you probably didn't before, and it will change you and what you want out of your academic career. Embrace that, and don't feel shackled by past decisions or current departments. Keep your CV current and never feel you aren't being transparent with your current employers by looking to see what's out there. There is little to lose in seeing if the grass is, in fact, greener elsewhere, especially when a department will drop you at a moment's notice, as you have no contract it needs to worry about violating.

As Christopher Newfield argues, the "Great Mistake" that academia made was to forget that higher education is a public good and to instead come to value profit over the social impact of the college experience for all involved (492). For now, though, while I expect the profit motive is here to stay, we must remember adjuncts are producers, not just consumers, in the higher education system. We do have power within it to carve out a niche that allows us to pursue an academic career within the sphere of adjuncting. Whether the benefits of working within the system are worth the pressures is entirely an individual choice, but if adjuncts leverage their individual choices and collective wills, there is still ample hope the profession's drawbacks can lessen and its benefits rise, not just for those who teach, but for everyone in higher education in the future.

Works Cited

"2021 Poverty Guidelines." *ASPE: Office of the Assistant Secretary for Planning and Evaluation*, https://aspe.hhs.gov/topics/poverty-economic-mobility/poverty-guidelines/prior-hhs-poverty-guidelines-federal-register-references/2021-poverty-guidelines.

"Background Facts on Contingent Faculty Positions." *AAUP: American Association of University Professors*, https://www.aaup.org/issues/contingency/background-facts.

Carrera, Catherine. "NJ Adjuncts Get 'Biggest Increase' Ever in Pay, While Full-Time Professors Vote to Strike." *NorthJersey.com*, 26 Nov. 2019, https://www.northjersey.com/story/news/2019/11/26/nj-colleges-adjuncts-get-big-raise-full-time-professors-strike/4300990002/.

Douglas-Gabriel, Danielle. "'It Keeps You Nice and Disposable': The Plight of Adjunct Professors." *The Washington Post*, 15 Feb. 2019, https://www.washingtonpost.com/local/education/it-keeps-you-nice-and-disposable-the-plight-of-adjunct-professors/2019/02/14/6cd5cbe4-024d-11e9-b5df-5d3874f1ac36_story.html.

Duncan, John C., Jr. "The Indentured Servants of Academia: The Adjunct Faculty Dilemma and Their Limited Legal Remedies." *Indiana Law Journal*, vol. 74, no. 2, 1999, pp. 513–86. *Indiana University Bloomington Maurer School of Law Digital Repository*, https://www.repository.law.indiana.edu/ilj/vol74/iss2/3/.

"Faculty Wellness and Careers." *Blog—Announcements*, Course Hero, 18 Nov. 2020, https://www.coursehero.com/blog/faculty-wellness-research/.

"Fidelity Investments and The Chronicle of Higher Education Study: More Than Half of College and University Faculty Considering Leaving Teaching, Citing Burnout Caused by Pandemic." *Fidelity Investments*, 25 Feb. 2021. https://newsroom.fidelity.com/press-releases/news-details/2021/Fidelity-Investments-The-Chronicle-of-Higher-Education-Study-More-Than-Half-of-College-and-University-Faculty-Considering-Leaving-Teaching-Citing-Burnout-Caused-by-Pandemic/default.aspx. Press release.

Finkelstein, Martin J., et al. *The Faculty Factor: Reassessing the American Academy in a Turbulent Era*. Johns Hopkins UP, 2016.

Finley, Laura. "Adjunct Professors and Workers' Rights." *Counterpunch*, 27 July 2015, https://www.counterpunch.org/2015/07/27/adjunct-professors-and-workers-rights/.

Flaherty, Colleen. "Barely Getting By." *Inside Higher Ed*, 20 Apr. 2020, https://www.insidehighered.com/news/2020/04/20/new-report-says-many-adjuncts-make-less-3500-course-and-25000-year.

———. "Congress Takes Note." *Inside Higher Ed*, 24 Jan. 2014. https://www.insidehighered.com/news/2014/01/24/house-committee-report-highlights-plight-adjunct-professors.

———. "More Faculty Diversity, Not on Tenure Track." *Inside Higher Ed*, 22 Aug. 2016, https://www.insidehighered.com/news/2016/08/22/study-finds-gains-faculty-diversity-not-tenure-track.

———. "New Data on Faculty Strikes." *Inside Higher Ed*, 28 Aug. 2019, https://www.insidehighered.com/quicktakes/2019/08/28/new-data-faculty-strikes.

Ginsberg, Benjamin. *The Fall of the Faculty: The Rise of the All-Administrative University and Why It Matters*. Oxford UP, 2011. *Oxford Scholarship Online*, https://doi.org/10.1093/oso/9780199782444.001.0001.

Hearn, James C., and Rachel Burns. "Contingent Faculty Employment and Financial Stress in Public Universities." *The Journal of Higher Education*, vol. 92, no. 3, 2021, pp. 331–62. *Taylor and Francis Online*, https://doi.org/10.1080/00221546.2020.1851570.

Hesli, Vicki L., and Jae Mook Lee. "Job Satisfaction in Academia: Why Are Some Faculty Members Happier than Others?" *PS: Political Science and Politics*, vol. 46, no. 2, 2013, pp. 339–54. *Cambridge Core*, https://doi.org/10.1017/S1049096513000048.

Kezar, Adrianna, and Tom DePaola. "Understanding the Need For Unions: Contingent Faculty Working Conditions and the Relationship to Student Learning." *Professors in the Gig Economy: Unionizing Adjunct Faculty in America*, edited by Kim Tolley, John Hopkins UP, 2018, pp. 27–45.

Lashuel, Hilal A. "The Busy Lives of Academics Have Hidden Costs—and Universities Must Take Better Care of Their Faculty Members." *Nature Careers Community*, 5 Mar. 2020, https://doi.org/10.1038/d41586-020-00661-w.

McNaughtan, Jon, et al. "Understanding the Growth of Contingent Faculty." *New Directions for Institutional Research*, vol. 2017, no. 176, 2017, pp. 9–26. *Wiley Online Library*, https://doi.org/10.1002/ir.20241.

Newfield, Christopher. "Have We Wrecked Public Universities? The Case of the American Decline Cycle." *The British Journal of Sociology*, vol. 69, no. 2, 2018, pp. 484–93. *Wiley Online Library*, https://doi.org/10.1111/1468-4446.12339_1.

Nye, Adele. "Building an Online Academic Learning Community among Undergraduate Students." *Distance Education*, vol. 36, no. 1, 2015, pp. 115–28. *Taylor and Francis Online*, https://doi.org/10.1080/01587919.2015.1019969.

Pettit, Emma. "'Now Comes the Hard Part': 20-Day Strike at Wright State Has Ended." *The Chronicle of Higher Education*, 11 Feb. 2019, https://www.chronicle.com/article/now-comes-the-hard-part-20-day-strike-at-wright-state-has-ended/.

Proper, Eve. "Contingent Faculty at For-Profit Institutions." *New Directions for Institutional Research*, vol. 2017, no. 176, 2017, pp. 97–110. *Wiley Online Library*, https://doi.org/10.1002/ir.20247.

Roscorla, Tanya. "Collaborative Course Design Helps Colleges Scale Online Learning." *Government Technology*, 11 Jan. 2016, https://www.govtech.com/education/higher-ed/collaborative-course-design-helps-colleges-scale-online-learning.html.

Salvatore, P., et al. "Recent Labor Victories for Adjunct Professors Signal Likely Uptick in Contingent Faculty Organizing." *Proskauer Labor Relations Update*, 16 Feb. 2021, https://www.laborrelationsupdate.com/nlra/recent-labor-victories-for-adjunct-professors-signal-likely-uptick-in-contingent-faculty-organizing/.

Schlaerth, Christian A. I. "Adjuncts Unite! The Struggle to Unionize, Administrative Response, and Building a Bigger Movement." *Labor Studies Journal*, vol. 47, no. 1, 2021, pp. 5–27. *SAGE Journals*, https://doi.org/10.1177/0160449X211028660.

Yang, Junfeng, et al. "Strategies for Smooth and Effective Cross-Cultural Online Collaborative Learning." *Educational Technology and Society*, vol. 17, no. 3, 2014, pp. 208–21, https://drive.google.com/open?id=1JMT6dVTuRoEJsAxdGIILIDBPw6uMKSam.

Part IV. Bye, Felicia

The closing section of this collection is a collection of pieces for readers who are considering leaving academia, partially or fully, for greener pastures. At one time, this was thought of as a failure. Some may still feel that way, which is highly regrettable. What individuals going into academic careers must realize is that it's not you that makes this work challenging—it's the scheme. The system is broken and prides itself on disposable, cheap labor. Therefore, if anyone can better themselves, or must better their circumstances, in terms of obtaining healthcare coverage, raising a family, buying a home, and so on, more power to them. It's not shameful. It's simply looking out for the greater good.

- In "Breaking Up with Higher Ed," Lee Kottner chronicles how she gave up on the freeway flyer lifestyle due to sheer exhaustion and poverty-like wages. She states, "I now work for a great non-profit, with fantastic colleagues, a better salary than I've ever made in my life, excellent health benefits, and a growing retirement fund. We just formed a union, too, for which I'm a shop steward."
- Andrea Verschaeve and Jason Porath were both ABDs in their doctoral studies when they realized an academic career wasn't the path they wanted to choose. They now both teach and work within the North Carolina state prison system, where they are happier, hold a great deal of professional freedom, and are compensated fairly.
- In "Contracting and Consulting: Crafting a Career," Ian S. Ray and Brandi Wren use their combined 25 years of experience as adjuncts and independent contractors to explore three areas in which adjuncts may find non-teaching, contract-based work: research support, educational support, and administrative support.
- Steven Yates explores in his chapter the history of anti-intellectualism and neoliberalism in the US and how those two forces have combined to create the academic precariat of today. He uses his personal story to show the similarities between working on the non-academic gig economy and working as an adjunct, and he advocates for creating a new network of thinkers willing to live and work outside of current exploitative systems.
- In "We Are the University," Debra Leigh Scott discusses her academic journey, where she found herself "teaching year after year on one-semester, low-wage, single-course contracts." She says, "Although my teaching wages were desperately low, I was able to cobble together an income by teaching at multiple universities." She advocates for contingent faculty leaving colleges and universities in a mass exodus, which would bring all higher education campuses to their knees overnight.

- BC Dickenson tells of adjuncting for many years with a side job of mowing lawns just to keep afloat. Then, at the age of 50, he accepted a tenure-track position to work with a group of kindred-spirit comrades at a small, unionized community college. Now, he issues a common-sense warning to those who are trying to "make it" in academia about making sure you love your work.

At this time in 2022, academia seems to be at a crossroads. The United States and other countries in the world are in the midst of what's being called the Great Resignation, caused by working conditions during the COVID-19 pandemic. Contingent faculty, no doubt, have felt this pinch more than anyone else in the academic ranks. Along with concerns about how well their health is being protected at work during the pandemic comes the constant pull between the heart (love of teaching) vs. head (can I support myself doing this?). I would not tell individuals what to do with their careers, but the current setup is that of an unethical and unkind business model. It is my hope this collection helps people, whether that's by inspiring them to carry on, strike, or find alternative work elsewhere. In the end, educators should know their worth, and they are deserving of all the support in the world.

Chapter 18. Breaking Up with Higher Ed

Lee Kottner
FORMERLY NEW JERSEY CITY UNIVERSITY
AND CITY UNIVERSITY OF NEW YORK

It's mid-January. I'm waiting for spring semester to start so I'll have a paycheck again. I am reading submissions for *Teaching Poor*[1] and just . . . weeping, for my colleagues and my students, for all of us. Right here in the coffee shop, surrounded by tenth grade teachers half my age, who make at least twice what I do. Not that I resent what they make; they deserve it and more. I resent the money-grubbers and corporate pirates who devalue the people like me who trained these teachers. It's the unions that ensure these young teachers are able to make a living, the unions that are starting to fight back against the high-stakes testing mentality that is robbing students of precious class time, and the unions that take a stand against the poverty that pushes so many of us out of a profession we love deeply.

More and more of my higher education colleagues are unionizing, too, but not with the traditional teachers' unions, AFT or NEA, because K-12 has its own struggles right now and its unions can't afford to divide their focus to fight for higher education at the same time. So, many of us have turned to the auto and steel and service workers' unions to fight for us. The reality is that unions are pretty toothless at this point in America's history and whatever concessions we win from what the adjunct/contingent/precariat movement calls badmin—a certain breed of overpaid, non-teaching, business-oriented administrator—will be won with as much blood, sweat, and tears as the Bread and Roses labor movement, fueled by the rank and file in the classrooms. We want to join unions that have experience with those kinds of fights because we know it's going to be dirty and ugly clawing our way back into the middle class. And we're not even talking about tenure here.

Tenure—what one contingent colleague calls the reward for surviving the feudalism of earning a Ph.D.—used to be the proverbial brass ring for post-secondary academics. It's not the sinecure that the public thinks it is, but it at least used to carry with it the promise of protected academic speech in return for the duties of teaching, research, and academic and public service. Physicist Peter Higgs, who proposed the existence of that elementary particle bearing his name, has rather shockingly stated that he probably would not get tenure now because the requirements have increased so much (Aitkenhead). It's becoming increasingly common for administrators, despite what colleagues might say about awarding tenure to scholars who've spent five or six years working in good faith toward that goal, to

---

1. *Teaching Poor* was the working title of the project I handed off to editor Dr. Natalie Dorfeld, who brought it to the finish line as the book you're reading now.

deny tenure for faculty members, making them start all over somewhere else, if they can even get another job offer after having been denied tenure once already. New blood is cheaper.

It's even easier to "fire" contingent instructors: just tell us there are no classes available next semester and hire someone far more pliable and submissive, some eager new graduate or an ABD (all but dissertation) who isn't fed up and desperate enough to cause trouble. Our contingent positions make us wary of trying new pedagogical techniques, make us afraid to push our students too hard or grade too stringently, make us less effective and rigorous than we want to be or should be, rob us of the time to prepare well or grade thoroughly. Learning is hard, frustrating, contentious, combative. Students often don't see why we ask them to do the things we do—to read this book, do this project, write this paper, look up that reference, give that presentation, come prepared to class, make sure those citations are correct—until years later.

We are too hard, assign too much work, expect too much, except when we're not and we don't for fear student "customer" complaints will cost us our job. The truth is, teaching is not about simply drilling facts into our students' heads; it's showing them what they can do with facts and information and how to find them. Little wonder our students are deemed not ready for the business world when we are constrained from challenging them to grow and think for themselves. And yet, ironically, it's the customer service model of education that is producing this result: student as customer, professor as salesclerk, diplomas and degrees as retail goods—all supported by cheap labor while admin is busy protecting the brand from anything seen as controversy, whether that's considering the situation of Palestine or acknowledging forms of discrimination on campus. It's hard to learn how to be a problem solver when people keep giving you the answers for the test to make their own performance data look better.

Little wonder I am weeping in the coffee shop.

By now, members of the public are starting to realize that our higher education system no longer conforms to either their cherished memories or their hopeful ideals. The cost of tuition has, according to one popular measure, risen 1,120 percent since 1978 (Shafrir), the year I graduated from high school and made my way, as the first in my dad's family to do so, to Chatham College, a small private women's college in Pittsburgh, now a university that has quadrupled in enrollment and cost. My years as a student are a stark contrast to what I endured as an adjunct professor. My tuition was equivalent to buying a new car each year, something my family could never afford, but I was given federal grants and loans as well as school grants and graduated with a mere $4,000 of debt.

But more importantly, that tiny liberal arts college of 600 students was an oasis of learning and community. I felt like a glutton at a banquet each time I registered for classes. My professors were accessible to the point of chumminess; in the English department, it wasn't unheard of to have Friday sherry with our profs or to sit in their offices for hours talking about books and the world. Some of my most formative learning experiences occurred in those out-of-class encounters with my professors, almost all of whom were tenured or working toward it. I had not even heard the word "adjunct" in connection with professors then.

In graduate school, I became one. Not only did I have a teaching fellowship at Michigan State University, but I was hired along with two of my fellow first-year colleagues to teach introductory composition at a nearby community college. I was just feeling my way into teaching, and I panicked, believing I was totally inadequate to the job. That I didn't turn out to be completely inept and that I learned over four years to be pretty darn good in the classroom was thanks to some expert tutoring and supervision by my full-time, tenured professors, who had time and means to be great mentors and who were even chummier than my undergrad professors.

We went to the same conferences, hung out in each others' offices, drank in the same bars, attended the same parties, and met up when travelling abroad over the summer. Class continued over beer and peanuts or wine and cheese. Life-long colleagues were cultivated over coffee. I was in heaven. I was being paid to teach, to learn, to think. The pay wasn't much, but there was the promise of more, of a steady career in which I could mentor my own students and nurture more intellectual relationships and personal friendships and learn more stuff.

And then there wasn't.

In the mid to late 1980s, full-time academic jobs dried up. I saw the writing on the wall and escaped without massive student debt by not finishing my Ph.D., which by then would have been in medieval history, a now-hopeless field for full-time employment. I bailed out of New York University, where I'd gone after switching fields, and took up the peripatetic life of a freelance, part-time editor, which, until the 2008 recession hit and work dried up in that field, too, had been paying fairly well. I went back to adjunct teaching because those jobs were still abundant. But the pay had barely changed since I'd last done the work 20 years before as a supplement to freelancing. I watched my savings dwindle, my retirement fund sputter and stall and nosedive, my bills pile up. Twenty-five years later, I was back in the same position I was in right after moving to New York City as a 26-year-old grad student: broke, with no prospects, and up to my eyeballs in credit card debt and back taxes I couldn't pay.

Like my cousins who worked on the factory line in Pontiac, Michigan, building cars, I found my career outsourced to cheaper workers, in this case, my own colleagues, both younger and older. Tenure lines, which once accounted for the majority of academic faculty positions, have been disappearing at an alarming rate over the last 30 years, until the ratio of tenured to contingent instructors (which includes full-time, untenured lecturers on one- to five-year contracts, graduate assistants, and adjuncts hired on a semester-to-semester basis full or part time) has completely reversed itself (Griffey). Now, approximately 75 percent of faculty everywhere in the country are contingent, and non-tenure track instructors are paid a fraction of what our tenured colleagues earn (*Data Snapshot*). We work without healthcare benefits, without retirement plans, without job security, all of which affect our ability to teach well.[2]

Students are paying ever-increasing tuition for instruction far inferior to what I received as an undergraduate and graduate student, not because the instructors are somehow worse or less intelligent, but because of time constraints imposed upon us by the scramble to make a living. Let me repeat: it's not that we're unqualified or inferior, it's that we're prevented from doing our best work by the lack of institutional support; faculty working conditions are student learning conditions. Contingent faculty members teach the vast majority of the so-called general education or foundational/introductory courses in most disciplines, the ones crucial to making further semesters successful. Yet we have no or little time to mentor or tutor the students who need it most. Too many of us teach as many as seven to nine classes a semester, online and in person, to make ends meet.

During the fall semester of 2014, I taught four different classes at three universities in two states, traveling an average of six hours a day just to get from one to the other. And I had it comparatively easy. Many of my colleagues drive hundreds of miles a week in their commutes, as so-called "freeway flyers" or "road scholars" (ha ha). My gross adjusted income? About $28,000, in New York City. Imagine trying to raise a child on that, let alone a special needs child as Brianne Bolin has done in Chicago (Quart).

I was never going to get tenure with just a master's degree (though that was once possible at a community college), and I was fine with that. It's one of the conditions that left me free to speak out about the ruination of higher education without fear. I had no career path to jeopardize. But that's one of the factors that keeps so many of us silent. Every now and then, one of us lands a tenure-track job, and it encourages the other doctors and all-but-doctors to engage in the kind of magical thinking that they, too, might get one, if only they don't jeopardize their chances, if only they freely share their painstakingly developed new class with a tenured colleague, if only they take this unpaid professional development course, if only they grovel prettily enough to the head of the department or the dean.

I, too, was fearful and silent for a long time, until I read Caprice Lawless' blog entry, "Teaching Poverty at the Community College." It wasn't a punch in the gut; it was a kick in the pants, a wake-up call like a three-alarm fire. *I am lying to my students. I'm lying about the efficacy of the education they're overpaying for. I am lying about my social class. I am lying about the American Dream. And I am perpetuating my own exploitation for the benefit of people who think my skills and experience are only worth $15 an hour.*

Not long after, I quit teaching at the College of New Rochelle, which was paying me less than $250 per credit for a six-credit class while charging $375 per

---

2. See also *The Chronicle of Higher Education Almanac, 2020–2021*, in which it is reported that tenured faculty members across all institutions are down to 23.3 percent of the total number of full-time faculty ("Tenure Status").

credit to each of the 28–32 students I taught. I took jobs at New Jersey City University (NJCU) and various colleges of the City University of New York and with the State University of New York system, which all had unions that paid three to four times as much but still left me without benefits or job security, even after I joined those unions. I started to tell my students that I was an adjunct and what that meant to them: that I wasn't available for office hours, that I didn't have as much time to grade their papers as thoughtfully as I should or give them as much feedback as I wanted to and as they deserved because I was teaching at two other schools, that sometimes my preparation wasn't as good as I liked for the same reason. And I broke a big taboo. I told them how much money I made for the class they were taking from me.

"You mean, like, a month, right?" one shocked student responded.

If only.

They couldn't fathom how my salary for teaching them was less than one percent of that class's tuition. Frankly, I still can't either.

From then on, I told every student in my classes exactly how much I made for teaching them. They were shocked, and increasingly, they were angry, too. They wanted to know where their tuition was going. There's still a great unawareness among college students of the consequences of being taught by professors who not only can't give their best but who also can't go to bat for students because they may lose their own jobs. This is their "New Normal," and as Bruce Cockburn sang, "The trouble with normal is it always gets worse." It's just hard to see how much worse it's gotten without the institutional history tenured faculty provide.

But because of many of my fearless colleagues like Lawless and Bolin, students and the public have at least become increasingly aware of the financial shenanigans going on in higher education: grossly overpaid presidents and provosts (Piper and O'Leary); administrative bloat so out of control that administrators now outnumber faculty two-to-one on some college campuses (New England Center); architectural empire-building that nearly bankrupts even wealthy private colleges like New York City's New School (Bellafante) and Cooper Union (Salmon); mismanagement of funds leading to the outright closure of small liberal arts schools like Lebanon College in New Hampshire (Kich); and worst, the deliberate impoverishment of America's intellectuals and educators in the name of so-called trustees' almighty bottom line.

Contingent faculty have told our stories in interviews (Quart; *Why Adjunct Professors*; *College Professors*), documentaries (*'Junct*), and comics (Whitney)[3]; created endless numbers of blogs; publicly petitioned the Departments of Labor and Education, the Pope, and the President; taken to Twitter to shame badmin's bad practices (see the many posts with the hashtag #NotYourAdjunctSidekick

---

3. Even Garry Trudeau has contributed to the adjunct comics collection. One example is his September 06, 2015, comic, which provides a satirical take on the semester job scramble.

and the account @ass_deans); and set up alternative schools of our own.[4] The comparisons between higher education and WalMart or McDonald's have been made crystal clear.

Many outspoken contingent faculty colleagues have been threatened with firing (Marvit), lost jobs in retaliation for organizing, or been forced out of their profession by poverty (a situation aptly described by Karen Kelsky in Quart). Not a few of them have gone into union organizing themselves (for example, the authors Balay, Bowman, Emmert, Gilmore, and Kovanen in this collection). Bringing their stories to light shows how a particular subset of people is destroying the promises of higher education and the lives of some of our country's best and brightest. Some days, after hearing yet another story, I feel a little like Allen Ginsberg in his opening lines of "Howl": "I saw the best minds of my generation destroyed by madness, starving hysterical naked . . . "

Our STEM and social science colleagues remind us that the plural of anecdote is not data, and that's true, but it's difficult to dismiss the repetition of the same facts and experiences over and over again as merely anecdotal. They are part of an under-researched, little-documented national phenomenon affecting every college and university in the country, as well as in Canada, the UK, France, Spain, and Australia, at the very least. That experience includes lack of respect, job precarity, grinding poverty, and the loss of a generation of scholarly research and thought, as well as the accompanying dilution of the quality of education.

If the stories begin to sound the same, it's because they are, whether we teach at community colleges, public or private four-year colleges, art colleges, technical colleges, non-profits or for-profits, or public or private research universities. The one sure commonality every edifice of higher learning in this country (and many abroad) shares is the presence of too many contingents on its faculty and their poor treatment. The differences are merely in degrees of awfulness and abuse.

Our stories reflect how long we've been adjuncting (long enough collectively for the condition to become a verb, anyway), and where we are in abandoning the magical thinking process that keeps us silent. These stories, however they are expressed, of what contingents go through as their temporary contracts stretch into infinity mirror the stages of grief: confidence, hope, disbelief, disillusionment, outrage, rebellion. Sometimes those stories end in death, as in the cases of Thea Hunter and Margaret Mary Vojtko (Harris; Kovalik).[5]

Many of the stories I know best are from my fellow English professors, simply because we are natural storytellers and writing is both a tool and a weapon

---

4. For example, the Brooklyn Institute for Social Research, a 501(c)3 non-profit that is "actively pioneering a new model for scholarship in the twenty-first century that integrates a commitment to pedagogy, research, and public programming" ("About").

5. Hunter and Vojtko represent the tip of the iceberg, and the COVID-19 pandemic has made and will continue to make it worse. There are many contingents I know who are still teaching and expect to die with their boots on. I certainly did.

for us. My sociology colleagues contribute especially biting analyses of the class war and hypocrisy embedded in the precariat struggle. I'm aware of many more stories of white, straight contingent faculty than of stories from people of color or LGBTQIA+ contingent educators. I wish this were not so because these stories likely carry an extra layer of precarity that needs to be emphasized. Without tenure protection, plain old bigotry has a much freer rein in academe.

The most silent professional population is that of contingent faculty members in the STEM fields, who suffer many of the same working conditions as those working in the humanities but framed in a slightly different way. Instead of perpetual semester-to-semester or one- to three-year contracts, contingent faculty members working in STEM fields often endure the endlessly repeated three- to five-five year postdoc contract originally meant to add a few years of experience to the CV and now used like the temp pool for laboratory workers (Powell). Postdocs, like contingent faculty members, often feel isolated from the university community and excluded from the decisions that affect their livelihoods (*Gender Equity Conversations* 10), but they often make more money than all but full-time contingents—but not much (Collins and Perez).

One reason for the silence of postdocs in STEM fields may be that they have more obvious options than contingent faculty members in the humanities and can more easily move into post- and alternative-academic positions in corporate research. But rest assured that contingent faculty members working in STEM fields do exist, teaching those introductory math, biology, chemistry, and physics courses or laboring away in tenured professors' laboratories.

The purpose of projects like *Teaching Poor* and the book you're holding now is to make the public—parents, students, and government policy makers especially—aware of the working conditions of the majority of the professors teaching in our centers of higher education and how the difficulties they endure affect the quality of our now very expensive education. Not on an abstract level, but on a personal, day to day level of existence.

Others have written well and eloquently—most notably in my opinion, Henry A. Giroux—about the consequences of market capitalism and neoliberalism in education and education policies. But there have been few stories about what contingent faculty member and author Alex Kudera calls "the long day" that every precarious instructor experiences: the jobs at multiple schools; the lost time on the road; the unpaid hours grading papers and preparing for class; the lack of professional courtesy or access to equipment; the student conferences in cars, cafés, and hallways; the necessity of applying for a new job every four months; the lack of paychecks or unemployment over the summer and the pittance we make during the year; standing in line at the social services office with your poorest students or serving them and their families fast food; lack of time to do your own research; staggering student debt too many contingents still carry; stagnation in your own career.

The heat death of higher education.

This story is about Pennsylvania's state negotiators calling contingent faculty members "teaching machines" and suggesting that our pay, such as it is, be reduced and our amount of work raised ("We"). It's about realizing that the unionized groundskeepers at our colleges make more money, get better benefits, and work fewer hours than contingents do. It's about a dean at NJCU saying "adjuncts are so desperate that they'll work for anything" while cutting our pay for professional tutoring from $27 per hour to $15 per hour.[6]

That last bit was part of the final straw for me. Not that I had much of a choice. My final summer of teaching, I worked in the writing center at NJCU, which was staffed by well-trained peer tutors and a few contingent professors like me. We weren't far into the summer semester when the dean summarily announced the college was closing the center—next week. Writing tutoring would be moved to a new centralized tutoring hub in the library, staffed by untrained undergrads. I won't detail the abbreviated, fierce but unsuccessful battle we waged. What matters is that suddenly I had no way to support myself over the summer and no chance of collecting unemployment thanks to the rules that exempt teachers from qualifying for it, even though few contingent faculty members have an assurance of re-employment between semesters. For the first time in my life, I was looking at bankruptcy and the welfare line.

Fortunately, for the previous five years, I'd been applying for jobs outside academe, and finally, one of them came through. That eleventh hour rescue was a job in graphic design and document production, skills I cultivated during my 20 years of freelancing. I now work for a great non-profit, with fantastic colleagues, a better salary than I've ever made in my life, excellent health benefits, and a growing retirement fund. We just formed a union, too, for which I'm a shop steward.

Two years into this job, I got out of the awful roommate situation my poverty had forced me into, moved to a great apartment, and started to breathe again. I'm finally clawing my way back into financial security, despite the pandemic. But I've watched my former colleagues suffer through that pandemic in a weekly Zoom meeting I set up for all of us. Some of them have lost jobs and all have had unreasonable expectations dumped on them in the haste to switch to remote teaching. The amount of stress they have been through is unbelievable, the compensation just as bad as it's ever been, the precarity even worse (Valbrun). And it makes me weep all over again, no matter how lucky I was.

The moral of this story? Let go of your magical thinking, colleagues. In all actuality, you have two realistic choices: get out as soon as you can, or stay and organize with a vengeance. Use the power of your numbers to grind the badmin juggernaut to a halt until you get what highly educated professionals deserve. It's already being done elsewhere. That would strike a blow for your students, for education, for all of us who love teaching and the academic life. But whatever you decide to do, save yourself.

---

6. Personal communication.

Works Cited

"About." *Brooklyn Institute for Social Research*, 2022, https://thebrooklyninstitute.com/about/.

Aitkenhead, Decca. "Peter Higgs: I Wouldn't Be Productive Enough for Today's Academic System." *The Guardian*, 6 Dec. 2013, https://www.theguardian.com/science/2013/dec/06/peter-higgs-boson-academic-system.

Bellafante, Ginia. "This School Was Built for Idealists. It Could Use Some Rich Alumni." *The New York Times*, 16 Oct. 2020, https://www.nytimes.com/2020/10/16/nyregion/new-school-nyc-endowment-layoffs.html.

Cockburn, Bruce. "The Trouble with Normal." *The Trouble with Normal*, Golden Mountain Music/Rounder Records, 1983/2002. Vinyl/CD.

College Professors in Poverty. *YouTube*, uploaded by Brave New Films, 26 Oct. 2015, https://www.youtube.com/watch?v=kbWFcqbefMs.

Collins, Francis S., and Thomas E. Perez. "Fair Pay for Postdocs: Why We Support New Federal Overtime Rules." *The Blog*, HuffPost, 18 May 2017, https://www.huffpost.com/entry/fair-pay-for-postdocs-why_b_10011066.

Data Snapshot: Contingent Faculty in US Higher Ed. American Association of University Professors, 2018. *AAUP: American Association of University Professors*, 2018, https://www.aaup.org/sites/default/files/10112018%20Data%20Snapshot%20Tenure.pdf.

Gender Equity Conversations: Strengthening the Physics Enterprise in Universities and National Laboratories, American Physical Society. *APS Physics*, 2022, https://aps.org/programs/women/workshops/gender-equity/sitevisits/upload/GE_CONVERSATIONS_Final.pdf.

Ginsberg, Allen. "Howl." *Howl and Other Poems*. City Lights, 1956.

Giroux, Henry A. *Neoliberalism's War on Higher Education*. Haymarket Books, 2014.

Griffey, Trevor. "The Decline of Faculty Tenure: Less from an Oversupply of PhDs, and More from the Systematic De-valuation of the PhD as a Credential for College Teaching." *LaborOnline*, LAWCHA: The Labor and Working-Class History Association, 9 Jan. 2017, https://www.lawcha.org/2017/01/09/decline-faculty-tenure-less-oversupply-phds-systematic-de-valuation-phd-credential-college-teaching/.

Harris, Adam. "The Death of an Adjunct." *The Atlantic*, 8 Apr. 2019, https://www.theatlantic.com/education/archive/2019/04/adjunct-professors-higher-education-thea-hunter/586168/.

'Junct: The Trashing of Higher Ed. in America. Directed by Chris Labree, 2255 Films. Post-production.

Kich, Martin. "The Warning Signs That a College Is in Financial Trouble." *Academe Blog*, 21 Aug. 2014, https://academeblog.org/2014/08/21/the-warning-signs-that-a-college-is-in-financial-trouble/.

Kovalik, Daniel. "Death of an Adjunct." *Pittsburgh Post-Gazette*, 18 Sept. 2013, https://www.post-gazette.com/opinion/Op-Ed/2013/09/18/Death-of-an-adjunct/stories/201309180224.

Kudera, Alex. *Fight for Your Long Day*. Atticus Books, 2010.

Lawless, Caprice. "Teaching Poverty at the Community College." *FRCC AAUP Founders' Blog*, 18 June 2013, https://coloadjuncts.blogspot.com/2013/06/.

Marvit, Moshe Z. "Duquesne's NLRB Filing Reads as a Brazen Threat to Adjunct Union Organizers." *In These Times*, 3 Aug. 2015, https://inthesetimes.com/article/duquesnes-nlrb-filing-reads-as-a-brazen-threat-to-adjunct-union-organizers.

New England Center for Investigative Reporting. "New Analysis Shows Problematic Boom In Higher Ed Administrators." *HuffPost*, 6 Feb. 2014, www.huffpost.com/entry/higher-ed-administrators-growth_n_4738584.

Piper, Julia, and Brian O'Leary. "Executive Compensation at Public and Private Colleges." *The Chronicle of Higher Education*, 15 Feb. 2022, https://www.chronicle.com/article/executive-compensation-at-public-and-private-colleges/#id=table_private_2019.

Powell, Kendall. "The Future of the Postdoc." *Nature*, vol. 520, 2015, pp. 144–47, https://doi.org/10.1038/520144a.

Quart, Alissa. "Hypereducated and on Welfare." *Elle*, 2 Dec. 2014, https://www.elle.com/culture/career-politics/a19838/debt-and-hypereducated-poor/.

Salmon, Felix. "The Tragedy of Cooper Union." *Disorientation*, 9 Nov. 2011–20 May 2013, http://freecooperunion.org/disorientation/the-tragedy-of-cooper-union-by-felix-salmon/.

Shafrir, Doree. "Why You'll Be Paying Your Student Loans Forever." *BuzzFeed*, 23 Jan. 2014, https://www.buzzfeed.com/doree/heres-why-youll-be-paying-your-student-loans-forever.

"Tenure Status of Full-Time and Part-Time Faculty Members, Fall 2018." *The Almanac, 2020–2021*, *The Chronicle of Higher Education*, 16 Aug. 2020, https://www.chronicle.com/article/tenure-status-of-full-time-and-part-time-faculty-members-fall-2018.

Trudeau, Garry. "Doonesbury," *GoComics*, 6 Sept. 1996, https://www.gocomics.com/doonesbury/2015/09/06.

Valbrun, Marjorie. "Lives and Livelihoods." *Inside Higher Ed*, 23 June 2020, https://www.insidehighered.com/news/2020/06/23/cuny-system-suffers-more-coronavirus-deaths-any-other-higher-ed-system-us.

"We Are Anything but 'Teaching Machines,' APSCUF VP Says After Difficult Session." *APSCUF: Association of Pennsylvania State College and University Faculties*, 29 Sept. 2016, https://www.apscuf.org/we-are-anything-but-teaching-machines-apscuf-vp-says-after-difficult-session/. Press release.

Whitney, H.E. "Adjunct World Comics." *Adjunct World*, 1 Apr. 2014–11 Feb. 2017, https://adjunctworld.tumblr.com/.

Why Adjunct Professors Are Struggling to Make Ends Meet. YouTube, uploaded by PBS NewsHour, 6 Feb. 2014, https://www.youtube.com/watch?v=Bz4pK8UP4PM.

Chapter 19. Where the Pipeline Ends: Teaching High School Equivalency in a Medium-Security Prison

Andrea Verschaeve and Jason Porath
INDEPENDENT SCHOLARS

Both Jason Porath, a special education educator at a medium-security state prison in North Carolina, and Andrea Verschaeve, a writing teacher at the same prison, saw the paths of their careers headed toward what doctorate degrees promised them: roles focused on academic leadership, scholarship, and research. Both had their professional dreams deferred, but they have found a real sense of purpose and fulfillment in educating students who are serving time for felony convictions.

In what follows, Porath focuses his story on the beginning of his journey down a path that led to education as a career in general, and prison education in particular. Verschaeve starts her narrative at the beginning of her teaching career and follows it through her current position, which, like Porath, is as a prison educator. After working together for some time and sharing their stories one day over lunch in the break room, both Verschaeve and Porath were surprised to discover that they had come to similar conclusions after leaving their doctorates unfinished: even though it feels like it at the time, it's not the end of the world. Really.

Mission, Passion, and Frustration: Jason Porath's Story

Education has been both my mission and passion for as long as I can remember. Since my first day of kindergarten, I have always had a desire for and a love of learning. During my second-grade year, I had my first experience "teaching" a student. This lit a fire within me that still burns brightly and intensely to this day. Becoming a teacher was now my life goal; an educational journey had begun.

When I entered junior high, I was approached by my aunt, a special education teacher, to become a peer tutor. Having accepted this position, I was now an official employee of a school district. My dream of becoming a teacher was beginning to come true.

The first students I worked with were a couple of first graders who struggled in both mathematics and reading. Although I did not know it at the time, these students were receiving special education services at their school in addition to the peer tutoring I was providing. Working with these students was both challenging and rewarding. Learning had always come easily to me. I thought everyone was able to learn if they just put in the effort and paid attention to the people who were teaching.

Working with those first graders opened my eyes to the world of special education. I began learning from my aunt as much as I could about learning disabilities, accommodations, and strategies for helping learners with special education diagnoses reach their full potential and achieve academic success. As time passed, the students I was tutoring began to understand the concepts we were working on during our sessions. Both their confidence and academic scores increased.

By the year's end, my students had increased their standardized test scores in both mathematics and reading. Most importantly, however, their confidence and love for school had increased. These students now came to sessions eager to learn, asked questions, and discussed how their school day had gone. Their final report cards indicated how much they had improved throughout the year.

I went on to be a peer tutor throughout my high school years. It was during this time that my career focus took yet another change. As a peer tutor, I had come to the decision that I wanted to become a special education teacher for elementary students with a focus on students with learning disabilities. When I began high school, my mother took a job as an educational aid in a self-contained classroom for emotionally impaired students. On a daily basis, we discussed her interactions with the students. Their behaviors and academic performance fascinated me. Then, one day, an event occurred that forever changed my focus.

School had just ended, and I headed home, eager for my daily conversation with Mom. However, this day was not going to be like any other day. When I arrived home, no one was there. This was quite unusual. Shortly after I arrived, the phone call came. Mom was in the hospital. While on a bus headed to a field trip, one of her students began threatening other students with a pencil. My mom instructed the student to hand her the pencil, to which he replied, "Go ahead and take it from me!" As she went to take the pencil, he grabbed her arm and wrenched it over the seat, causing an injury that required surgery and resulted in permanent nerve damage. Due to the severity of the injury, my mom was unable to return to work for the rest of that year and was never able to do that job again.

Immediately upon hearing of my mom's injury, my brother and I became furious and were ready to "destroy" this kid. We demanded she tell us this kid's name, as we already knew what school he attended. The answer she gave us was a complete shock. Not only did she not tell us his name, but she told us that she was not angry with this student and did not wish for anything to happen to him. She sat with us and calmly explained how this student had a number of behavioral, academic, social, and emotional issues that were most likely the reason that he attacked her in the manner that he did. Initially, I was not buying any of that. Then, I began to think and wonder about what she said. I needed to know more. That is when I decided that I wanted to become a teacher of students with emotional impairments.

In 2001, I graduated from Northern Michigan University with a degree in education certified to teach special education in grades K-12 and endorsed in emotional impairments for grades K-8. Upon graduation, my intention was to teach in an elementary self-contained classroom for special needs students. After a few unsuccessful interviews, I was informed of an opening for a special education teacher at a detention/treatment center. Although the student population was youth aged 11–18, not the elementary age students I was hoping to work with, I was intrigued by the position. After consulting with my then fiancée and my mother, I decided to apply for the position.

Despite my educational background and my completion of a teacher preparation program, I was nervous about this position due to the age group of the students I would be teaching. Also, these students were one step away from jail and/or prison. Many people I discussed my new position with could not believe I would want to work with "those" kids. This was extremely frustrating to me, and I had a difficult time listening to people discuss my students as though they were barely even people due to being in what many called "kiddie jail."

Not long after I began teaching at the facility, I knew I had made the right decision. The students I worked with were, in fact, worthy of having people believe in them and help them better their lives. Many of my students came from backgrounds that included broken homes and exposure to physical, emotional, and sexual abuse. Victims themselves, they had become victimizers. During my time as a teacher there, I was able to play a part in aiding over 78 students obtain their high school diplomas, several students earned GEDs, a few went on to earn college scholarships, and most all were able to realize at least three grade-level gains in both mathematics and reading. Most importantly, however, many students realized and vocalized that there are people who truly care and that because of this, they realized they were able change and become healthy, productive members of their home communities.

After ten years of teaching at the facility, shifts in politics and leadership caused the mission to change and the focus of the facility to be lost. Youth were not achieving the successes that once had occurred, staff was leaving, and the program was falling apart. At this time, I decided that I needed to take action. I could not watch our program and my kids suffer. So, I enrolled in a doctor of educational leadership program at Central Michigan University with the intention of becoming the director of the facility and bringing success back to our program.

Coursework went smoothly, and I made it to the dissertation phase of the program. This is when the problems began. There was a three-year delay for approval to use data from the facility in my dissertation. Once I finally received approval, I had lost both momentum and desire to complete the paper. Then, after several promises that I would be made program manager and ultimately director of the facility were broken, I was discouraged and ready to give up.

At this time, my wife and I decided it was time for a move. I began searching for positions in North Carolina. Having worked with juveniles for the previous 14 years, I began looking for positions at youth centers, and then I saw a few openings at prisons. Remembering what my mentor teacher once told me, I decided to apply to the prisons. A few weeks later, I was hired at a medium-security men's prison to teach special education classes.

This change of scenery was what I needed to bring my focus back to my dissertation. With renewed enthusiasm, I began working on my paper, only to be derailed once again: my mother was diagnosed with multiple sclerosis (MS). The MS was fast and furious, and within a year, my mom had lost her battle. Prior to her passing, I was on alert to head back to Michigan at a moment's notice. As a result, I once again lost focus on my dissertation. Unfortunately, the university-imposed clock on time to degree completion had expired. I could re-take classes that had expired, but I came to realize that my place is "in the trenches," working with students where I can have a direct impact on academic, emotional, and social growth.

Finding Professional Freedom: Andrea Verschaeve's Story

I knew this job would be different when I was on the phone to set up an interview and the human resources representative on the other end of the line said, "Make sure not to wear an underwire bra." I had thought about working in a prison before when I was applying for teaching jobs after I graduated from college without a teaching license, but at that time, I ended up accepting a teaching assistantship and getting my master's degree instead. I didn't consider prison education again for more than 20 years.

When I began full-time teaching, first for a year in a rural Virginia high school, then for nine years in two different rural Virginia middle schools, I loved teaching, and I also wanted to continue my own education. During this time, I was accepted into Indiana University of Pennsylvania's doctoral program in composition and TESOL. I completed the rigorous coursework and had begun working on dissertation research when the local university hired me as a full-time lecturer.

The lectureship had an expiration date. I could stay in the position for a maximum of six years. It paid $40,000 a year when I began in 2008, which was less than I had been making as a middle school teacher, and when I left six years later, I still made $40,000 a year. I thought in that position it would be a little easier for me to work on my dissertation because I would be gaining experience teaching the level of students I would be qualified to teach when I finished my doctorate, so I thought accepting the position, even with a pay cut, would be a win-win.

Unfortunately, teaching at the college level was not as rewarding for me as teaching eighth graders had been. For one thing, I didn't connect as easily with college students. They didn't spend as much time in my class as middle school students had, who I taught for a full year rather than just one semester, and they were busy and preoccupied in a way the middle school students were not. In short, college students weren't interested in forging relationships with me, and because this was an important way I developed a sense of community to foster learning in my classroom, I didn't enjoy teaching at the college level as much.

In addition to the lack of connection, I didn't feel creative or inspiring as a university lecturer, whereas I felt that most of my eighth-grade students looked forward to my class and probably characterized me positively to their friends or parents as "fair" and "nice" and "funny" and "smart." I doubted my students at the university were talking about me at all, but if they were, I felt characterizations of the time they spent with me might include words like "boring" and "uninspired."

Although I thought it would be easier to research and write my dissertation in the university setting, even though the lectureship had a 5/5 teaching load, I didn't really know what I was doing. I didn't know the questions to ask to navigate dissertation research, so I fell further and further behind until I saw no way to move forward. In addition to feeling like I was drowning in inability, I also realized I was no longer invested in the degree because the door that degree would open—a tenure-track position at a university—no longer appealed to me.

When I emailed my dissertation advisor with my intent to drop out of the program, I felt fear and shame but also relief. I was fearful that I wouldn't find fulfillment in education anymore, that I would have to start all over in a different field. I didn't have any ideas about how to do so. I was ashamed that I was quitting, that I was letting down my advisor who believed in me, and that I was letting down the people who had invested in my journey with me—friends, family, and colleagues. I dreaded telling people about my decision, and I ended up having to tell it over and over again, in the grocery store, in the hallway at work, in the writing center where I was working as part of my lectureship, through email conversations.

Sharing my decision to drop out of the Ph.D. program stopped being dreadful only when I stopped equating it with failure. It was the best decision for me, and I often had to reassure others of that fact. When people reacted with disappointment and distress, I felt like I was letting them down, but I was careful not to internalize their disappointment. When I left the university, it was to teach high school, first at a public school in Virginia, and then at a charter school in North Carolina. When I needed a new challenge, I applied to teach at a medium-security correctional institution, one of four in North Carolina that has a dedicated school for the offenders it houses.

Now, I teach writing with an eye towards preparing my students to pass the writing portion of ETS' HiSET (High School Equivalency Test). To get to my classroom each morning, I enter a gatehouse through one side of a sally port, scan my work badge, and pass through a metal detector before proceeding through the other side of the sally port. In the main building, I pass through a second metal detector and a cell phone detector. A correctional officer peruses my clear bag of belongings—the day's lunch, a book, and a file of papers—and I am patted down before proceeding through a second sally port.

Now inside the prison complex proper, I pass the visitation area on my left and the chow hall on my right before heading upstairs where the school, chapel, medical and dental facilities, and diagnostic testing area are all housed. From the four slivers of window in my classroom, I can see the gym and outdoor basketball court, the dormitory housing units, the single cell housing units, and the high security housing unit.

My classroom has no internet connection, neither my students nor I have access to cell phones during the school day, and the only things I am able to give my students—ever—are the pencils and lined paper provided by the state. The irony of it is not lost on me: that my job at a medium-security North Carolina state prison is the first one I've held as an educator that has a significant amount of professional freedom.

Conclusion

Both of us agree the time we spent pursuing a doctorate wasn't wasted. Although we became part of the number of students who enter doctoral programs without completing the degree, we recognize that an important part of our professional identities stems from the knowledge and insight we gained in those programs through taking part in a variety of deep classroom discussions, completing rigorous coursework, and growing close with a cohort of fellow doctoral students.

Neither of us would be picked first for a team you'd bet on being successful and resilient prison educators, but we have experienced success in classrooms populated by men and women dressed in identical tan pants and grey t-shirts, serving anywhere from a few more months to more years than they want to count. We do exactly what others in classrooms at every level across the country do every day: we encourage, entertain, cajole, and discipline. We tell stories and jokes and make connections. Sometimes we argue. We hope we are inspiring our students. We participate on committees and attend faculty and department meetings. We grade papers, and we make plans for tomorrow.

Chapter 20. Contracting and Consulting: Crafting a Career

Ian S. Ray and Brandi Wren
University of Denver and Independent Scholar

Faced with an ever-shrinking academic job market, many contingent faculty members supplement teaching incomes with other contract-based employment (or transition entirely to contracting). In this chapter, we discuss examples of non-teaching contract work that contingent faculty members engage in, raise general issues and research challenges that can arise when contract faculty members work multiple jobs, and suggest ways around these challenges.

Using our combined 25 years of experience as adjuncts and independent contractors, we first explore three areas in which adjuncts may find non-teaching, contract-based work: research support, educational support, and administrative support. Examples of contract-based research support work include GIS and statistical analysis and consulting; manuscript editing, proofreading, or copyediting; grant writing and contracting; and research interview transcribing. Educational support work includes designing curricula, delivering trainings and workshops, offering writing support, providing remote text interpreting, or tutoring. Administrative support work may involve program evaluation or grant evaluation.

Second, we examine the phenomenon of contingent faculty members working multiple jobs. While this practice is not inherently negative, the fact is the vast majority of them do so because of financial pressures. Many contingent faculty members are constantly faced with the choice of whether to take on "just" one more contract job (and the stress it places on their wellbeing) or to limit their work schedule to attempt work-life balance (at a financial cost).

Next, we explore the challenges contract faculty members face when conducting scholarly research. When contracts are short term and ever changing, it becomes difficult to maintain the institutional support necessary for obtaining grants, accessing research resources, and covering publication fees. Even professional development opportunities can be limited because adjuncts often have scheduling conflicts due to working multiple contracts, are not made aware of opportunities, or are not eligible for them. As a result, they can be left feeling like they and their research are stuck in quicksand, sinking deeper and deeper into obscurity.

In the last section, we provide what we call hacks for adjuncts to use to overcome obstacles. Many have written on the solutions that educational institutions could and should enact, most of which would solve these problems. Until that happens, we hope our suggested hacks can help other adjuncts like us survive and, possibly, even thrive.

DOI: https://doi.org/10.37514/PRA-B.2022.1589.2.20

Types of Contract Work

Despite years of quality teaching experience, positive evaluations, and scholarly publications, many adjuncts remain on the academic contract teaching circuit indefinitely. How can we manage to make a living? We have adopted the approach of contracting and consulting to supplement the meager income generated by the adjunct life. Specifically, we have been contracting within, and adjacent to, the academy. Ian has been completing short-term research gigs and evaluation projects while Brandi has been working in the realm of student and disability services. In this section, we'll explore three areas in which adjuncts may find contract and consulting work: research support, educational support, and administrative support.

Research Support

Depending on your prior academic training, freelance research support work is a way to sustain yourself while filling an adjunct or contingent faculty role. Several online services exist to assist both freelance contractors and potential clients, such as *Fiverr*, *Upwork*, and *Guru*, to name a few. Services requested or offered in relation to research projects may include IT support (such as website development, survey creation and administration, or programming), specific creative outputs (including maps, charts, graphs, or graphics), or data analytics (text analysis, qualitative coding, or statistical analyses and interpretations).

Snagging research assistant positions can be challenging because academia doesn't run on tuition dollars. Professor Farnsworth of the television series *Futurama* put it best: academia is "powered by dump trucks of flaming grant money!" ("Reincarnation"). Offering a few times a semester to do any grant-related work has proven to be a pseudo-reliable way of finding short-term salaries. For example, Ian worked for a summer evaluating the concurrent enrollment program at one of the community colleges where he is an adjunct. Even though it was a short-term job, nonetheless it was a $20 per hour, 20 hour per week supplement to his adjunct salary.

Academics know grants and technical writing better than anyone out there, so we suggest putting that knowledge to work. It can be worth offering to help other researchers with grant writing, manuscript editing, and other research related tasks. Grant writing work may or may not be paid, but it can be useful if it requires limited time and later leads to a research assistant or analyst position that is paid.

Beyond writing actual grants, there are opportunities to provide other grant subcontracting services. These include transcribing ethnographies or research interviews or completing other research-related tasks that researchers may be looking to contract out. Another way to work with other researchers is to serve on research advisory boards. These roles sometimes can be paid via grant funding and tend to involve reviewing surveys or other data collection instruments before live deployment or reviewing research results prior to publication or presentation.

Educational Support

Areas where adjuncts can contribute educational support include tutoring, working in student support services, and designing educational materials. For example, work may be available for private tutors or research mentors/pseudo-advisors. Funding for research design advising and tutoring may or may not be tied in with the grant process but can be particularly useful if students need support beyond what the institution is offering. Ian has been a private tutor and statistical consultant for 15 students to date, with several stating openly that they would not have been able to finish their dissertations without the extra help.

Student support services may also be provided by third-party contractors. Brandi provides remote text interpreting services for students with disabilities, working for multiple agencies as an independent contractor. As an academic with graduate degrees, she has been able to charge premiums for interpreting for graduate level courses and other advanced content. There are also opportunities for multilingual individuals to serve as interpreters or translators of important documents or course materials. Study abroad programs, international campuses, and specific academic programs may be in need of these kinds of services. There may be opportunities to interpret research documents targeted at specific populations as well.

Academics can also act as subject matter experts (SMEs) for publishing and other companies on a contract basis. This work may involve advising on any number of projects, with one of the most common being production of educational materials like textbooks or documentaries. SMEs are also hired to write test banks or create presentation slides to accompany textbooks. Both of us have been approached via professional networking platforms and email to advise or act as SMEs on such projects.

Content creation and freelance writing of educational and other materials is another area in which adjuncts find contract employment. Editors and writers are needed for a wide variety of specialized content about which adjuncts are often highly knowledgeable. Another option that overlaps both educational and research services is editing of professional manuscripts, including academic journal, thesis, and dissertation manuscripts. Some academics earn relatively competitive pay performing these services for students and faculty such as early career researchers or individuals looking to publish in their non-native language.

Another area to consider is providing supplemental training for other professionals. Most of these training programs require a great deal of upfront work, but once they have been conducted a few times, they are much easier to modify on the fly. Some trainings we have been involved with have included

- professional development for K-12 teachers (such as "How to Google-fy Your Classroom" or "Schoology101")
- implicit bias training for admissions interviewers at professional schools
- culturally responsive teaching methods training for fellow adjunct instructors

Even better, these trainings can be converted to *YouTube* videos and other specialized resources, then generate passive income via AdSense or marketing via a personal website. You're unlikely to become the next multimillionaire via these strategies, but you will at least have a passive income stream to supplement your adjunct pay.

Administrative Support

One type of administrative support that contractors can offer is program evaluation. Program evaluation is one of the most under-appreciated activities within academia. At its core, evaluation is applied research. The outcome is intended to answer the question, "Was this program successful?"—with the answer to this question often determining if a grant is re-funded or extended. Evaluations can be performed for specific programs, as part of a larger grant, or potentially as a retrospective for philanthropic foundations. Getting started in evaluation work requires a relatively low investment, as much of the required training has already occurred in graduate school. Most evaluations will require the evaluator to develop a plan based on specific questions. The short version of this scenario is to replace the word "evaluate" with "research" and suddenly the whole scope of work makes much more sense.

Learn to Juggle! (Working Multiple Jobs)

Contractors (and, by extension, adjuncts) often work multiple jobs. This isn't inherently negative, but a problem arises when faculty members are forced to work multiple jobs to make ends meet. This is overwhelmingly the case with adjunct faculty. The most recent nationwide study of the adjunct experience in the US revealed that a whopping 85 percent of contingent faculty members struggle to pay their basic expenses (*An Army* 1).

We have to remember that contract jobs do not look the same across all institutions or businesses. In higher education, they may be labeled as anything from adjunct instructor to visiting professor, contract instructor to limited term lecturer, and more. The same applies in industry, where a job posting may be for a "research scientist" or a "content writer," with the contractual nature only revealed in the fine print. For some of us, contract teaching means teaching one class a semester while working other jobs. For others, it means teaching six classes a semester at four different institutions. We have both met adjuncts all along this spectrum. One common thread is that the work is not consistent. Adjuncts lack the job security of knowing that we will be teaching a given number of classes every semester or academic year (and on the rarer occasions that we do, they are still on a contract basis, so renewal each year is contingent on a number of factors).

Having income and work options that are flexible in nature to supplement adjunct income is a requirement for many adjuncts, at least those who try to actively prioritize teaching over other contract work. Contract work has allowed both of us to teach when teaching opportunities are available and still have other work and income when it is not. For example, Brandi has spent over a decade cobbling together work schedules consisting of teaching, transcription, and field course instruction—all on a contract basis.

One thing to consider as an adjunct is how much time you will have for your other jobs. We all know how demanding teaching can be. This means having limited time and energy for other jobs, making it difficult to work in some industries. As a result, creating your own contract-based employment means you can schedule work that fits your needs. More importantly, it means you can charge rates that provide a living wage.

Research Challenges for Adjuncts

Maintaining an active research program (a phrase commonly seen on the academic job market) becomes increasingly challenging as a long-term adjunct. Research programs require support of various types that is often provided by higher education institutions to full-time, tenure-track faculty members, but not to adjuncts. For example, of the three higher education institutions Brandi has taught for, only one allows a temporary contract instructor with a Ph.D. to serve as a principal investigator (PI) on a research project. This is common practice at many, if not most, colleges and universities; when adjuncts are allowed to serve as PIs, it is only with special approval from the department chair and, often, a dean as well. In many cases, a co-PI who is a tenure-track faculty member at your institution is needed. Functionally speaking, adjuncts have to have supervisors—administrative babysitters, if you will—to maintain active research programs. This means the direction and pace of our research programs are often characterized by zigzags and stalls depending on the level of commitment and support we get from tenure-track faculty members. (There is a way around this, which we will discuss in the next section.)

Applying for research funding without the support of your academic institution is another obstacle faced by adjuncts trying to maintain a research program. Many research grants require institutional affiliations. As we just discussed, as adjuncts, if our affiliations do not allow us to serve as PIs on projects, then we cannot apply for grants as PIs through our institutions; this means that to apply for grants, we must essentially ask tenure-track faculty members to support us and serve as PIs or co-PIs. Not only does this entire system limit adjuncts as independent researchers and scholars, but it places an unnecessary burden on those tenure-track faculty members who do attempt to provide support for adjunct colleagues.

Now is probably a good time to stop and remind ourselves of the contingent nature of adjunct work. Some contract teaching positions in higher education are one-year positions, but many are only semester assignments. Anybody familiar with the process of research—including grant cycles, field seasons, and revise and resubmit periods—knows that it is rarely possible to complete a scholarly project within the time span of a temporary contract appointment.

Imagine it now: You are adjuncting at two schools, teaching three classes, and working another job to pay the bills. In your spare time, you design a study, prepare and write grant proposals (whose submission dates align with your one-year appointment's schedule), conduct the research and analysis, and submit manuscripts about the work to journals—all within the six- or twelve-month contract appointment. Ludicrous daydream, right?

Contingent affiliations often provide few resources for adjuncts, certainly less than provided for tenure-track faculty members and arguably less than provided for graduate students. Often, contract faculty members are not eligible for professional development programs, support for conferences, departmental research funding, and other institutional support, such as coverage of publication fees. When contract faculty members are eligible for such opportunities, we often do not know of them because often we are not included on institutional or departmental listservs. This is especially discouraging for those adjuncts who stay within academia wanting to make contributions in both teaching and research.

All of these factors together result in what we call "adjunct quicksand." It is not merely a fear but a reality that the more we adjunct, the more we can lose touch with our research. It becomes more and more difficult to contribute to and maintain relevance in our academic fields when we are distracted by piecing together affiliations that must be renewed or replaced each year or each semester, trying to find a tenure-track faculty member to support our research and serve as co-PI, and working on research entirely outside our full 40-plus hour work week. Further, the longer one adjuncts, the less likely they are to ever be offered a tenure-track position ("The Status").

Improving Adjunct Working Conditions: Hacks versus Solutions

In this final section, we provide hacks for adjuncts to navigate the higher educational system. By hacks, we mean tips for adjuncts on finding ways around the systemic barriers to developing their careers. These hacks stand in contrast with solutions, which would result in actual changes to the academic and higher education systems. We focus here on hacks, not solutions, as precious few adjuncts are in a position to actually enact systemic change.

Our first recommendation for those who lack consistent or quality research support is to join an organization that provides independent researchers with resources. For example, the National Coalition of Independent Scholars (https://www.ncis.org) provides adjunct academics and other non-tenure-track scholars with research support they would not otherwise receive. Such organizations offer not only a route for adjuncts to serve as PIs on research projects but also the opportunity to apply for research grants that require institutional backing, as these organizations can serve as the required institutional affiliation.

Another option is to negotiate a permanent visiting scholar appointment in an academic department. These unpaid positions can provide library access and other basic research and academic resources. This provides an uninterrupted academic email address as well, especially important when confronted with constantly changing academic affiliations through temporary visiting assistant professor or visiting lecturer positions.

If research is your forte—your calling, your passion—and adjuncting is just a means to that end, cut out the middleman. Many grants and fellowships are open to small business owners. If you're committed to research, it might be worth diving into the business world as a "recovering academic." For example, the National Science Foundation allows small businesses to apply to many of its research grant programs, with preference given to small, woman-owned, and/or minority-owned businesses.[1] Additionally, independent institutional review boards (IRBs) are available to provide the federally mandated oversight that colleges and universities offer to their affiliated faculty members,[2] and collaborations with "real" academics can still enable your research to continue.

Another tactic for making a living as a contractor is to keep control of the rates you charge for services. When you are starting out, you may be compelled to accept low rates (particularly if work comes through existing grants), but that should not be your long-term rate. Industry professionals earn raises and promotions; contractors increase their rates periodically and as they gain skills.

While hacking the system, be sure to keep your websites and personal and professional social media accounts current with your professional skills. This can be helpful for attracting contract employment and for demonstrating that you are competent (e.g., by displaying an e-portfolio of your work). Do not hesitate to let your colleagues know about your contract-based services and share your web presence with them.

---

1. For more information on these opportunities, see the "Programs for Small Businesses" page on the National Science Foundation website at https://nsf.gov/funding/smallbusiness.jsp.

2. For a partial list of such independent IRBs, see the "CIRB Members" page on the Consortium of Institutional Review Boards website at http://www.consortiumofirb.org/cirb-members/. A *Google* search using the term "independent IRB" returns a sizeable list as well.

Depending on your background, it may be beneficial to reach out to professional organizations, schools, or businesses to discuss any needs they may have for training or workshops. By providing such services, you can increase your portfolio size, bring in much-needed income, and build connections for future contracting work. Further, this can even out the income, since long-term (six-month-plus) contracts can ensure you still are getting a paycheck over the summers.

Works Cited

An Army of Temps: AFT 2020 Adjunct Faculty Quality of Work/Life Report, American Federation of Teachers, 2020. *American Federation of Teachers*, https://www.aft.org/sites/default/files/adjuncts_qualityworklife2020.pdf.

"Reincarnation." *Futurama*, created by Matt Groening, season 6, episode 26, Comedy Central, 9 Sept. 2011.

"The Status of Non-Tenure-Track Faculty." *Reports and Publications*, AAUP: American Association of University Professors, June 1993, https://www.aaup.org/report/status-non-tenure-track-faculty.

Chapter 21. After Adjuncting: Questioning Academia's "Big Club"

Steven Yates
INDEPENDENT SCHOLAR

"It's a big club ... and you ain't in it!"

– George Carlin

When learning of this project, I was caught between conflicting impulses. I could write a semi-autobiographical narrative about my career trajectory in the academic precariat[1] and about how I escaped—or I could dive more deeply into the disaster American academia has become. The former might make good "quit lit," as it's now called. The latter, though, would prove more useful.

The impoverishment of the "New Faculty Majority" hasn't happened in a vacuum, after all. A latent anti-intellectualism has long permeated American society from top to bottom. I'm not referring to religious fundamentalists or some such group nowhere near the societal locus of power. Efforts to socially engineer obedient workers and compliant consumers via public schooling and mass media go back a very long time.[2] Once, generations ago, the damage was minimal. The centralization of the American political economy that came about after the Second World War did much to change this.[3] Then came globalization, and the prevailing ideology driving capitalism—neoliberalism—evolved to support both.[4]

---

1. The term precariat has gained currency, as it refers to a core phenomenon of 21st century neoliberal political economy. Adjunct faculty members are just one species of precariat. For a definitive account, see Guy Standing's *The Precariat: A Dangerous New Class*.

2. The reader unfamiliar with the true history of the shaping of primary and secondary education in the US and wanting a quick overview might consult Paolo Lionni's *The Leipzig Connection*. The most comprehensive treatment I have seen, though, is John Taylor Gatto's *The Underground History of American Education: A Schoolteacher's Intimate Investigation into the Problem of Modern Schooling*. Gatto spent 30 years boots-on-the-ground in New York City's toughest schools, winning a New York State Teacher of the Year award in 1990. Then he quit and embarked on an independent research mission that included following money trails and investigating the role of foundations such as The Rockefeller Foundation using very deep pockets to shape the modern public school paradigm. I have no doubt he knows what he is talking about; if he is not an "expert," no one is.

3. To get a sense of how *long* this process has been underway, see C. Wright Mills' *The Power Elite*.

4. For a good accounting of the rise of neoliberal ideology, see Philip Mirowski and Dieter Plehwe's edited collection, *The Road from Mont Pèlerin: The Making of the Neoliberal Thought Collective*.

One consequence was the erosion of upward mobility as we moved toward a deindustrialized, techno-feudalist global marketplace of "gigs" instead of stable, reliable, long-term employment. Aspiring professors were just one casualty of these long-term trends. Atop this system is a small ruling class of neo-feudal plutocrats, having gained far more wealth from investments and passive income than real, productive work; next come their top administrators and technocrat enforcers; and finally is a protective encirclement of well-financed upper-echelon media, tenured-class academics, and think tank-based shills.

Below all these is the new peasantry, or serfdom. That would be *us*. We were never invited into the "big club." We tilled the academic soil of the "gig economy" plantation that stands at the end-road of deindustrialization and the neoliberal business model. Adjunct pay may be as little as $2,500 per course, which means earning under $20,000 per year after taxes. Earning this little may mean going into debt to pay utilities or suffering the stress of choosing to go hungry so one's children can eat the ramen noodles—especially for those without parental support or a spouse with a real salary. All while praying for no health or car emergencies.

On the other hand, college and university administrations—academia's techno-feudalist enforcers—have seen their numbers swell and their pay explode over the past three decades. Few adjuncts are positioned to expose and challenge this abusive system, for despite efforts at adjunct unionization that are sometimes assisted by organizations, such as the Service Employees International Union (SEIU), there is no established (i.e., properly funded) powerbase from which adjuncts can operate and draw on resources where necessary.

I am one of those who graduated with his doctorate in philosophy and high hopes, given three publications in refereed journals (another forthcoming) and presentations at national meetings. These were properly specialized, carefully footnoted, calculated efforts to push the right buttons. I knew I faced stiff competition for tenure-track academic employment, but basically I trusted the system.

My hopes were gradually dashed by a multiyear job search as I moved from institution to institution to institution (six in all in ten years). Because of the onerous process of writing position-specific cover letters, getting three letters of recommendation, and assembling any other requested materials—a job in itself often occupying over 40 hours per week—while teaching as many as four classes—I'd set aside scholarly projects, in many cases indefinitely. Finally, I left university teaching to seek other opportunities. I had already withdrawn applications for part-time teaching positions due to what I considered insultingly low pay.

I then discovered another harsh truth about the neoliberal/proto-technofeudal era we are being pulled into. It's not "nicer" outside academia than it is inside, unless you can retrain and retool in a hurry as some kind of entrepreneur. The gig economy is ubiquitous. Moreover, despite my earning an additional professional degree (in public health promotion and education), more than one nonacademic job interview ended with the subtext OVERQUALIFIED.

"Why would someone with your education want to work here?"

The answer, "*Even smart people need to eat, pay rent, and put gas in their vehicles,*" didn't seem to suffice. After drawing unemployment for six months, I lowered my head and removed those advanced degrees from my resume. I then wrote obituaries for a couple of years, ghostwrote a couple of books (work I had to keep secret but which paid *well*), and wrote a technical report for a cancer research group supported by money from the U.S. Centers for Disease Control and Prevention (CDC).

Writing was clearly my superpower and still is. I returned to academia when the technical writing gig ended (the CDC pulled the plug) and because I saw no other options: you can be the best writer around, but if you can't sell it in a marketplace hostile to anything written above a seventh-grade level, you're screwed.

What I discovered when I returned to academia was that while I'd been away, the adjunct zone had more than doubled in size. I stepped back in. Thus began seven years of freeway-flying sometimes hundreds of miles per week: I worked at four *more* institutions beyond the six I had previously worked for in four cities/communities overall, working on six campuses total during that period.

By this time, I'd made uneasy peace with my status as an outsider—someone who would not only never be invited into the big club but who had also started to look askance at it. Having studied the authors and subjects I had studied, I realized that a solid case could be made that academia had been seriously off course for a very long time and that the adjunct zone was only one manifestation of a system rife with corruption.

What/who had I studied? Philosophers in my own area, such as Thomas S. Kuhn and Paul Feyerabend, who in different ways stressed the social embeddedness of knowledge and, in the latter's case, forcefully questioned the "scientis*tic*" (not scien*tific*) methodology that permeates Western institutions, including higher education, like water fills a sponge.

In other areas, my reading ran the gamut from neoconservative Straussians like Allan Bloom to left-leaning thinkers like Russell Jacoby, Cary Nelson, Noam Chomsky, Richard Rorty, and Robert Frodeman and Adam Briggle. These authors—and others too numerous to cite individually—collectively threw cold water on the idea of academia as a "safe space" for the pursuit of truth, and for reasons quite different from those currently being bandied about. The problems *are* structural, in addition to just plain awful ideas floating around, and come down to perverse incentives driving adjunctification and administrative bloat.[5] Were there space here, we could delve into the causes of excessive inequality more broadly, the corruption of a financial system designed to benefit billionaires, the decomposition of American politics (both parties) that birthed Trumpism, and more.

---

5. For an up-to-date account, see Jason Brennan and Phillip Magness' *Cracks in the Ivory Tower: The Moral Mess of Higher Education*. It should be noted that the authors are not sympathetic to adjuncts' plight.

For my part, back around the turn of the millennium, I began to take more chances with my work, developing and defending theses that were interdisciplinary instead of specialized, thus sometimes venturing outside the narrow, paradigmatic boxes academic philosophy supplied.

One result was a couple of heavily footnoted pieces that were rejected by journal after journal. The rejections often came without referees' comments—although one came from someone who had outlined the paper, clearly showing that they'd read it and understood it but recommended its rejection anyway. They did not supply a reason for their decision to reject.

Philosophy supposedly trades on arguments, evaluations of their cogency, and their ability to contribute usefully to ongoing conversations. Really significant contributions often began new conversations. Absent sound assessments from others that my material was lacking, I came to a realization that made those hopes I mentioned previously seem naïve and the life I'd been leading shallow and inauthentic.

Survival in academia was not about making sound arguments at all. It was more about not pissing off the local big club: tenured faculty and administration. I'd left temporary positions in the past with a distinct sense of having become a threat to superiors. Teaching was similar: in my experience, philosophy adjuncts were typically assessed on their ability to entertain students for an hour (or two or three) by cross-pollenating Socrates and Seinfeld.

"Unexciting in the classroom" came back on one of my evaluations by a senior faculty member. The truth: *academia is not a meritocracy*, and it probably never was, neither in scholarship nor in teaching. Meritocracy is, by and large, a myth. There are Horatio Alger stories out there, of course. But the drama surrounding such narratives is a dead giveaway of their outlier status.

Many of the dominant tendencies of the past century—and the present one—are more the products of intellectual inbreeding and in-house political sympathies than advancing insight. *Novelty* has become an end in itself. What "succeeds" is what has the institutional capability to bully alternative points of view off stage. Or, to use a trendy recent term, to *cancel* them.

This stage was set years ago when humanities and liberal arts departments kept churning out Ph.D.s with no end in sight after the job market collapsed in the 1970s. A "buyers' market" creates an environment in which conformists are hired and dissidents are weeded out. A few of us who defended unorthodoxies learned (sometimes the hard way) to keep our heads down if we wanted academic employment. We tried to avoid rocking boats on campus.

The internet did much to break up the consensus-reality narratives that had dominated before, especially about how "our democracy" really functions. Its new platforms exposed how major media and academia are controlled endeavors designed to turn out a certain kind of scholar, voter, and consumer: one who believes and does what he/she is told and does not question the consensus or the authority of "the experts."

Eventually I presented some of my findings in a book—for which I created my own "publishing collective" with a few close friends who supplied valuable assistance. I was sure no academic press would touch it (I did not try).[6] With that book in hand, I asked my department chair for a raise one last time. After I was turned down flat, I resigned and prepared to move overseas (a small inheritance helped), assisted by friends who were vacating also, one by one, an America in cultural and political-economic decline and becoming expats.

I became an entrepreneur of sorts, trading in ideas. I learned copywriting and copyediting and did more ghostwriting. I worked for a handful of clients, some of whom were native Spanish speakers needing help with English and some of whom needed help with other kinds of writing.

Since my departure (in 2012), things in academia have gotten worse.

It was clear all along: there are too few free minds in academia to make a difference. Someone with a *free mind* questions dominant narratives, especially those about how power really operates in this world, who has it, how it transcends abstract political economy, how we're encouraged to believe lies, and what we can do about this.

We had high hopes for the internet, but with "Big Tech" censorship in place, that hope is now dwindling. I sometimes find myself looking back wistfully at what could have been . . . and I follow the latest tendencies. Do I see a massive brain drain from present-moment academia, or is it just sour grapes? I don't think it's sour grapes.

Philosophy has clearly suffered. Where are the present era's Bertrand Russells, its Ludwig Wittgensteins, its Jean-Paul Sartres, or even its Thomas S. Kuhns and Paul Feyerabends and Richard Rortys? With rare exceptions, those purporting to replace them leave *much* to be desired. *Anyone* can produce automatic writing calling Trumpism nascent fascism. Would such authors try explaining how the American political system got into this mess? Which of "our" premises and narratives collapsed, and why?[7] That is going to take *work*.

For my part, I've survived. I'm still in a foreign country, living in a condo in a place where the cost of living is half of what it is in the US. I do not use heat during winter months, though. Nor do I jet off to conferences every year like I once did (thank God for Zoom). I earn income through ghostwriting, editing, and occasional English tutoring.

I have no employer and am not seeking one. Have we not learned, *employees are expendable?* And the larger the employer, the less relative importance you have and the more expendable you are. That's the adjunct situation in a nutshell.

---

6. The finished product appears as *Four Cardinal Errors: Reasons for the Decline of the American Republic.*

7. If you want to find answers to these questions, I'd begin with Rorty's *Achieving Our Country*, as Rorty has been credited—correctly, in my view—with diagnosing *some* of the conditions that led to Donald Trump's victory in 2016.

The employer pays starvation wages because of the systemic, built-in assumption that you have nowhere else to go. And because it *can*.

This is due to the still-ridiculously overcrowded and therefore hostile academic job market. There are no easy answers. Surely there is something to the claim that higher education has produced and is *still* producing too many Ph.D. degrees. This is because of perverse incentives: the more Ph.D.s a department graduates, the greater its prestige.

I wonder how many of those Ph.D.s still see academia as a refuge from that equally hostile gig economy out there filled with Uber drivers and Amazon worker bees?

Unraveling the conundrums the adjunct crisis points toward isn't possible in a piece of this brevity.[8] Arguably, academia is a microcosm in a world where wealth is concentrating, inequality is worsening, and basic freedoms—however understood—are diminishing: these are those proto-techno-feudalist developments I mentioned at the outset.

Those of us who put down our academic peasant's plows and walked away did not abandon our ability to think nor the will to use it. Thus, we can still ask pointed questions and make a few constructive suggestions. It is in this spirit that I offer this piece and the companion material available online.

The most constructive suggestion I have is that we need a new and bold network of philosophers—and folks in cognate areas who want into our "little club" (if you will). We've been misled and lied to, to an extent that we need to go *back to basics*, review what we should be doing, and do so in a *parallel environment* of our own design.[9] This can be done in the spirit of the free and open discourse my generation once championed, such as during the original civil rights movement, and directed also against the past and more recent destructive foreign wars of choice.

While present generations face multiple challenges and an admittedly much worse situation than mine encountered, I would invite its members to ask themselves the following: Do you really want to commit your abilities and lives to institutions that *daily* confess their indifference to your dedication? Is the recent pall of censorship and cancelation a direction you want to go in—or be dragged in? And finally, in a divided nation, how much of what we see and hear from both sides of the political aisle is *theater* (critical race theory advocates *and* obsessives, I'm talking to *you*!), distracting from the geopolitical and geo-economic realities I described in my second and third paragraphs of this chapter: *things we had better start paying attention to while we still can!*

Works Cited

---

8. I expand on some of them in my Substack article "Stale Breadcrumbs from the Academic Dinner Table: Notes of an Ex-Adjunct."

9. I elaborate on these points in chapter six of *What Should Philosophy Do? A Theory*.

Bloom, Allan. *The Closing of the American Mind: How Higher Education Has Failed Democracy and Impoverished the Souls of Today's Students*. Simon and Schuster, 1987.

Brennan, Jason and Phillip Magness. *Cracks in the Ivory Tower: The Moral Mess of Higher Education*. Oxford UP, 2019. *Oxford Scholarship Online*, https://doi.org/10.1093/oso/9780190846282.001.0001.

Carlin, George, performer. "The American Dream." *Life is Worth Living*, directed by Rocco Urbisci, MPI Media, 2005. *YouTube*, uploaded by YouTube Movies and Shows, 1 Aug. 2013, https://www.youtube.com/watch?v=i_mCmIJDnZE.

Chomsky, Noam. *The Chomsky Reader*, edited by James Peck, Pantheon Books, 1987.

Feyerabend, Paul. *Against Method: Outline of an Anarchistic Theory of Knowledge*. New Left Books, 1975.

Frodeman, Robert and Adam Briggle. *Socrates Tenured: The Institutions of 21st Century Philosophy*. Rowman and Littlefield, 2016.

Gatto, John Taylor. *The Underground History of American Education: A Schoolteacher's Intimate Investigation into the Problem of Modern Schooling*. Oxford Village Press, 2001.

Jacoby, Russell. *The Last Intellectuals: American Culture in the Age of Academe*. Basic Books, 1987.

Kuhn, Thomas S. *The Structure of Scientific Revolutions*. 2nd ed., U Chicago P, 1970.

Lionni, Paolo. *The Leipzig Connection*. Delphian Press, 1988.

Mills, C. Wright. *The Power Elite*. Oxford UP, 1956.

Mirowski, Philip and Dieter Plehwe, editors. *The Road from Mont Pèlerin: The Making of the Neoliberal Thought Collective*. Harvard UP, 2009.

Nelson, Cary. *Manifesto of a Tenured Radical*. New York UP, 1997.

Rorty, Richard. *Achieving Our Country: Leftist Thought in Twentieth-Century America*. Harvard UP, 1998.

Standing, Guy. *The Precariat: A Dangerous New Class*. Bloomsbury Academic, 2011. *Bloomsbury Collections*, https://doi.org/10.5040/9781849664554.

Yates, Steven. *Four Cardinal Errors: Reasons for the Decline of the American Republic*. Brush Fire Press International, 2011.

———. "Stale Breadcrumbs from the Academic Dinner Table: Notes of an Ex-Adjunct." *The Clarity Factory*, 7 Oct. 2021, https://stevenyates.substack.com/p/stale-breadcrumbs-from-the-academic.

———. *What Should Philosophy Do? A Theory*. Wipf and Stock, 2021.

Chapter 22. We Are the University

Debra Leigh Scott
Hidden River Publishing

History shows that whenever vast empires decline, barbarians appear who threaten and destroy the age's culture, art, and learning. Against this onslaught, there are those who fight at great risk to their own well-being in order to guard and rescue what is to be treasured. We are, once again, in such an age, and our institutions, including those institutions of education, have been under attack for decades.

For these last 50 years, what I call the corporate colonization of higher education in the United States has captured and destroyed authentic academic culture. Our campuses are no longer gathering places where scholars and students dedicate themselves to the rigorous pursuit of learning. Instead, far too many of these spaces have come to closely resemble theme parks for the "college experience"—complete with lazy rivers, climbing walls, state of the art gyms—where both learning and teaching are more performative than real. Armies of administrators with little to no experience in or respect for education or educators now control universities' decisions.

This managerial class has taken over our universities to the extent that they now outnumber faculty on every campus across the nation and are very close to outnumbering the students. Although cleverly concealed by public relations staff and marketing agencies and the glossy logos, branding statements, and brochures they produce, the goal of these functionaries is profit for the corporate university, and the result is poverty for both faculty and students. This poverty finds its expression not only in the unlivable working conditions and compensation of faculty but also in the debt burden of students. It finds expression in a poverty of the mind as well.

Background

Nearly 25 years ago now, I found myself teaching year after year on one-semester, low-wage, single-course contracts. Although my teaching wages were desperately low, I was able to cobble together an income by teaching at multiple universities. My efforts to find a full-time position in academia met with failure, so I continued to work on those humiliating adjunct contracts for years, often teaching courses that were administration-designed, many with some new, nonsensical, "best practices" theory behind them. With common syllabi and pre-ordered book lists, such courses offered little possibility for the kind of sovereignty that the academics of past generations claimed in their classrooms. I felt frustrated and angry that, after over ten years of graduate work, I was never able to design and teach courses in the areas and disciplines in which I had studied and trained.

This is the reality for those teaching on adjunct contracts. We find ourselves in a kind of edu-factory, working on an academic assembly line, teaching the ever-increasing number of "core" courses that have little to nothing to do with our areas of specialty. Core courses, in fact, have everything to do with the kind of standardization that makes a factory run efficiently; the idea is to make it possible for these courses to be pre-packaged and then taught by nearly anyone. What happens to all the possible courses taught in a more intellectually rigorous, ongoing pursuit of knowledge by all those specially trained scholars? They never happen. The most important work of those scholars is never born. The very reason for the existence of a university is smothered.

That is the state of dysfunction presently found in universities in the United States. The incalculable waste of intellectual training + the mind-numbing sameness of conveyor belt core curriculum = academic fraud and educational malpractice. The sense of failure, of frustration, and of isolation experienced when doing this kind of work often convinces us that our own personal choices are at fault. But this is not a personal failing; we are the majority faculty. Approximately 75 percent of all American faculty is now itinerant. The truth is that what we've experienced as lonely and exploited low-wage academic "untouchables" (a phrase borrowed from Pablo Eisenberg) is a widespread and shared suffering.

The plight of the majority of scholars in the US is the result of very intentional actions and impositions put into place in a takeover of academia by corporate interests and business culture. It was a systemic change, a massive shift away from true academic culture, that began with the now infamous Powell Memo of 1971. Hundreds of articles and essays on its devastating effects can be found.

The resulting corporatized universities have been rebuilt on a factory model where the abused and exploited faculty work the conveyor belts on which student after student rolls by—and while far too little is given *to* students, much is extracted *from* them. The truth of the corporatized university is that it operates on the model of vulture capitalism. It extracts, it strip mines, it outsources, it depletes. It sells off what was once a thriving intellectual ecosystem for parts.

When the time came and the majority of faculty members finally, as a growing chorus of voices, attempted to call attention to issues like our labor exploitation, we discovered that there existed already a very effectively painted picture, constructed and depending largely on the "ivory tower, useless professor" myth. The general population too often believed that a professor was someone who worked barely a few hours a week for only thirty weeks a year, then spent the rest of their time at leisure. The general public imagined that faculty members spent hours each day sipping sherry in a well-appointed study or library, reading obscure texts nobody cared about, then giving dinner parties with other erudite but useless professors, where obscure texts were discussed over more sherry. In short, our corporate enemies had gotten to the population before us and had successfully planted a powerful narrative that was very well-delivered and too often accepted.

The "overpaid, overindulged" intellectual class was painted so well, and mocked so thoroughly, that it was a hard image to dispel in order for us to tell our own truths. Who would care if this class of smug and self-important louts was finally facing its comeuppance? Let them go out into the real world and find real jobs. Then, when this narrative became connected to the lie that all skyrocketing costs of college are tied to the bloated salaries of these loutish do-nothings, however could we successfully expose the deceit?

Raising Awareness

It was about ten years ago that I began with my co-producer, filmmaker Chris LaBree, to record interviews with a variety of faculty members, union representatives, think tank policy makers, and legislators, starting our efforts to put together a documentary about all the issues surrounding corporatized academia in order to raise awareness of what was *really* going on beneath the pretenses that were accepted so easily.

During this decade, it has been my honor to meet some truly amazing people who are working to fight back against the corporate functionaries on our campuses. Chris and I met and spoke with those involved in unionizing efforts—largely with those involved in the United Steelworkers (USW) and the Service Employees International Union (SEIU)—new to the higher education battles. They were passionate about succeeding where the traditional education unions had failed after their many decades of ignoring the growing casualization of faculty labor. I'm sorry to say, however, that in these ten years, with all the earnest unionizing attempts—some still ongoing, some that resulted in unionizing—we have not been able to restore our academic profession.

The same percentage of America's faculty are still subjected to work on short-term, low wage, adjunct contracts. Most of this "new faculty majority" are still without job security, benefits, and health insurance. Most are still unable to design and teach courses in their academic areas of specialty. And the unionizing efforts have never addressed, nor are they designed to address, the larger issues of the corporatized campus—issues like exploding tuition costs, student debt, corporate partnerships that drive book assignments, or the ways in which our largest financial institutions dictate how financial aid officers are trained to entice students into taking out higher loans than they need. So, beyond the issues of the academic profession, there are many other ways in which the corporate university is out of control. It has become a nearly impregnable predatory institution, a many-headed dragon—and we are fighting with plastic picnic forks. How long can anyone endure in such circumstances?

During these past ten years, a genre of academic literature nicknamed "quit lit" has appeared—stories of those individuals who could finally take the abuse and poverty no longer and who left academia to find alternative career options. These career options are often called "alt-ac" choices, "alternative" choices when academia becomes untenable. Many took jobs in publishing, in consulting, in tech, in entrepreneurial enterprises. Anything that offered some job security, a steady and respectable paycheck, and an end to the terrors of financial ruin is considered preferable. I am one of those who left.

I've known people who took jobs managing clothing boutiques, who bartended, who drove for luxury limousine services. Every one of these people expressed relief and gratitude that they no longer had to lie awake at 3:00 a.m. tasting blood in their mouths, fearing their next electric bill or rent increase. But not one of them would say that they didn't grieve being forced to give up what felt like a calling. When you are called by love to a profession, your heart and spirit break when you finally admit the truth: that you are being abused by the institution to which you had dedicated so much of yourself and in which you will never have the career your heart still yearns for. And, while every one of these alt-ac jobs is a respectable and honorable form of employment, there is no one sounding the alarm over the loss of those millions of highly trained and extensively educated individuals who are not providing our society with the benefits of those years of study.

I want to declare that, despite the false narrative about our uselessness, academics are an essential class. What we trained for matters. We are a professional class that provides real benefits and that meets real needs. Every healthy, thriving society needs a robust and engaged intellectual class as much as it needs doctors, accountants, or lawyers. We serve not only as teachers, writers, and scholars, but also as the collective of minds made available in service to society at large.

And yet, we've become part of what I call the diaspora of the learned. As solitary academic objectors, we are scattered throughout society, exiled and isolated from others of our former profession, unable to fulfill the calling that had been our lives' goal. Our departures for these alt-ac positions, while essential for our material survival, too often mean we sacrifice our training and education and possible contributions to ongoing academic discovery. Those fruits die on the vine.

Moreover, those quit lit stories of individuals leaving bring us right back to where I started this chapter, to the story I told of my experience 25 years ago—quit lit stories are solitary stories. It is the individual making the difficult choice to leave their chosen profession, to abandon their calling. We are abandoning our calling to those who wish to see academia die.

Yes, the number of those leaving academia continues to rise, but not in a way that alarms the corporatized institution. In fact, our departures increases its strength. When we leave a university as an individual, we are replaced in a heartbeat by another desperate individual willing to endure the abuse that finally drove us away. It reinforces the certainty all corporatized universities have that we are of little value, entirely and easily replaceable.

I received a panicked call at 9:00 one morning from the chair of an English department in one of the several universities for which I taught humanities classes. She wanted to know if I could step into a class that met beginning at noon that day. The person who had been contracted for the course had left abruptly. I asked about the course. Was it an area in which I was experienced, in which I had trained to teach?

"Oh, that doesn't matter," she said. "I just need a warm body."

That was one of the most unveiled, succinct declarations of our worthlessness that I had ever heard. It was also horrifying to realize that the chair of an English department cared not a whit about the quality of the English courses being offered because her goal wasn't to assure quality of pedagogy or rigorous educational material but to avoid canceling the course and refunding tuition. She had abandoned her loyalty to her discipline and become a functionary of the corporate bosses. But she is not alone.

Anyone working on an adjunct contract bears responsibility for what has happened to our academic culture. Working in the edu-factory places us squarely in collusion with the corporate values, willing or not. And, as necessary as we find it, when we leave as individuals, we fail to end this conveyor belt abuse of faculty and student. There will always be more "warm bodies" who can be shoved in to do your factory work.

Am I saying that we are wrong to depart? Of course not. I'm simply pointing out that our individual departures, my own included, increase the power of the corporatized campus model. I want to declare, therefore, that it is our duty, as the scholars and intellectuals of our country, to act beyond our own self-preservation. It is also our duty to destroy the edu-factory. So, instead of or in addition to our individual departures, I propose we help to plan and execute a mass exodus. I'm not talking about a strike or a walkout or a shutdown. I'm talking about the permanent departure of a majority of faculty members across the entire country.

A mass exodus.

Solutions

Why would a mass exodus of faculty members be the most effective way to respond to the crisis in academia? Because, despite the corporate college's very carefully maintained illusions, without the scholars, every campus becomes a ghost town overnight. Classrooms sit empty. And those hordes of administrators who have outnumbered both faculty and students on our campuses are suddenly powerless against our permanent absence. We would destroy the corporatized factory campus in a New York minute.

This truth is simple, but powerful: We *are* the university. We carry within us all the necessary experience, learning, training, and abilities required to bring academic pursuits and the intellectual training of our youth back to its fullest and most pure expression.

We are not tethered to the ruins created by these corporate usurpers. Those chains are illusory. We ourselves have made the mistake of believing that our true work lies in the built environment of a campus, now wholly conquered by a hostile culture. Our wars, up to now, have been fought over the wrong property. Our gifts, talents, and abilities don't need real estate. Ours is intellectual property, and we must awaken to that truth—an epiphanic blinding truth—that this has always been ours and will always be ours and that all we have to do, as a large class of extremely gifted people, is walk away and take the ark of truth with us. We ARE the physical embodiment of that ark.

So deep has our misunderstanding been, that even before our individual departures, we lived as exiles within what once we perceived of as our own land, our own sanctified space. For a half century now, we haven't so much labored in these ruined halls and classrooms as we have *haunted* them.

To be clear, I'm not talking about this as a negotiating strategy. The days for negotiations are long, long past. Think about it this way: the American Declaration of Independence acknowledged many previous attempts to negotiate with the British Crown but declared, in this document, that there would be, of necessity, a permanent severing of the bonds—the United States declared itself to be free and independent. THIS is what I'm talking about: a Declaration of Academic Independence and Sovereignty, which should be written and circulated as such. Put another way, when Moses led his people out of Egypt, it was not with the intention of going back if Pharoah promised better benefits and fewer abuses. It was a march forward.

Yes, in both these examples, the march forward was a march into the unknown, as ours will be. But we don't go alone. We are surrounded by the spirits of those who have refused injustice and abuse through human history. And we don't go empty-handed. We carry with us not only the values and principles and truths of our training but also the highest ideals of our species. We are some of the best-educated people in our country. It is most certainly within our capacity to envision and create new spaces, platforms, and models of higher learning.

That's one of the most important things to keep in mind: this exodus wouldn't be only a march *away* from a captured and ruined culture but also a march *toward* a new, better expression of academic culture in the pursuit of wisdom and the discovery of truths.

The individual flights may have saved us individually. But a mass exodus will save academia itself while simultaneously destroying the corporate colonizer. And, of great importance, it will save our students. Let's return briefly to the story about the English department chair and her search for that "warm body." Her attitude toward the faculty was horrifying enough, of course. But what does it say about her attitude toward the students? If her goal was to put someone, anyone, into the classroom, the primary purpose was the avoidance of canceling the class and losing tuition money.

This is a managerial attitude that sees nothing wrong with taking a student's tuition for a low-quality—or a no-quality—educational experience. In fact, it is preferable to holding out for quality when tuition money is at stake. This, as I have already said, is educational malpractice. It is academic fraud. Our mass departure means that our students will no longer be victims of such fraud and malpractice. Why? Because we, as the living embodiment of the university, will be building and offering new alternatives. WE are the highly preferable alternative.

Finally, our exodus would be for the good of our chosen academic disciplines. Millions of academics over this half century have been prevented from doing their most expansive work in service and support of their disciplines. The continuation of the research, teaching, and writing of scholars in generations past has been halted and silenced by the poverty of the precarious conditions under which we have suffered. A massive departure and the wide, collaborative ways in which we rebuild academic platforms will also provide us with intellectual possibilities long smothered by want of ability, time, and opportunity. We can restore and reinvigorate the work of all disciplines. In other words, our mass departure will save and restore authentic academia.

A saying attributed to George Eliot, "It is never too late to be what you might have been" (qtd. in "George Eliot"), is true, no matter who may have said it. The truth is that we owe it to ourselves, to our disciplines, to academia, and to the youth of our country to be the visionaries that we were always meant to be. We can fulfill all those duties by a mass exodus.

We've spent decades in a struggle against the corporate takeover of our universities. We are never going to win. We will never be able to fight these powers for the full restoration of a true academic culture if we limit ourselves to the current campuses. We will always find ourselves on the collapsing end of a bargaining table. So, let them keep the real estate. It will crumble to dust around them once we depart. One of Buckminster Fuller's most famous quotes is applicable here: "You never change things by fighting the existing reality. To change something, build a new model that makes the existing model obsolete" (qtd. in "Green Wave"). That is our job now: depart *en masse*, declare intellectual liberation for ourselves and our students, and restore the pursuits of the mind and the joys of mental rigor. This will quickly render the edu-factory obsolete. The possibilities here are so vast that we may very well be standing at the beginning of a new Renaissance.

We, the diaspora of the learned, can create something new, something global, in combining traditional, even medieval methods of learning, with tutorial rather than classroom models, with independent study and mentoring and the benefits of technology. Imagine restored intensity and focus, restored rigor, in a more highly individualized pursuit guided by mentors and scholars from around the world.

The possibilities of interdisciplinary, international work done by scholars who have reclaimed sovereignty over their work. . .what could be more dazzling? The kind of learning that could be achieved, the ways in which our youth could be supported in their own discoveries and epiphanies, the ways the global communities could be brought together and a new world born, all beginning with the liberation of the scholars. . .can you feel the glorious promise of such a new world? Can you see that this is how we defeat the barbarians?

Works Cited

Eisenberg, Pablo. "The 'Untouchables' of American Higher Education." *The Blog*, *HuffPost*, 25 May 2011, https://www.huffpost.com/entry/the-untouchables-of-ameri_b_629815.

"George Eliot Quotes." *BrainyQuote*, 2022, https://www.brainyquote.com/quotes/george_eliot_161679.

"Green Wave." *Buckminster Fuller Institute*, 2018, https://www.bfi.org/challenge/2015/greenwave/.

Powell, Lewis F., Jr. Confidential Memorandum: Attack on American Free Enterprise System to Eugene M. Sydnor, Jr., Chairman, Education Committee, U.S. Chamber of Commerce, 23 Aug. 1971. *Washington and Lee University School of Law Scholarly Commons*, https://scholarlycommons.law.wlu.edu/powellmemo/1/.

Chapter 23. Escape This Neoliberal Shit Show Now

BC Dickenson
INDEPENDENT SCHOLAR

I envision you, dear reader, as a focused, motivated, intellectually-curious person who possesses a diverse array of interests and abilities. These are the odds. Right? Moreover, because I have found that most educators care deeply about their students and their subject, I imagine you by and large to be kindred spirits who would tend to inspire me to do my best. Given all of this, I look upon the task of giving you any sort of advice with reverence. It is from that of deep place of respect and gratitude that I endeavor to help you consider your career choices. Does that make sense?

Despite the fact that you possess all of the qualities I've just described, you may very well be living under the poverty line or close to it while preparing America's youth for their bright futures. And you may be earning half the salary of a tenured professor. In any case, thank you for reading this. I am writing because I care, and I hope that my story and ideas can be valuable to you. I aim to persuade you that if you don't love this teaching world, go forth into the night and use your prodigious talents elsewhere.

Context

In the spring of 2021, I was in one those Hollywood Squares Zoom meetings with which we are all now so familiar. It was a board of trustees meeting, and the playas were all there! My square was lit because I was speaking against our president's $20,000 yearly raise during the worst pandemic of our lifetimes, which was implemented without informing the faculty or the union (I don't even think they told the accountant) in a time when enrollment had plummeted and adjunct class hours were being cut. I and others showed up with our union Zoom backgrounds to make the statement that we were united. A few of my many brave and eloquent colleagues spoke with an honest clarity that evoked a perfect combination of heart and mind, the best of communication. It was an important moment of solidarity, as we were collectively steadfast in our indignity. So, damn. Right?

Let's zoom out. In 2016, at the age of 50, I accepted a tenure-track position to work with a group of kindred-spirit comrades at a small, unionized community college. It was the 50th anniversary (get the synchronicity?) of the institution, which was initially dubbed the "college without walls," having been started by a group of idealistic intellectuals, teachers who traveled to gymnasiums and high schools in nearby farming communities to teach required college liberal studies prerequisites (the 101s and 201s) to the nearby farming communities.

The college has a distinctively friendly feel to the campus, supportive colleagues, and hard-working students, and the course load is manageable; it is a wonderful place to teach. 1 However, despite this goodness, a stale, dysfunctional, neoliberal, three-layered, inequitable dynamic remains ever-present at all institutions, mimicking in microcosm the larger capitalist structures in the economy. This dynamic looms over all of us and creates tensions that underlie the surface friendliness, tensions that exist not only between the faculty and administration but also between adjuncts and the full-time faculty, and these tensions logically play out and cause all of us to be broken in a way, which begs the question of how we can better navigate out of these stale layers.

Imagine, hundreds of good, hard-working, high-achieving people being baked into a stale multi-layered cake. The inequities that we face are systemically embedded within a corporatized system. In other words, there is no escaping the shit show of higher education, and the school without walls of course now has walls aplenty and is awash with capital projects, including stylish dormitories and a learning center with so many windows one feels permeable with the volcano off to the east. Both are LEED certified. This reminds me in microcosm of my overcapitalized home institution even though it's much smaller, the place that just slashed divisions and programs because declining enrollments merged with overcapitalization.

That said, I love my colleagues and my students, and I'm glad that at age 50, I accepted my first and likely only tenure-track position at this institution. My now adult sons laughed that I finally got my first real job. I am fortunate, healthy (I say as my heart skips a beat), and, after decades of meditation, would not trade my current consciousness, as bumbling and fault-ridden as it manifests, for all the money or power in the world. It's all an illusion.

This job, though, as my friend Jane, who works as an adjunct and is married to my best friend of 35 years, who is also an adjunct, said to me when I lived with them for six months when I first moved to take this position, consumes my life. My job is my life. I do love it. It's the only paid work that I have loved, and it's arguable that it's the only job that I have been good at. However, my message throughout this chapter is that if you don't love your job, if you're somehow doing this for any other reason, get out now. This work will consume you. As mentioned, I have allowed myself to be consumed by this work, and after I finish writing this on a Friday, I have more reading that attests to such consumption.

Our state higher education system has been smart during COVID-19, as faculty have not been forced back into the classroom like so many of my friends

---

1. Moreover, administration, faculty, and students all seem to be devoted to anti-racist pedagogy, to curing our equity gaps, to doing our parts for a more sustainable future on this planet, though there have been signs that administration is furthering another sort of agenda in the name of anti-racism.

and colleagues have across the country. Our union is strong and would work to protect our health if needed, though our new contract seems to attenuate the faculty's collective power, particularly the power of those in the arts and humanities, by agreeing to dissolve divisions in favor of giving the power to individual department chairs, which would seem to make our departments more dividable and conquerable in an age when top-down forces seem to steering our students away from a life of the mind and into a life of the more quantifiable components of a failing neoliberal capitalist structure.

A Love Affair Begins

For a long time, I was at the bottom layer. Now, after earning a Ph.D., which took time and weekends away from my children during their childhood and teen years, I am probably on the penultimate layer from the bottom. In 2001, at the age of 35, I walked into my first class as a teacher. The Center for Lifelong Learning at Mt. Aloysius College, a small Catholic school in the hills of Western Pennsylvania, sent me a contract for $1800-ish to teach a three-credit composition class, a textbook, and sample syllabi.

At the time, I was working a full-time human service job at $20,000 per year supervising a home-based program for adults with intellectual disabilities. I remember being scared and insecure when I was thrown into my first teaching assignment in 2001. On the 40-minute drive, through the foothills of the Alleghenies, I was so nervous that I was popping valerian root tablets (the calming herb, du jour) the whole way there. My heart was beating so fast that I feared it would explode. *How I am going to do this without blowing a gasket before I start my class?* I wondered. *Is this worth it?* I remember thinking. All this angst for only $1,800 for a three-credit class. At the time, though, I was trying to support a family and needed the money.

I don't remember much about that first class. I remember holding the textbook and gesturing at the students with it. It was before I knew anything about teaching composition or cultivating group work; my ideas were guided by the processes and current-traditional modes presented in the textbook. I remember feeling a sense of elation or at least less fraudulent when some students looked interested or laughed at an attempted joke.

During that first class, a non-traditional student—a tough looking middle-aged guy—sat in the back, scowling at me with a furrowed brow. I taught the entire class assuming that he must hate the class and that he wanted to kill me or even worse. Maybe he was some sort of spy from the college administration and had recognized me as an obvious fraud. I pictured him calling security and saying, "An inexperienced hack has snuck into our hallowed halls and seeks to fill our non-traditional students' minds with a potpourri of nonsense! Come now! And bring the guillotine!" Class drew to a close, the rest of the students seeming to enjoy it.

As I said my goodbyes to the talkative, cheerful students in the front, the guy from the back—the scowling one—approached. I didn't know what to expect. He was expressionless. I pretended to be looking in my grade book. During class, he had asked a couple of terse questions, but that was it. I feared that my charade was over—he had my contract in his pocket ready to rip into pieces, or maybe he just wanted to punch me for wasting his time. He looked to be deadly practical, a working man who had little time for whatever I was talking about. I looked up as he reached the table.

"BC" he said, "thanks for keeping things interesting; I hated English class in high school, but I think I'm going to really like this class."

From that moment on, I was hooked. This was the job I loved. For the next few years, I taught at a local college's branch campus where many of the students were LPNs and laid-off coal miners working on nursing degrees. I taught at least two, sometimes three, courses a semester, supplementing my $20,000 per year human service job with roughly $10,000 in income for teaching five to six classes a year in what I now know is a three-quarters load. Then, it didn't feel like that. I just noticed that I didn't have as much time and that my fiction writing was replaced by paper reading.

In 2004, when my human service job was eliminated due to a budget cut, I got lucky and landed another job—a one-year, full-time, temporary position as instructor at my home university where I had received my master's degree and where, because tuition was suddenly "free," I was able to begin taking courses toward my Ph.D. I signed a contract for $40,000 and took the first sustainable-wage job I had ever had. I remember when I got the surprise call (I was 12th on the finalist list) from a medievalist who was the chair of the department. I felt like I had won the lottery. I was sitting in the kitchen having a beer with my best friend and my wife. I enjoyed this moment, this feeling that I had "made it" somewhere.

Needless to the say, I learned a lot—trial by fire. The students and the assistant chair pointed to numerous flaws in my pedagogy. After that one-year contract ended, I stayed on as an adjunct. All the adjuncts were placed on a ranked list for consideration for future full-time openings, and after a less-than-stellar observation the next year, I was bumped to 20th on the list. Over the years, I was placed all over this list that determined whether I needed to be on unemployment and/or needed to accept the additional meager wages offered by the language institute on campus.

In the summers, I had many jobs. For instance, one summer I carried bricks. One of more consistent gigs was helping my friend with his lawn care company two or three days a week. Charles and I had followed remarkably similar trajectories. Both of us were writers and environmentalists and both were too principled to sell out to any sort of corporate job. We had both lived out West, loved the West, but returned to rediscover our home region of Appalachia with its opportunities for camping and its natural beauty. Charles would look at my crookedly mown lines on the country club lady's lawn and say, "Dickenson, that's what I get for hiring a scholar to help me mow lawns."

Earlier that day, we were mowing on scorched-earth areas near campus with garbage everywhere—students need to think about appreciating a sense of place. I waved to a couple of my students walking by. They looked confused at seeing a professor who mows lawns.

Think of merging lawn care and academia: "At University of the Future, we've thrown away all the hierarchies! Not only are our faculty members well-published in their fields, but also they are responsible for all lawn maintenance duties, hedge clipping, etc. In fact, several of our courses are taught by faculty members while they do lawn maintenance. You'll find yourself pruning and clipping hedges with some of the best scholars in their fields."

Fortunately, my family had a sense of humor. "Why don't you get a real job?" my then 13-year-old son, Brendan, teased after a recent three-day paper-reading binge. He showed his irony through his low, quasi-parental voice. Anyway, I sustained our family financially through odd jobs like this until the hard-fought sustainable work of adjuncting dried up when the university went to the business model of using TAs as almost free labor.

By this point, I had worked myself into being a seasoned professional with a Ph.D. I was generally on the top of the adjunct list, but that list, along with the jobs, disappeared. Fortunately, while my eldest son was going through college, I had managed to string together a few years of steady work, and he was able to graduate by taking advantage of the free tuition offered to university employees. Don't ever work in an institution that is not unionized. That is the lesson here.

The System Feeds Upon Us Easy Marks

In a way, I was an easy mark for adjunctification. "Come be an academic bohemian with me," said my high school acquaintance, whom I had always admired and who was now a safety science professor. A lot of us are easy marks—progressive, somewhat anti-capitalist—but mostly not enough to make any of us uncomfortable. That's telling, right? We're succumbing to a subculture run by profiteers.

My two cents? Run away now. Run away if you don't love it. And if you don't know if you love it, you probably do not. I am not trying to put words in your mouth, but I am trying to give you advice if you're wavering between two fields. Many of us progressive-minded educators who have sought rich lives rather than rich bank accounts are easy marks for adjunctification. From college onward, I was resistant to the environmental and economic atmosphere wrought by the Reagan-era deregulation of the 1980s. Thus, even though I had a business degree, it was safe to say that I was an anti-capitalist.

But the capitalist system creates many insidiously pernicious circumstances. For instance, I am now 55 years old and making over $80,000 in one of the most expensive areas in the country. This is a lot of money for a hippie bohemian, but because of the expensive cost of living in my region and because all those years of adjuncting at low wages left me without much savings, moving out here to an economic boomtown caused me to raid all of my previous retirement funds to afford a down-payment on a home, and I am feeling the financial strain.

But even by today's standards, my education level, and the fact that I work far more than the 35 hours weekly for which I am contracted, I feel guilty because my adjunct colleagues are still making far less money than I am. I fear that my friend down the road who works as an adjunct is being worked to death. He seems to have twice the responsibility that I have. Even when I lived with him when I first moved to take this job, I noticed that he didn't sleep much.

This colleague, let's call him Sampson, who is an adjunct and who has never cared about money, has expressed his concern about the inequities he has experienced, saying that when he taught six composition classes per year (seven is a full load) over a period of years, he earned only $30,000 per year while his full-time colleagues earned over $60,000. Thus, we have in place a system of guilt for full-time faculty members.

I have a job in which I earn what I am worth, whereas my colleagues who have the same skillset are making in the neighborhood of three-fifths of what I earn. This problem is changing on my campus and on others. We are finding new ways to deal with the problem of adjunctification. For instance, an institution in another part of the state has no adjuncts or tenure. Everyone is hired as a full-time employee, and their union has a created a system in which individuals can persist equally.

To everyone who is struggling in the field, my advice is this. One, if you don't want to give everything over to a failing system that is reliant upon you being overworked and underpaid, run away. If you have a graduate degree, you have skills. I know nonprofit and government employees, and they report happiness at being able to attend weekend events and not having to worry about their next paycheck.

Two, if you want to continue to teach, you might consider redrafting or recrafting your cover letter to fit a community college rather than a university. Community colleges, at least on this left coast, are looking to promote equity. They are trying to diminish the gaps caused by adjunctification. That said, try to find stable work. Don't relocate unless you land tenure-track, tenured, or full-time work. Best of luck to you.

Conclusion. Labor-Informed Graduate Education

Amy Lynch-Biniek
Kutztown University

When Natalie invited me to write the conclusion for this collection, she asked me to consider two questions. Given your experience, research, and organizing, would you do it all again? Would you advise others to pursue a career as a higher education faculty member?

I am tempted to answer "yes" to the first question, as I have been so fortunate. I recognize that I embody so much unearned privilege that made a career in higher education a bit easier. I'm a cishet, able-bodied, childless, White person. I have a supportive partner with a well-paying job and an extended family who contributed to our success. This means that, while the odds were still stacked against my status as a tenured full professor, I had significantly fewer hurdles to overcome in a system still riddled with sexism, racism, ableism, and homophobia. I enjoy many aspects of my job: I teach courses I like that I had a hand in designing, and I feel supported in my research and scholarly goals.

At the same time, I struggle to do my job well as public higher education is defunded and as administrations begin to serve corporate forces more than educational ends. Nancy Welch's description of the effects of neoliberalism on higher education has always stuck with me as particularly apt: "The work of education is to be carried out by angels in the austerity's architecture, shepherding programs without monetary support and formal workload recognition" (137). As part and parcel of that, I must also reckon with the fact that my success is in part endowed by the exploitation of the majority of workers in my profession: historically, too many tenure-line faculty members have been willing to sacrifice the compensation and stability of contingent colleagues in the fight to secure their own. The COVID-19 pandemic has only underscored the effects of this exploitation, as we see many protections and services offered to full-time faculty members not extended to adjuncts, from the ability to move sections online to the availability of free testing on campus.

The second question—would you advise others to pursue a career in higher education—is trickier, but it's one I've had to answer often. I teach in my campus' Master of English program, and many of our students hope to adjunct or already are adjuncting at local community colleges. Some plan to apply to doctoral programs with the goal of being professors. Every semester, at least one undergraduate student emails me asking if we can chat about how they might do what I do. I feel compelled to educate our students on two fronts as they decide whether to pursue a career in higher education: a labor-informed view of academic careers, and the necessity of organizing for labor justice in that sphere.

Labor-Informed Preparation

I have always been honest with my students and colleagues regarding how much of my career has been dependent on good fortune. While I am smart, hardworking, and dedicated, those adjectives describe most of us in higher education. How then, given the context and challenges described by the authors in this collection, did I become a full tenured professor?

While I was teaching ninth and tenth grade English, my father, also a high school teacher, suffered a heart attack. He had long been supplementing his income by adjuncting at local colleges. His medical event meant he needed coverage for his evening college courses; he told his chairs that he just happened to know someone with a master's degree who could step in. I taught the remainder of his courses that semester, and one of the campuses offered me an adjunct position the following year. So, my first gig in higher education was due to the coincidence of emergency need and familial relationship. As Natalie says in her introduction, I was in the right place at the right time. I was convenient.

When I decided to make the leap from working in secondary education to working in higher education full time, I did so with no knowledge of its systemic labor practices. I was able to perform well and even really to enjoy my work despite my ignorance of the problems described so well in this collection in part because my partner had a well-paying job that extended health coverage to me. I knew nothing, really, about the employment structure of my chosen career beyond what my contract told me. I didn't know about attacks on shared governance, the replacement of tenure-line jobs with adjunct positions, or the systemic defunding of higher education.

A year into adjuncting, though, the cracks began to show. Despite teaching four courses across three campuses and directing the writing center at one of them, I was making less money than I had as a high school teacher. I found practicing good pedagogy challenging in the spaces I was allowed to use. How was I supposed to hold one-on-one conferences in an office with two desks and one computer shared by fifteen adjuncts? (No exaggeration, I promise.) When a full-time position opened at the community college employing me, I was overjoyed at the potential for upward mobility—until I realized that all fifteen adjuncts working in my department were applying and that outside candidates were being interviewed as well. (I didn't get the job.) Another employer offered to clear out a literal closet to make me an office, as I was teaching on two part-time contracts on that campus and seemed to need a home base. I was invited to exactly one department meeting. A tenure-line colleague asked me why I hadn't attended the university's holiday party. I had to explain that as an adjunct, I wasn't invited. "You're an adjunct?" he asked in disbelief, "But you're here all the time!"

I decided to go back for a Ph.D. with the naive sense that it would of course lead to a tenure-line job with better circumstances. It was only when I began the doctoral program that I learned the degree would be no guarantee of more stable employment. I read Henry A. Giroux's *The University in Chains: Confronting the Military-Industrial-Academic Complex*, James Sledd's *Eloquent Dissent: The Writings of James Sledd,* and Marc Bousquet's *How the University Works: Higher Education and the Low-Wage Nation* and discovered that the time, money, and passion I was throwing into the doctorate would likely result in the same piecemeal teaching jobs and low pay I was already experiencing.

My coursework completed, I continued adjuncting as I dissertated. I applied to a tenure-line opening at Kutztown University on a lark, never expecting to be offered the position. It was just the sort of job I wanted, but I was ABD and had only one publication under my belt. They wouldn't want me. This was a *practice* application. Sure enough, I was not invited to be interviewed that fall. That spring, however, I heard from the search committee: the position was open again; was I still interested? I was the fourth-place candidate who got the job only because numbers 1–3 said *no, thank you*. I didn't mind. I made the most of my good luck, and I didn't have to worry about childcare or chronic pain; no one questioned my sexuality or demeaned me for the color of my skin. I have been mansplained and denied promotion, but I've persisted.

As many of the authors in this collection demonstrate, sustainable tenure-line positions are in the minority; most of us persist in non-tenure-track jobs of many flavors, each with their own challenges and opportunities. This is why I share the story of my career with graduate students and with you, why I think that collections like this one are important to share and assign. Many graduate students begin as naively as I did, imagining the path to and experience of *professor* very differently than the reality. I think we have an ethical obligation to prepare all graduate students to enter academia with eyes wide open, armed with knowledge of the systemic issues higher education faces.

Specifically, I assert that graduate coursework should familiarize students with the teaching and employment contexts they are likely to encounter after graduation. As my co-writers and I—Anicca Cox, Tim Dougherty, Seth Kahn, Michelle LaFrance—explain in "The Indianapolis Resolution: Responding to Twenty-First-Century Exigencies/Political Economies of Composition Labor," "we relish teaching students who love the subject to which we have dedicated our own careers, but the responsibility to prepare them for the material realities that come with a graduate degree or an academic career in English is clear" (57).

First, we need to educate graduate students about the range of positions and institutions in which they may work. Too often, if graduate programs mention careers at all, it is to mark employment at R1 universities as the only respected goal. And yet, David Colander and Daisy Zhou, writing in Pedagogy, report that "overall, slightly fewer than 50 percent of the graduating students from all programs get tenure-track jobs, and about 20 percent get non-tenure-track teaching positions" (140). Little attention is paid in graduate education to careers in community colleges and teaching-intensive institutions (like the one where I work), or to professors of practice and part- and full-time non-tenure-track positions.

Labor-informed preparation also concerns acknowledging the hurdles to teaching well in an academic culture that still values scholarly work above teaching. Most graduates will move into teaching-intensive positions, yet teacher preparation has long been minimized in much of graduate education, relegated to a single course, a workshop, or a seminar. Even more rare are programs that consider the contexts beyond the teaching assistantships that fuel them; Colander and Zhou documented that graduates are more likely to teach in programs ranked lower than that from which they graduated, with a focus on teaching undergraduates (141–42). Even so, too many graduates must rely solely on the experience of teaching in a context that will not match the jobs they will hold after graduation, with limited coursework and guidance in how to teach students across contexts. Graduate students should be made well aware of the challenges they may face in the classroom that have nothing to do with their skill or dedication and everything to do with the material conditions on their campus and the specifics of their contracts.

The second prong of the Indianapolis Resolution calls for pedagogy that "draw[s] explicit attention to the reality that material conditions are teaching and learning conditions—that current labor conditions undervalue the intellectual demand of teaching, restrict resources such as technology and space to contract faculty, withhold conditions for shared and fair governance, and perpetuate unethical hiring practices—as the central pedagogical and labor issue of our times" (Cox et al. 40). It is not the employment status or the title of professor per se that affects teaching but the support, respect, resources, and pay given them.

A 2013 study by the National Bureau of Economic Research "found that new students at Northwestern University learn more when their instructors are adjuncts than when they are tenure-track professors" (Figlio et al.). What's more, we know that contingent faculty members are often productive scholars and perform a great deal of campus service, even though both are often unsupported and unreported in their departments (Doe et al. 438–42). They are succeeding *despite* their working conditions, not because of them.

That faculty members regularly inspire students, create original research, and just keeping coming back is testament to how much they love education. That love drives many of us to work hard despite discouraging circumstances. But that love doesn't pay rent or provide healthcare coverage. Teaching graduate students about the labor structure of higher education admittedly doesn't change that system, but some instruction in advocacy and organizing might contribute to change.

Organizing for Change

During graduate school, when I was first learning about the intricacies of the employment system, a scholar of academic labor spoke at a campus event. During the meet and greet with graduate students afterwards, I expressed my excitement about perhaps organizing adjuncts like me on my campus. "Don't do it," was his reply. He said I'd lose my job, that organizing wasn't worth it. For a long time, I was angry with him; while my adjunct status made me more vulnerable, to be sure, the advice to do nothing denied my agency and my right to fight for my own well-being. The many successful instances since of graduate students and contingent faculty members organizing demonstrate that this agency is real and powerful.

As a tenured professor now, I think I understand that scholar's warning, although I still think it was unhelpful. He was aware of the fragmentary way that labor is addressed on campuses, the way in which tenured faculty members often ignore or pay lip service to the need for a more just campus without doing anything to address it, the fear of reprisal that grips untenured faculty members, and the genuine risks that contingent faculty members take when organizing.

Even so, I have come to see labor organizing as a key component of my job, even though it is not in my job description. If I am to teach well, serve students, be fair to my contingent colleagues, and take care of my own health and well-being, I have no choice but to embrace advocacy as integral to every aspect of my job—service, scholarship, and teaching. I feel this responsibility acutely given my beginnings as an adjunct and my privilege as a tenured professor. While I have long and loudly argued that tenured faculty members especially have a moral obligation to do this work, I have also come to understand that this work must be intersectional and collective, uplifting and protecting the most vulnerable among us. The work of organizing for workplace equity should be the responsibility of all faculty members, not simply the purview of the most vulnerable; at the same time, those most empowered by the current, broken system should not center themselves. This is why Seth Kahn and I argue that we need organizing—collective work grounded in worker solidarity—rather than activism—often focused on individual work or leadership (Kahn and Lynch-Biniek).

In a conversation with Seth Kahn, I lamented the enormity of addressing systemic labor issues in higher education. He observed, "Working for change isn't hopeless, but it is *hard*." We have a lot of hard work ahead of us. Indeed, I believe that one way we teach is by modeling *how we work*. We do this, in part, by standing up for ourselves and each other when working conditions are precarious so that we can work well, serve students, and take care of ourselves, too.

Works Cited

Bousquet, Mark. *How the University Works: Higher Education and the Low-Wage Nation*. New York UP, 2008.

Colander, David, and Daisy Zhuo. "Where Do PhDs in English Get Jobs?: An Economist's View of the English PhD Market." *Pedagogy*, vol. 15, no. 1, 2015, pp. 139–56. *Duke University Press*, https://doi.org/10.1215/15314200-2799276.

Cox, Anicca, et al. "The Indianapolis Resolution: Responding to Twenty-First-Century Exigencies/Political Economies of Composition Labor." *College Composition and Communication*, vol. 68, no. 1, 2016. pp. 38–67. *NCTE: National Council of Teachers of English*, https://library.ncte.org/journals/CCC/issues/v68-1/28754.

Doe, Sue, et al. "Discourse of the Firetenders: Considering Contingent Faculty through the Lens of Activity Theory." *College English*, vol. 73, no. 4, 2011, pp. 428–49. *JSTOR*, https://www.jstor.org/stable/23052350.

Figlio, David N., et al, "Are Tenure Track Professors Better Teachers?" *The Review of Economics and Statistics*, vol. 97, no. 4, 2015, pp. 715–24. *MIT Press Direct*, https://doi.org/10.1162/REST_a_00529.

Giroux, Henry A. *The University in Chains: Confronting the Military-Industrial-Academic Complex*. Paradigm Publishers, 2007.

Kahn, Seth. Personal communication with the author. 5 May 2022.

Kahn, Seth, and Amy Lynch-Biniek. "From Activism to Organizing, From Caring to Care Work." Labor Studies Journal. Forthcoming.

Sledd, James. *Eloquent Dissent: The Writings of James Sledd*. Edited by Richard D. Freed, Boynton/Cook, 1996.

Welch, Nancy. "First-Year Writing and the Angels of Austerity: A Re-Domesticated Drama." *Composition in the Age of Austerity*, edited by Welch and Tony Scott, Utah State UP, 2016, pp. 132–45.

Contributors

Nooshan Ashtari has spent the last two decades of her life teaching languages, graduate/undergraduate courses, and conducting research in various countries around the world. Her main research interests include virtual reality (VR) in teacher training, reading in SLA, and heritage language development. She gets frustrated by any kind of injustice in the world and the lack of collective actions to confront unfairness. Her only artistic talent is in martial arts. Once in a Tae Kwon Do competition she got yelled at furiously by her coach because she thought her opponent had excellent technique and deserved to win.

Anne Balay is the author of *Steel Closets: Voices of Gay, Lesbian, and Transgender* Steelworkers (2014) and *Semi Queer: Inside the World of Gay, Trans, and Black Truck Drivers* (2018). Balay has a Ph.D. in English but has never found stable academic work. In addition to academic gig work, she has been a car mechanic and a truck driver. She now organizes adjunct faculty members for SEIU Local 1 in St. Louis, Missouri.

Devan Bissonette received his doctorate in 20th century American media history from Binghamton University in 2009. Previously, he earned a master's degree in telecommunications from Michigan State University, as well as a bachelor's degree in political science. His most recent publication, "'Modern Day Presidential:' Donald Trump and American Politics in the Age of Twitter," appeared in *The Journal of Social Media in Society*. His current research interests include the study of visual news narratives and the impact of anonymous discourse in cyberspace. He has been teaching fully online since 2009, primarily in history, humanities, and film studies.

Andrew (Andy) Bowman is a Ph.D. candidate in the Center for Writing Studies at the University of Illinois Urbana-Champaign. His scholarship reconstructs the rhetorical histories of campus student activism. His current project examines the work of queer students on the University of Illinois campus during the AIDS crisis and the response to their push for inclusion. Andy is currently co-steward for the English department in the Graduate Employees' Organization and was formerly stewards' chair; officer-at-large; and a member of the communication, personnel, and work action committees. He also serves as a staff organizer for the Campus Faculty Association at UIUC.

Daniel S. Brown earned his Ph.D. in English literature in 2012 from the University of Florida. After many years of diminishing returns on the contingent faculty circuit, he decided to fall back on a library science degree earned in 2001. He spent a few years editing content for ProQuest databases before securing a position as electronic resources librarian at the University of the South Pacific, a regional university overseen by 12 member nations, with its main campus in Suva, Fiji. Currently, he is head of a technical services department at Lincoln Memorial University. In his spare time, he enjoys scuba diving, discussing books and films, and taking pictures of his cat.

BC Dickenson (pen name) teaches way, way out on the left edge of the continent. After being an adjunct for 15 years, he finished his dissertation in 2013. In 2016, at age 50, he landed a full-time position at a small, unionized community college. He works long hours but loves his students and some of his colleagues, works on the scholarship and creative work of his choice, and currently holds tenure. His dissertation and scholarly work has dealt with eco-composition. He is currently working on a study relating to anti-racist assessment ecologies and metacognition.

Natalie M. Dorfeld earned a B.A. in philosophy, a B.S. in English with a specialization in writing, and an M.A. in English at Slippery Rock University. She also has a Ph.D. in English with emphasis on composition and TESOL at Indiana University of Pennsylvania. She is currently an associate professor of English at Florida Institute of Technology. Her research on contingent labor has featured in *Forum: Issues about Part-Time and Contingent Faculty*, *CEAMAGazine: Journal of the College English Association Middle Atlantic Group*, *The Quint: An Interdisciplinary Quarterly from the North*, *Reflections: A Journal of Community-Engaged Writing and Rhetoric*, *Inside Higher Ed*, and *The Chronicle of Higher Education*. In her spare time, she paints, surfs, and rescues stray animals.

Jeff Dories is currently an assistant teaching professor of English at the Florida Institute of Technology. His primary research interests are the British romantic period, ecocriticism, and science fiction. He has given many conference presentations and published articles on 18th and 19th century British literature, ecocriticism, science fiction, and contemporary Chinese writing, primarily the work of Cixin Liu.

Michael Dubson has a been a teacher of developmental writing, college writing, and literature since 1990. He has worked as an adjunct at many colleges in the greater Boston area, and he is now a tenured, full professor at a Massachusetts community college. In addition to his teaching, he has been a writer, a journalist, a publisher, a playwright, a producer, and an actor. When not working, he loves reading, listening to music, and singing. He is grateful to Tim, Daniel, Beau, and especially Cooper for the joy and comfort they have brought.

A. Kay Emmert is a senior lecturer and interim co-director of the program in professional writing at the University of Illinois Urbana-Champaign (UIUC) where she teaches composition, business writing, and creative writing. Born in rural Oklahoma and generally having lived in Southern rural states, her first encounter with unionism occurred at UIUC in 2012. She quickly became involved in the efforts to unionize faculty at UIUC; is one of the founding members of NTFC Local #6546 (AFT/IFT, AAUP), the non-tenure-track faculty union on campus; and served as lead negotiator for the union for both the first and consecutive collective bargaining agreements. Through collaboration and training, she has shared her knowledge with other union leaders on a variety of subjects, including union leadership, organizing, communication, grievance, and bargaining.

Belle H. Foster teaches exercise science classes in the northeastern United States. She is a cynical, and maybe even bitter, adjunct professor, who works in a variety of institutions of higher education in any department that is desperate enough to hire her.

Constance H. Gemson is a former adjunct lecturer at LaGuardia Community College. She taught creative writing to cancer survivors and dementia patients and served as a career counselor and hospice social worker. Her essay "In the Spaces of Strangers" was included in the magazine *Month to Years*, and her recent article "12 Gates to the City" was published by *The West Side Spirit* weekly newspaper. Her play *A Cigarette Girl in the South Bronx* was produced by the Working Theater, an off-Broadway venue. She teaches workshops on resiliency and coping with change. She resides in Manhattan.

Shawn Gilmore is a senior lecturer in English at the University of Illinois Urbana-Champaign (UIUC) and writes on comics, prose, film, and the like and teaches the same. He is a past president and current secretary of NTFC Local #6546 (AFT/IFT, AAUP), chair of the university statutes and senate procedures committee of the UIUC academic senate, and a member of the American Association of University Professor's committee on college and university governance. In addition, he is the editor of *The Vault of Culture*, a public scholarship site that features work by a range of scholars and lay writers about a variety of cultural objects, from comics to film to novels to video games and everything in between.

Jennifer K. Johnson teaches first year composition and various upper-division writing courses in the writing program at the University of California, Santa Barbara, where she also works with new teachers of writing. Jennifer holds a Ph.D. in composition and TESOL from Indiana University of Pennsylvania. Her work has been published in several edited collections, including *What We Wish We'd Known: Negotiating Graduate School* (2015), *A Minefield of Dreams: Triumphs and Travails of Independent Writing Programs* (2016), and *Standing at the Threshold: Working Through Liminality in the Composition and Rhetoric TAship* (2021). Her research interests include TA preparation, independent writing programs, genre theory, writing about writing, and the relationship between composition and literature.

Lee Kottner is a New York City-based writer, editor, former college professor, and education activist. She earned her B.A. at Chatham University and an M.A. in English at Michigan State University. Her poetry has appeared in literary journals, anthologies, and a hand-bound, hardcover artist's chapbook from Blue Stone Press called *Stories from the Ruins*, which is part of the permanent collections of both the Museum of Modern Art and the Detroit Institute of Arts. She's currently working on her next poetry collection (*Water from the Well*) and a novel (*The Angels in Orion*).

Bruce Kovanen is a Ph.D. candidate in the Center for Writing Studies and the English department at the University of Illinois Urbana-Champaign. He has been actively involved in the Graduate Employees' Organization (GEO Local 6300), where he served as grievance officer, officer-at-large, and co-president. In addition, Bruce was a member of the GEO's bargaining team and strike committee in 2018 when graduate workers went on a 12-day strike. He is currently a vice president of the Illinois Federation of Teachers and a member of the American Federation of Teachers' higher education program and policy council.

Sarah Lonelodge is an assistant professor in the English department at Eastern New Mexico University. She completed her Ph.D. in rhetoric and writing studies at Oklahoma State University in 2021. Her research interests include religious rhetoric, propaganda studies, and composition and technical/professional communication pedagogies.

Amy Lynch-Biniek works on writing pedagogy, literacy studies, and labor studies. She is co-editor with Seth Kahn and Bill Lalicker of an anthology, *Contingency, Exploitation, and Solidarity: Labor and Action in English Composition*, that explores the ways and means of labor reform on college campuses. She has published in the journals *College Composition and Communication, Teaching English in the Two-Year College,* and *Academic Labor: Research and Artistry*. She is a former editor of NCTE's *Forum: Issues about Part-Time and Contingent Faculty*.

Dustin Michael received a master's degree in English from Southeast Missouri State University and a doctorate in English from the University of Missouri. He has been working as an adjunct instructor of English in some form or another for his entire teaching career with no end in sight. When he was little, his dream was to become a paleontologist. Never settle, kids.

Kimberly M. Miller earned her B.S. in writing and her M.A. in English from Slippery Rock University and her Ph.D. from Indiana University of Pennsylvania. She began working as an adjunct at Grove City College and eventually was hired on as a full-time faculty member in the communication department. In the spring semester of 2018, she took on the role of interim chair, which led to her assuming the position of chair in the fall of 2018.

Pamela Minet-Lucid has been teaching English to international students and MAT students for many years in California, Hawaii, and Oregon. She holds degrees from Stanford University and the University of Hawaii and is a doctoral candidate in educational leadership and educational psychology at the University of Southern California. Her research interests are autonomy and learning, inclusive practices and language for transgender and gender nonconforming students, and teacher education in TESOL that is inclusive and equity driven.

Jason Porath has been teaching for 18 years, having begun his career at a juvenile detention/treatment center in Michigan. There, he taught special education classes and served as state testing coordinator and GED test center director. Currently, he is the exceptional education coordinator at a North Carolina prison for male offenders. He is also the exceptional education coordinator/teacher at a North Carolina prison for women. Teaching and providing opportunities for both social and academic growth for at-risk student populations has been and continues to be his passion.

Contributors 227

Christian L. Pyle earned a BA from Centre College and an MA from the University of Kentucky. He is an adjunct English professor at Bluegrass Community and Technical College in Lexington, Kentucky. His work has appeared in *Science Fiction Film and Television, Reconstruction: Studies in Contemporary Culture, Review of Communication*, and *Postmodern Culture: An Electronic Journal of Interdisciplinary Criticism*.

Ian S. Ray is a broadly trained social scientist and educator with professional experience ranging from anthropology and sociology to biology and chemistry. He earned a B.A. and an M.A. from Ball State University, received an M.Ed. from Regis University, and is completing both a Pg.C. in GIS and a Ph.D. in applied statistics at the University of Denver. Ian has taught a wide range of courses at the secondary to graduate levels and is actively researching and publishing in the biological and social sciences. Ian enjoys role-playing games (virtual and tabletop), reading nonfiction books, and listening to space opera audiobooks.

Katie Rieger works at University of Missouri. She is an English Ph.D. candidate with a focus in technical/professional communication and writing studies. Her research interests include intercultural communication and programmatic topics.

Debra Leigh Scott taught humanities courses in literature and religion for over 20 years in Philadelphia universities. She is currently a writer, playwright, and filmmaker. She is the founding director of Hidden River Arts (http://www.hiddenriverarts.com) and the editor-in-chief of Hidden River Publishing. A current project-in-process is a docuseries about the corporate colonization of American academia called *'Junct: The Trashing of Higher Ed. in America* (http://www.junctrebellion.com).

Maria Shine Stewart is a Clevelander by birth and a lover of all classrooms, from the one she held in the basement for the neighborhood kids, to workplace seminars, to collections of memoirists gathering in coffee shops. She is a fan of reading and of all alphabets. The daughter and sister of displaced people following the devastation of World War II in Europe, she learned early about intergenerational transmission of trauma—and moments of transcendence. She works as a writing teacher at two community colleges, as a mental health counselor, and as a weekly columnist.

Marjorie Stewart teaches English composition, journalism, and creative writing at Glenville State University in Glenville, West Virginia. She is a playwright with more than 20 productions, and her poetry and essays have appeared in *The Pittsburgh Post-Gazette, Time of Singing*, and *Composing Ourselves as Writer-Teacher-Writers: After Wendy Bishop*. Her recent paintings can be seen in the August, September, and October issues of *Beyond Words Literary Magazine*, and "I Drive Killer 65," a short play produced as an episode of Rachel Love's *AirPlay 21* show, which airs on the New Earth Television *YouTube* channel, available at https://youtu.be/DG7NxCwGawk.

Andrea Verschaeve has taught for 25 years in middle schools, high schools, and colleges in Virginia and North Carolina. Currently, she teaches HiSET (the

High School Equivalency Test by ETS) writing at a medium-security state prison in North Carolina. Her free time is spent with friends, family, dogs, bees, and books.

Nicole Warwick is a full-time lecturer in the writing program at the University of California, Santa Barbara, where she teaches a variety of lower- and upper-division courses and mentors TAs. Her research interests include TA preparation, assessment, transfer and metacognition, and narrative study. She has presented research at the Conference on College Composition and Communication, the Council of Writing Program Administrators conference, and the Writing Research Across Borders conference, among others. She has work appearing in *The Journal for the Assembly for Expanded Perspectives on Learning* and the collection *Writing Assessment, Social Justice, and the Advancement of Opportunity*.

Joanna Whetstone earned her B.S. in writing and her M.A. in English from Slippery Rock University and her Ph.D. from Indiana University of Pennsylvania. She began teaching as an English adjunct in 1998, working at four institutions in three counties each semester. After nine years as an adjunct, Joanna transitioned into a full-time tenure-track position at a community college in Ohio. In 2019, she took on the role of co-chair of her department, working with 11 other full-time and over 50 adjunct faculty.

Ann Wiley (pen name) received her M.F.A. from Southern Illinois University Edwardsville and her B.F.A. from Indiana University of Pennsylvania. She is an award-winning artist with a national exhibition record. Her career as an adjunct instructor started in 2008 and continues today at multiple locations in the St. Louis region. In her not-so-spare time, she is a mom to her two young children, enjoys spending time with her college-aged stepdaughter, works at the YMCA part-time, loves volunteering, and tests her sanity through her tedious art practice.

Brandi Wren is a behavioral ecologist and education professional with a background in primatology, anthropology, field biology, veterinary medicine, international field courses, and disability services. She studied anthropology and biology for her Ph.D. from Purdue University and for her M.A. and her B.A. from Ball State University. She has taught as a contract lecturer in higher education and also contracted as a remote text interpreter, both for over a decade. Her work has examined primate-parasite ecology, the biology of social behavior, primate population distribution, and human-wildlife interactions. She currently lives in Colorado and in her free time enjoys hiking, playing with her pets, roller-skating, and traveling.

Steven Yates earned his Ph.D. in Philosophy in 1987 and taught philosophy both full and part time at various institutions in the Southeast. His specialties range from philosophy of science and epistemology to political-economic philosophy; his primary teaching area was logic. After adjuncting at one institution for seven years, he resigned, left academia, and moved to Chile, where he has resided since. He has taught English and done copywriting, freelance editing, and ghostwriting while continuing to write philosophy. The author of several articles and book reviews in journals, his latest book is *What Should Philosophy Do? A Theory* (Wipf and Stock, 2021). He lives near Concepción, Chile.

www.ingramcontent.com/pod-product-compliance
Lightning Source LLC
Chambersburg PA
CBHW020525080526
44583CB00013B/734